MUCH TO BE DONE

MUCH TO BE DONE

Private Life in Ontario from Victorian Diaries

*I hope something very important
will happen before long because
I want to make my journal interesting.*
DIARY OF HELLEN BOWLBY, 15 MAY 1867

FRANCES HOFFMAN
RYAN TAYLOR

NATURAL HERITAGE / NATURAL HISTORY INC.

Published by Natural Heritage/Natural History Inc.
P.O. Box 95, Station O, Toronto, Ontario M4A 2M8

Canadian Cataloguing in Publication Data

Hoffman, Francis
    Much to be done

Includes bibliographical references and index.

ISBN 1-896219-07-1

1. Ontario - Social conditions - 19th century.*
2. Ontario - Social conditions - 19th century -
Sources.* . I. Taylor, Ryan. II. Title.

FC3068.H64 1996   971.3'02   C96-930477-3
F105.H64 1996

Design by Norton Hamil Design
Cover hand-tinted photograph of Mary Ellen Crysler by Notman, dated 1895, which was likely the date of printing. The original was probably taken many years earlier. *Upper Canada Village*
Back cover drawing titled *Residence of Chas Ed. Walker. Esq.* by Gertrude Nicholson, diarist. *Collection of Clair C. Chapman*

Natural Heritage/Natural History Inc. acknowledges with gratitude the assistance of the Canada Council, the Ontario Arts Council and the Association for the Export of Canadian Books.

PRINTED AND BOUND IN CANADA BY HIGNELL PRINTING LIMITED, WINNIPEG, MANITOBA

Notes to the Reader

IT WAS THE ORIGINAL INTENTION of the authors to include in this publication only writings from the diaries of women living in Victorian Ontario. However, as the pleasure of discovering and reading diaries progressed, it became clear that there would be some input from men. In addition to writings of fifty women, the reader will discover those of six men: Forbes Geddes, whose diary contains his frank and often entertaining observations; L. H. Wagner, who documents the tragic struggle of his wife, Mary Staebler, during her final illness and who provides a vivid picture of the Victorian sickroom; William Maccaulay, who writes of his concerns with domestic details, particularly with reference to servants, during the illness of his wife, Ann Catherine Geddes (sister to Forbes Geddes); Thomas Adams, whose diary was sometimes written by his daughter; James Geddes, no relation to Forbes and Ann Catherine, who was a lay preacher and who often wrote within the context of his pastoral duties; and, Samuel Cormany, who provides documentation on the work of a midwife during his wife's confinement.

Women's names presented a dilemma. At least two of the diarists married and changed their names during the course of writing their diaries. To avoid confusion, we decided to use names under which the various collections are catalogued at the institutions which houses them. For instance, Matilda Bowers, who married Aaron Eby is under Matilda Bowers Eby.

The biographical sketches which appear towards the end of this publication will provide the reader with some indication as to which socioeconomic group these people belonged. Some had to watch their pennies very carefully. Some were from quite affluent backgrounds.

It is clear that Victorian Ontario contained people from all walks of life. They ranged from the poorest homeless beggar, to that group amongst the wealthy who were in a position to thumb their noses at propriety. However, it is the normal everyday events that convey the average concerns and way of life of most people. The writings contained in this publication which include diaries, a few extracts from letters, in addition to quotations from other publications, will present the reader with a glimpse into a bygone age.

The quotations reproduce the diarists' writings exactly as they recorded them, including what we might regard as spelling or punctuation errors.

Contents

Diaries

This day like all other days has left few traces
Old father time Wings us speedily on to eternity.
DIARY OF MATILDA BOWERS EBY, 1 JUNE 1863

A s THE NINETEENTH CENTURY neared its end, the Millbrook Reporter devoted an editorial to the keeping of diaries.[1] It had a jaundiced view in regard to this common habit:

> ...the plan for keeping throughout the year a daily journal in which shall be set down all the trivial routine of one's life is not a good one.

The editorialist was, however, in favour of keeping a journal if the reasons for doing so were the right ones. He suggested four reasonable purposes:

1. a temporary expedient for training one's memory
2. to record a special purpose
3. to remember a special event, such as a trip
4. jotting down in its proper place any remarkable occurrence whose exact date & description may be a matter of interest at a subsequent time.

He had forgotten that most typical of reasons for journal keeping, namely self-improvement.

> I commenced writing this journal thinking that I would make some improvement in writing, but I think it will prove a failure. Well, it may make some improvement in my spiritual welfare. (Diary of Catherine Bell Van Norman, 5 January 1850)

The editorialist's musings have the high-minded quality of much Victorian wisdom, but they neglect the fact that, for most diary-keepers, it is the recording of their own activities which is of primary interest. He does end with the acute observation that "a diary is an intolerable taskmaster, but a very convenient and useful servant."

The writing of journals and diaries during the Victorian era was not only a fashionable pastime, but also served as an important emotional outlet. During this age, when rules of behaviour were firmly entrenched into the pattern of life, very little room was left for free-spirited creatures with nerve enough to test the bounds of respectability. The diary, therefore, often became a way in which writers were able to vent frustrations and record their innermost feelings, without fear of compromising discretion.

> My beautiful new Diary Book! I am ever so pleased with it and have been examining & admiring it for ten minutes. The lock too. My Diaries as Miss Bernard did not need such precautions but then I was an insignificant young spinster & what I might write did not matter now I am a great Premier's wife & Lady Macdonald & "Cabinet Secrets & mysteries" might drop or slip off unwittingly from the nib of my pen. that is they might do so—if my pen had any nib or if I knew any cabinet secrets which I certainly don't. but then a locked diary looks consequential & just now, I am rather in that line myself…Well in this house the atmosphere is so awfully political that sometimes I think the very flies hold Parliament on the kitchen table clothe!…(Diary of Lady Macdonald, 5 July 1867)

The diary not only enabled the writer to work through difficult personal times, but also permitted criticism of others without fear of repercussion.

This evening Daniel Zimmer brought me a letter and paper from the post, sent by Jacob. I was greatly pleased with the contents of his letter. Some surprising news such as "received a letter from Eliza Jane a little more than a week ago." Who ever heard of such a thing as a would be young lady writing a letter to a young man without the solicitation of doing so? When will girls learn to be wise? It appears to me that girls are becoming more silly every day, instead of wiser as they ought to. (Diary of Matilda Bowers Eby, 17 March 1863)

Most diarists tried to write a few lines each day. However some led such busy lives that they were not able to do so.

I have intended keeping a Diary ever since I came to Port Arthur in July, but have neglected doing so. I have had so many pleasant days and evenings amusements that I wanted to keep a note of them so that I might enjoy them again in the reading of them. (Diary of Belle Kittredge, 2 December 1891 [first entry])

No matter who the diarist was, the activity presented an opportunity for unburdening the mind, as well as providing a space in which thoughts could be collected and the difficulties of life worked out.

Again I sit down to make note of a few particulars that have transpired and also a few stray thoughts, that may happen to come in my mind. It is a great comfort to me, to have you my diary to confide in. To you I can tell my thoughts, without fear. (Diary of Matilda Bowers Eby, 9 July 1863)

The reasons for keeping a diary were as varied as the women who wrote them. Lady Macdonald perhaps thought it important for her to do so because of her position of great distinction as the Prime Minister's wife. Others may have thought the effort worthwhile since they enjoyed sharing their diaries with friends.

I will have to take my journal down to Caledonia with me for I am going to let Em see mine and she is going to let me see her journal. (Diary of Hattie Bowlby, 5 May 1874)

In fact, Marion Chadwick wrote "public property" in large letters on the front of each volume of her frank and funny diary. There is evidence inside that other family members read it, commented on it and may even have written in it too—a communal record.

For Mary Brown, the diary was a mixture of account book and domestic memorandum. Victoria Campion registered her longing for friendship, while Annie Cragg recorded her household accomplishments, pausing only occasionally to note the emotional side, as when no one remembered her birthday. When her sister left the family home, and when her cat died, the personable Emma Laflamme wrote about the events in heartfelt honesty. The personal nature of all the entries allows the modern reader to hear the voice of the long-dead writer. Even in the brief entries of Margaret Emma Griffiths' farm journal, there is a sense of the woman behind the pen. These diarists will remind us of the varied natures, interests and lives which were theirs.

There is the danger of thinking that all women in nineteenth century Ontario led lives of domesticity only. There were always women whose circumstances led them down different paths, sometimes ones exciting or demanding in other ways.[2]

Anna Loretta Gallivan (formerly Carey) was married for only 34 hours when her husband died. She was a dressmaker in Ottawa for her entire working life. Photo by S.J. Jarvis, Ottawa. *Author's collection*

Amelia July, for example, spent her days in the early 1860's plying the Great Lakes (Ontario and Erie), the Welland Canal and the Detroit River aboard the Brig 'Mayflower', where she acted as Cook. Her husband Peter was Captain. The remainder of the crew were men. She received $156 per year, paid intermittently, perhaps only when the brig made money itself. Her husband's salary was $480.[3]

Emma Cooper of Oshawa, whose father died soon after the family arrived in Canada in 1873, was brought up by an aunt and uncle. She never married and had to find outside work for her living. She was employed at a furrier's in the winter, and in summer in a canning factory, where she rose to forewoman.

After her husband's death in the early 1860's, Mary Rau of New

Hamburg continued to operate the family brewery.

The keeping of small stores, especially those selling baked goods or candy, was an alternative which required a great deal of work. Often the children were able to assist in this enterprise.

Peter Susand died c.1863 and his widow, Elizabeth who was white, opened a candy and fancy goods store. Her sons also helped to support the large family by selling pop and ginger beer at picnics. Mrs. Susand became a well-known business woman because of her molasses taffy, which was known as "Susand's Taffy" and a favourite of the local children.[4]

Clearly, Amelia July, Emma Cooper and Elizabeth Susand were not stereotypical Victorian shrinking violets. We have discovered that most of the diarists you will encounter here were not, either.

As the century neared its close, the growth of office work opened a new door for women who wanted or needed to work outside the home. The position of "type-writer," as a stenographer or secretary was called, was felt to be suitable. Many young women took advantage of the new technology to start themselves on an adventurous path. For Belle Kittredge, it meant moving from Strathroy to Port Arthur to work in a relative's office. She soon became quite proficient.

> Yesterday I made my first fee outside the office. I wrote 35 letters on the type-writer for Mr Maitland for 1.00. That is far below regulation price of 10c a folio, but I was glad to get the dollar. (Diary of Belle Kittredge, 17 May 1892)

For Belle, her earnings as an office worker were to pave the way to the university education which was her dream. She longed to teach kindergarten using the Montessori method, and eventually realized her ambition.

Edith Bowlby of Windsor received a letter discussing the future of an unmarried cousin, who was also taking advantage of new technology, this time in photography.

> Ethel is again at Dr Ball's office & does her retouching there so she "Killing two birds with one stone." She takes charge of Mr Simpson's (the photographer's) books & office & will also do the office & will do the retouching as well there by obtaining a good salary.[5]

For the majority of women, however, life ran along fairly traditional lines. The Barrie Magnet offered this male-dominated view of what a woman's life should be:

A Receipt for a Wife

As much of beauty as preserves affection—
As much of cheerfulness as spurns dejection—
Of modest diffidence, as claims protection;
A docile mind, subservient to correction;
Yet afor'd with sense, with reason and reflection;
and every passion held in due subjection;
Just faults enough to keep her from perfection;
Find this, my friend, and make your selection.[6]

The simpering and lifeless person drawn in these lines does not appear in the writings we found. Society restricted the diarists with a great many rules, but their writings show them to be people living by their own clear vision. Their concerns, as reflected in correspondence and diaries, were very much taken up with the business of daily life. During the early and mid-Victorian years, many Ontarians were still living a pioneering style of life. Women were predominantly preoccupied with the home, food and the health of their families, tasks which left little time for frivolities. Later on, as people gained a degree of financial stability, life became more sophisticated and women were presented with more options.

Courtship and Wedding

Love—A sweet contagion, which attacks people with great severity between eighteen and twenty-two. Its promontory symptoms are sighs, ruffled shirts, ringlets, bear's grease, and whiskers. It feeds on moonlight and flutes and looks with horror on "biled pork" or baked beans.
The Spirit of the Age, 15 JUNE 1859

THE MYSTERIES OF LOVE AND ROMANCE have always intrigued us and captivated the imagination. The Victorians were certainly no different in this respect. People found young love both interesting and amusing, as long as it was not too serious. Jokes were made about this topic.[7]

> A girl who had become tired of singleblessedness thus wrote to her intended: 'Dear Jim, come right off if you're comin' at all. Edward Kelderman is insistin' that I shall have him and he hugs and kisses me so continually that I can't hold on much longer.'

Real life, of course, provided its own humour, and most were as quick to sum up an amusing situation as they were to pass judgement on an unsuitable match.

> Young Hilliard Cameron who has matriculated at Christ Church Oxford is staying nominally at "Dundurn" but in reality at the Rectory. He is desperately smitten with Hannah

there—but it is only calf love, he is just 18. That constant "lover" F. Ritchie is awfully far gone in that quarter and I fear it is reciprocated—such taste!! The gentleman actually appeared at Church in a pair of canvas shoes—no better indication is needed of his being a snob. He was roasted about them—did not like it at all. (Diary of Forbes Geddes, 3 August 1862)

Charles Grasett from Berlin here—he is desperately smitten with Hannah who does not reciprocate. (21 August 1862)

Hannah's attractions were perhaps a little uncomfortable for her parents, for in the autumn of 1862 she was sent to visit relations in England for several months. Fred Ritchie did not let her absence keep him away from the Rectory, however, where he was still a constant visitor!

Aggie & I started for Toronto But the weight of aggies love for a young man on board the boat broke the rudder & nearly sunk the boat his was very good looking & if she was standing to minutes he would always make his appearance up behind her especially if she was going up steps I guess he wanted to be there so that if she tumbled down the stairs he would be there to catch her in his arms made extra strong to save his sweet little lady love from harm. It was painful to see him at times his noble lips (Diary of Bertha Harnden, [undated] September 1895)

Because of the long distances and slow transportation, if young folks went out in the evening, they were often not home until day was dawning. In the case of Daisy Brown and Ernest Smith, his visits from London to Hamilton were rare enough that they sat up all night together, and alone, after which he would leave almost directly to catch his train home. We view the Victorians as being so strict, but in this they were not, and sometimes the house or farm work fell by the wayside while they caught up on their sleep.

Sarah told us there was to be a concert at Aylmer. It was twelve miles there...We had a gay time and did not get in until 9 o'clock in the morning. We did not take breakfast untill 1 o'clock in the afternoon. (Diary of Hellen V. Bowlby, 3 July 1867)

At about eight Aaron came. John went out swimming so we were left all alone. (Diary of Matilda Bowers Eby, 27 June 1863)

People were understanding about the requirements of courting couples, perhaps more than we would expect, given the Victorians' reputation of prudishness.

We had a very pleasant evening. Maria & Mr Jarvis got lost after a while. They were in the hall. (Diary of Belle Kittredge, 20 January 1892)

Most young women, however, were fairly cautious regarding their entanglements with the opposite sex. They knew that their behaviour, should it be anything other than exemplary, would become the talk of the town.

After tea, Eby called. We took a stroll down the river as far as the islands where we amused ourselves hunting shells and nice little stones for a short time when we retraced our steps. It was past dusk when came back. We are raising quite a commotion in this illustrious village. (Diary of Matilda Bowers Eby, 9 July 1863)

Some were drilled so thoroughly in the social proprieties that any breach, however inadvertent, caused them genuine upset. In December 1892, Belle Kittredge enjoyed a concert practice and dance at the armouries, but:

When it came time to go home Birdie & I found ourselves going alone. There were not enough men for all and we were the ones alone. I never was in such a position before & never will be again…that night I bawled & the next day if I thought of it I cried. It was terrible. (Diary of Belle Kittredge, 9 December 1891)

Looking back on it a few years later, she wrote in the margin:

this makes me smile now but I won't tear it out

During a Leap year, society pretended to turn a blind eye to women who indulged their romantic inclinations. During such a year it was permissible for a woman to make a proposal of marriage. However, note was certainly taken of the number of engagements which took place.

> February has one day more this year. Leap year seems to have a great effect on the young folk. It is astonishing how many are changing their state, for the better I hope. Single blessedness seems to be a burden to some. I am at a loss to know whether the girls take the advantage of it to such an extent or if the young men are the cause. No doubt both parties are too blame. I sincerely wish them all happiness and joy to the end of their lives. (Diary of Matilda Bowers Eby, 29 February 1864)

Watching the opposite sex has always been a pastime of the young.

> I watched the fellows all after noon but there wasnt one good looking one. (Diary of Bertha Harnden, 26 May 1895)

> didn't do much of anything but watch the men on the road digging post holes they are a rum set and woppers too the master is a nice looking man but hes married like all the rest. (21 June 1895)

Sometimes there were insufficient numbers of young men.

> I went to Fan Varies party last night it was just an evening party. no tea or anything. We had a pretty good time considering there were five boys and ten girls. There are more girls than there is boys in this town. (Diary of Hattie Bowlby, 29 April 1874)

If your friends were popular, comparison with your own chances might make you unhappy. When Bessie Scott's roommate at college was asked to a big campus function, but she was not, Bessie felt all of her nineteen years keenly.

> Mr MacP called on Geen—asked her to go to "Conversat"— she is quite un-decided over the whole affair—dear child, I

feel as if I were some old maid who had long ago gotten over all such things—no body ever wants me to go anywhere. I hope she will have a good time. (Diary of Bessie Mabel Scott, 21 January 1890)

The most elementary of social problems could arise. In the case of Belle Kittredge, she met one of them head-on, refusing to allow it to spoil a happy social occasion with two young men.

We had raw onions for dinner & as we were staying at home helped to empty the dish. After dinner however the telephone called us & it was Mr McKibbon to know if he could come up to see us and bring Mr Schricker. I said we would be glad to see them if they would eat raw onions & he agreed so I went into the kitchen cut up some onion & bread & butter & set on the table for them. When they came I marched them into the dining room & they ate them & *seemed* to enjoy them. Then we adjourned to the drawing room. We played "nap" for a while, had some music & then had some butter-nuts & apples after which we made the two men sweep the floor & shake the cloth (Diary of Belle Kittredge, 6 January 1892)

Some young women managed to maintain an impressive number of male correspondents.

Annie is writing to Dr Bridgman, she is always writing to some feller but you know they are all cousins, quite convenient sometimes. (Diary of Hellen V. Bowlby, 8 June 1867)

Sometimes news of love was not exciting.

she told me that Mr Taylor said there was a Farmer out there that was dead in love with me forget his name. (Diary of Annie Elizabeth Cragg, 2 April 1888)

Most young people naturally felt a certain amount of modesty and even reservation when it came to the art of love. The idea of courting undoubtedly had its attractions. But for many young men, the prospect may have been a little intimidating. It is not clear whether the following item was kept as a joke or for instructional purposes.

Whichever the case, it interested John Perrin sufficiently to copy it, perhaps from a newspaper, into his journal in November 1862. He was twenty at the time.

> People will kiss yet not one in a hundred knows how to extract bliss from lovely lips, any more than they know how to make diamonds from charcoal. And yet it is easy, at least for us: First know whom you are to kiss. Don't make a mistake, although a mistake may be good. don't jump up like a trout for a fly, and smack a woman on the neck, on the ear, or on the corner of her forehead, on the end of the nose, or knock off her waterfall [hairpiece]. The gentleman should be a little the tallest. He should have a clean face, a kind eye, and a mouth full of expression. don't kiss everybody. don't sit down to it; stand up. You need not be anxious about getting in a crowd. Two persons are plenty to corner and catch a kiss: more persons spoil the sports. Take the left hand of the lady in youre right; let your hat go up—any place out of the way; throw the left hand gently over the shoulder of the lady, and let it fall down the right side toward the belt. Don't be in a hurry; draw her gently, lovingly to your heart. Her head will fall lightly upon your shoulder and a handsome sholder strap makes! Don't be in a hurry; send a little life down your left arm. Her hand is in your right. Let there be an impression to that, not like a grip of a vice, but a gently clasp, full of electricity, thought, and respect. Don't be in a hurry. her head lies carelessly on your shoulder. Your nearly heart to heart look down into her half closed eyes. Gently brave, but don't be in a hurry. Her lips are almost open. Lean lightly forward, with your head not the body. Take good aim; the lips meet—the eyes close. The heart opens—the soul rides the storm; Troubles and sorrows of life [disappear]. don't be in a hurry. Heven opens before you. the world shoot under your feet as a meetor flashes across the evening sky don't be afraid the nerves dance before the erected alter of love as Zephyrs dance with the dew trimmed flowers the heart forgets its bitterness and the art of kissing is learned. No fuss no noise fluttering and squirming like hook impaled worms. Kissing dont hurt it dont require a brass band to make it legal.[8]

Age was never a barrier when it came to flirtation. Although it may have caused momentary embarrassment to the participants, it provided great entertainment to observers.

> Still day we cannot *get out* It is quite amusing to see how attentive Mr Neugent is to Mrs. Moberly more tender than a sons attentions & she seems delighted with him. this evening they were both sitting *in* the *seat* which has long been called the flirting chair when Agnes was cruel enough to inform them of its name. Mrs. M. said she never has been a flirt & would not be one in her old age. Mr Neugant remarked as he tenderly pressed her to remain "when you are old" she sat down quite on the edge of the seat & far away from him & it took three moves for her to get quite comfortable by his side & to commence a most interesting conversation about the creases in the palms of each others hands to tell their fortunes by but I thought the eyes told them much better. (Diary of Mary Hallen, 18 December 1851)

Those who speculated on the possibility of this relationship developing into something serious were not disappointed. Five months later the Hallens learned of an interesting piece of news.

> Yesterday we called on the Miss Hodgetts they told us they have heard from their father who is in Toronto that Mrs. Moberly & Mr Nugent are going to be married (Diary of Mary Hallen, 14 May 1852)

Mary Hallen seldom lost her composure, but a romantic gesture caught her off guard on this occasion.

> Mr J. had a rose in his button hole which he gave my Mother to smell he afterwards gave it to me & I very composedly took it & put it in the glass with the other flowers which caused them all to laugh very much & me to blush he modestly said it would last as long as the rememberance of Mr Jane. (3 July 1851)

When a large garrison of soldiers, including a number of wealthy English officers, came to Hamilton in 1862, it caused no end of excitement in town.

She has caught the Military infection now raging in Hamilton—and who can wonder at it—The Officers form the almost sole topic of conversation—and each fair one dreams of her chance (however small) of becoming a Soldier's bride. (Diary of Forbes Geddes, 16 March 1862)

Phipps-Geddes wedding, Hamilton, 1868. *Hamilton Public Library*

The first union between an officer and a Hamilton woman was the source of much interest, especially as the bride was the daughter of William P. McLaren, a wealthy grocery wholesaler.

The 1st of the Officers of the "Rifle Brigade" have been "hooked" by a Hamilton girl with a silver hook—Miss Jane McLaren is now the fiancee of Captain Playne. The retired and distinguished ex-seller of sugar and tea gives his darling pounds 1000 in hard cash—her prospects in addition are considerable. She was congratulated right and left...(Diary of Forbes Geddes, 9 July 1862)

At Jane's wedding later that year, upwards of three hundred guests danced in a tent with a board floor set up in the back yard of the McLarens' house. The honeymoon was spent in Niagara Falls, New York City and with the captain's family in Gloucestershire.

In fact the town was wedding-mad. Every action of the affianced parties was noted by society.

Miss Minnie Margaretta Mills was married to Major Dillon of the 30th Regt by the Rector of Christ Church today. Hannah & Kitty Mills were bridesmaids. Capts Singleton & Brock of the 30th best men. There was a clergyman at 12 o'clock. Some interest (more than ordinary) was exhibited to witness the ceremony there being some doubt whether the gentleman would come up to scratch having on more than one previous occasion jilted his fiancee. The church was crammed. (Diary of Forbes Geddes, 17 June 1862)

Miss Street married at Church of Ascension—a Choral Service—the usual interest displayed by a host of forlorn spinsters, who no doubt pray their turn may come next. (11 September 1862)

A mother had mixed feelings when it came to the marriage of her last daughter.

Sabbath at home. reading all day my eyes are a little better. much anxiety of mind about different things, none immediately belonging to myself. Maryan fixing to get married, the last of our Girls my children likely to be far away from me. all those things are against me. however, I am determind, God being my helper, to submit with resignation to His devine will, all things. this is and has been the most remarkable winter I ever remember. (Diary of Eliza Bellamy, 20 January 1855)

Pleasant weather Tuesday 20th Maryan Bellamy has married

to James Dowling in the presence of her nearest connection by the Rev'd R Boyd of Prescott. Our Company number'd about 50 every thing pass'd off well. at 12 Oclock prayer and the company dispersed. next morning, felt very tired, however much was to be done. (22 February 1855)

Fathers often did not consider the promising bachelor quite good enough for their daughter—no matter what her own view of the matter might be. His approval being essential, they were forced to wait.

Bella's engagement with Wilkinson remains "in status quo." Allan wont give swain a decided answer. (Diary of Forbes Geddes, 5 October 1862)

When Adam Brown was asked for permission to marry his daughter Daisy, he refused on the grounds that the man had no house nor prospect of one. The suitor wisely won over the prospective bride's older brother, and a few weeks later tried his luck again. This time he was successful, and Adam Brown wrote to his son Frazer in Montana on 12 June 1889:

I gave my consent to her lover Mr E B Smith of London provided he won her, he has a good grocery business in London retail & jobbing, does $160,000. his brother supplies him with most of his goods. he puts $3000 in Daisy's name & $7000 he has yet to get from his Father's Estate also in her name—he insured his life for $10,000 & put that in her name.[9]

A wedding settlement of this magnitude would have been the lot of only a very few brides.

In fact, parents or guardians could make the progress of any romance difficult simply by preventing the parties from meeting or by obvious disapproval when they were together. The comfort of young peoples' lives was so dependent on their elders.

Josephine Ketchum of Colborne had no mother to guide her and her father was frequently absent on business. Her aunt ran the house in which she lived, and she was not sympathetic when Josie's heart turned to a young man she calls "W.L.R." Josie's diary entries are very brief, but she makes a note of everything she hears of W.L.R.

W.L.R.'s birthday (21) (Sent him a card) (Diary of Josephine Ketchum, 11 January 1886)

Thought I saw W.L.R. but guess I must have been mistaken. (15 February 1886)

Emily told me W.L.R. is coming to town to-morrow. (28 March 1886)

W.L.R. has not arrived yet. (30 March 1996)

W.L.R. comes to town. (21 April 1886)

W.L.R. calls to say good-bye—he goes by the evening train. (22 April 1886)

I hear that W.L.R. has come but I don't know if it is true. (12 May 1886)

W.L.R. calls in afternoon. (19 May 1886)

Went to church twice and played the organ. Saw W.L.R. in church also H. (23 May 1886)

W.L.R. call & asks me to go driving with him but I refuse by necessity— (25 May 1886)

I'm in Em's & Aunt's & Gran's black books all the time about W.L.R. but I don't care. (29 May 1886)

W.L.R. comes down in afternoon. (31 May 1886)

W.L.R. comes down and brings me a bit of Mozart that I admire (7 June 1886)

W.L.R. comes down in afternoon & we have a little practise. (i.e., on the piano; 10 June 1886)

W.L.R. goes away to Toronto. comes down in afternoon. (11 June 1886)

Pack my things in trunk ready for Toronto. Go by seven train & get there 11.30. (15 June 1886)

Invitation & call from WLR (16 June 1886)

home by 8 train. WLR & JDT at station also P. Smith & Herby. (18 June 1886)

WLR decides had better steer clear of me & I agree. very hard though. Practise at Miss Will's in afternoon. Play tennis at the Griers in evening. Deuced cross! By Jove! (28 June 1886)

WLR goes to Toronto. I get a terrible rowing up by aunt because WLR turned the lamp down. (7 July 1886)

WLR arrives home. (17 July 1886)

I miss somebody very much. (21 July 1886)

Perhaps her interest in WLR was not too serious, for she begins to notice another young man and WLR is not mentioned for a time.

TDJ arrives (19 July 1886)

Have not yet seen TDJ (21 July 1886)

I have a big flirtation with a certain Mr. Heart just to tease Goo who is as cross as a bear. In some ways I have been horrid to TDJ & am reaping my reward a very sore heart. (22 July 1886)

See TDJ at a distance but he could not come across the road it is too far. (24 July 1886)

See TDJ at a distance. (25 July 1886)

The summer romance is only temporary, for WLR returns to Colborne.

W.L.R. arrives home & brings some gent with him. (4 August 1886)

See W.L.R. at the gate for a minute. (25 August 1886)

Go to cricket match. WLR walks home with me & comes in for few minutes. Aunt raises a row cause I ask him to bring my music. (18 September 1886)

On that unhappy note WLR disappears from the diary. A few weeks later, Josie died at the age of 18.

Proposals of marriage were received with great joy, providing they came from the right quarter. However, sometimes a young woman was not quite certain of her feelings. Matilda Bowers did not immediately consent to marry Dr. Aaron Eby. But she did not take too long to decide, for they were married almost a year to the day later.

This morning I got up rather late, and then I did not feel so good as if I had gone to bed two hours earlier and got up so much sooner. Keeping iregular hours puts me out of time considerably. Fanny went away soon after breakfast. Eby stayed, to wait on a Gentleman with whom he intended to go out electioneering, but was disappointed. It commenced to rain at nine o'clock. Jacob was in the store with John so Eby and myself had matters all by ourselves. He watched a favourable opportunity, when he asked me if I would marry him. I informed him, that that was a very serious question. He said he did not expect me to answer it right away but on some future occasion. It made me feel very strange for awhile in fact it affected me more than I thought anything of that kind ever would. But any modest girl would blush at having such a question put to her. Something of such serious nature is not to be treated lightly. I gave him some encouragement. (Diary of Matilda Bowers Eby, 30 May 1863)

Siblings or other relatives were not above adding their two cents worth when it came to forming an opinion of a new "beau."

Mr S was telling Mother he was in love with Frank [her sister]. He is 6ft 5 & looks more. (Diary of Annie Elizabeth Cragg, 26 January 1888)

As we hear no more of this suitor, Frances Cragg must not have reciprocated. He was wise to start by talking to the mother, however.

Jack surprised us by announcing his engagement to Aymis Hewat. He is a foolish boy as she is much older than he is & very delicate & he has not known her quite two months. Of course it is not received very cordially by any of us as it is so utterly absurd. (Diary of Avice Watson, 29 November 1886)

…Our fears are realized & Bertie has confirmed his engagement to Mary Parsons. Mama heard all about it from them both on Sunday. Poor boy I pity him most heartily. (16 January 1888)

On the other hand, the Hallen family were thrilled when their son, Skeeter, announced his engagement to Elizabeth Mary Fitton.

Miss F and Skeeter went for a long walk and it ended in their being engaged; we are all so pleased. (Diary of Sarah Hallen Drinkwater, 23 January 1863)

Superstitions flourished when it came to matters matrimonial.

Well I do believe something is going to turn up, for I heard Miss Pusey was going, to be married Wednesday and Bell Mc-Call be bridesmaid. Bell better be careful, this is the third time and the old saying is "three times a bridesmaid, never a bride." (Diary of Hellen V. Bowlby, 21 May 1867)

A woman was able to break off the engagement without explanation. People would talk, of course, but she did not have to give a reason. If she did it too often, however, she would get a reputation.

Ellen Grasset Powell of Niagara, who danced so often with the Prince of Wales during his Canadian tour was married to John Ogilvee, merchant, of Montreal, on 30 January. It was her 3rd or 4th Engagement she was a desperate flirt. (Diary of Forbes Geddes, 5 February 1862)

Miss Hill returns from Scotland with her trousseau and will soon be married to Mr Lethbridge of North Douro. Her friend Miss M. Counsell has forgotten her old love, Mr Lane in less than a year and in December will be married to Ed

Martin, Lawyer. It is, in a worldly point of view a better match than the other but is only another instance of woman's inconsistency. (Diary of Forbes Geddes, 1 October 1862)

As with most young people of her time, Marion Chadwick went to church twice most Sundays (morning and evening), often at different places. In the morning, you attended your own congregation, but in the evening you could "try out" other places, not only for the religious reasons but also for who you might see and what you might hear.

In the evening Mrs. Muntz gave a sitonthegrassandtalkto-yourpartnertillthebellringsandthenchangeplaces party. It was awfully Jolly & afterwards we took a walk on the breakwater to the light of the moon that was behind a cloud. (Diary of Marion Chadwick, 11 August 1892)

...& then "Oh bliss!" we went for our first ride in the new electric cars down Church St—it really was most exciting...walked home the beach way "to meet the men coming home"—that is not my innocent little thought—we didn't meet any of course. D_ _ the luck. (31 August 1892)

I went to Methodist Church in forenoon to the S[alvation] A. Army in afternoon to Presbyterian church in evening (Diary of Fanny Goodfellow, 21 December 1891)

When interest was piqued, life offered excitement.

About two weeks ago little Jont and Long Tom were up here visiting, just two of the nicest chaps you ever did see, especially Jont who I expect to see a good deal after this year, but dont tell anyone. (Diary of Hellen V. Bowlby, 1 May 1868)

I enjoyed the afternoon very much on the whole. In the evening John went to Singing School Mr Eby accompanied me home, stayed till John came. He told me a few things that astonished me a little. (Diary of Matilda Bowers Eby, 17 May 1863)

One story told over the years was of the daughter of a Presbyterian elder who refused to come down (to the parlor) to the waiting bridegroom. Besides all the virtues demanded of an elder, her father was known for his perfect truthfulness and his perfect courtesy. But he was painfully tried at market the following Saturday when a neighbour woman said, "Tell me, Mr. X. why wouldn't Mary Ellen come down to be married?" "Well, Mrs. Y.Z.," he replied slowly, "You've done more than I did. For I never asked."

Such living consideration was Mary Ellen's good fortune throughout life. For next year, when she was ready, the same bridegroom who had been left standing in the parlour the year before married her.[10]

Women who were thought to be marrying for money did not escape criticism. The Hallen and Moberly families did much socializing together. So when a Moberly girl married into aristocracy, everyone was filled with tremendous curiosity.

> Mary Sarah Moberly married to James Jones Bridges, baronet; they say she is just marrying him for his title and money, what a dreadful thing. There were five brides maids. Sir B. has settled pounds 500 a year on the bride, poor thing. (Diary of Sarah Hallen Drinkwater, undated [June 1854])

Sarah's sister, Mary Hallen, also made note of this event in her diary, having learned details of the wedding from her younger sister, Agnes, who apparently was one of the wedding guests.

> Agnes has enjoyed herself very much & all the rest of the party excepting the poor Bride, it must be a melancholy thing for her marrying without love has she as done. I can conceive nothing more dreadful, but peoples tastes are not all the same & I have heard some people say that those sort of matches turn out happyer than love marriages but I cannot fancy it & think it far too great an experiment to be tried but I do not know what business I have to think any thing about it but I think I am becoming a regular old Gossip. The ceremony took place on the 10th in the morning. There were between 40 & 50 people present. Mr Ardagh began by publishing the bans of marriage between Harford James Jones Brydges Baronet, Bachelor & Mary Sarah Moberly, Spinster. who ever heard of such a thing & the unfortunate creatures had to say

all those tiresome names in the ceremony. There were 5 Bridesmaids dressed some in white & some in pink. The Bride wore a white watered silk dress with a [illegible] bonnet of the same with orange flowers & white roses under it. After, an elegant breakfast at Mrs. Moberly's Sir Ashford proposed that all the party should accompany them to the [illegible] landing on bord the boat they accordingly did & had a merry journey in spite of the rain they danced on the lower deck Mr Ardagh permitted the Miss Ardaghs to join in the [illegible] dance" which was wonderful as he entirely disapproves of it. Sir Hartford has settled 500 a year on his wife. (Diary of Mary Hallen, 10 September [year not indicated])

Young women would put away a few things toward the day when they would be mistress of a house themselves.

I also got a letter from Julia explaining the present she sent. she sent a pair of kid mittens for Birdie & one for me. In one of mine there were two solid silver teaspoons. I suppose she is thinking when I start housekeeping for myself I will have some silver spoons to begin with. (Diary of Belle Kittredge, 26 December 1891)

Widowers, left with a number of small children to look after, were usually anxious to find another bride.

Mrs. Ross' funeral sermon is this morning. the service must be nearly through as it is now half past eleven—a number of cutters have passed by but I do not think it is quite through as the bell would surely toll if it were. What a number of mourners there will be—Mrs. R had so many cousins. Already some have mentioned the Widow Suffield as a probable Successor, but I must say his former conduct gave rise to talk & I presume people think he will court in haste again. (Diary of Emma Laflamme, 27 March 1888)

Often a second marriage worked well, but sometimes it did not. Mary Hallen and W.A.R. Gilmour, M.D., a widower, were married on 13 January 1875. Mary was then fifty-six years old and had not been married previously. The marriage did not last. Although one seldom learns the true reason for marriage failure, one might speculate that, in this case, inheriting such a large family may have contributed towards some degree of marital stress.

> Mary was married to Dr. Gilmour. Tom drove me up to the wedding; it took place on Jan. 13th. Dr Gilmour is a widower with 2 girls and 5 sons. (Diary of Sarah Hallen Drinkwater, 5 April 1875)

Extract from a letter by Sumner:—
> "The Dr. found her very hard to spark, her heart seemed impervious to Cupid's bow, for it took 2 years to accomplish it. 999 men out of 1000 would have thrown up the sponge in despair long before that time, but I suppose he kept the saying fresh in his memory 'faint heart never won fair lady.' "[11]

> My father has left Penetang; I forgot to mention Mary has returned to my Father as no longer living with Dr. Gilmour. (Diary of Sarah Hallen Drinkwater, 9 September 1876)

Mary Hallen may have endured an unhappy marriage before returning to her Father's home, but so far, no diary recording this period of her life has been found. Mary did however make note of an acquaintance who found herself in a very awkward predicament.

> Mrs. Frazer called & spent the day. The Miss Atteralls came & I finished their likenessess. Poor Mrs. Frazer is looking very thin. She feels Mr Frazers conduct very much he does not treat her as his wife but is living with another woman who he was married to last Summer in the States. (27 March 1850)

In the weeks before her sister's wedding in the fall of 1886, Emma Laflamme's attention turned to that perennial topic, "What shall I wear?"

> I'll be left as they say unless I hasten my work for there is my dress to make. I dare not bring it out until Kate leaves for being light colored would wake suspicions. I do not apprehend any difficulty with that unless fitting waist and lace trimming will cover wrinkles & such like. (Diary of Emma Laflamme 1 September 1886)

Finished lace last week and it is beautiful. Have commenced dress. shirt is nearly done an hours work will finish it.
(5 September, 1886)

Sent for cream gloves to Mary (15 September 1886)

Should I wear some color to relieve my cream dress? And what? (17 September 1886)

Mary sent me postal last night asking for sample of shade for gloves, I stupidly forgot to send it, so I wrote again & sent money for ribbon or some thing to wear at my neck. (19 September 1886)

I gave my present to Maggie Friday while we were alone, the next three days the house will be full-lace for her neck & sleeves and a $10 bill. Am making her too, a couple of brack-

Louise Ewart in her wedding gown, 1874. *Archives of Ontario*

ets but I could not possibly finish them in time.(19 September 1886)

Finally the big day itself arrived, and Emma gave a full description:

M. was married Wednesday Sept 22nd at about half past six P.M. A few moments before that time Wes took his place in front of sitting room window then Maggie came through sitting room door leaning on papas arm & was led to Wes' side. they were married under a horseshoe of white flowers by Rev. Mr McDonald of Osmond. M. had on white dress of India muslin heavily trimmed with oriental lace & point lace at neck—orange blossoms at neck and hair, veil of illusion, white kids [kid gloves], white lisle thread stockings & white satin slippers—Wes in black suit white tie & kids—We had supper shortly after ceremony—table was prettily decorated with flowers—we had cold sliced pressed chicken, cold sliced ham, pickles & catchup. Apple jelly tarts, raspberry & strawberry preserves, chocolate & cocoanut layer cakes, cornstarch cake, Spanish buns, bride's & wedding cake. Coffee & tea—pears & grapes. Shortly after supper M changed her dress for a travelling one of blue cloth, trimmed with striped plush—with jacket to match, hat of blue felt trimmed with striped ribbon & a wing, blue kids, Ed drove happy pair to Morrisburg in cab—they started about 9 P.M. to catch midnight train for West taking in Chicago, Toronto, Minneapolis & St Paul. (4 October 1886)

A few weeks later, she lists the wedding gifts:

28 Nov 1886: it may be pleasant to refer to—
Father—Bridal trousseau,
Mother—cream shawl,
Emma —Point lace & $10,
Edwin —Silver cake basket,
Walter—hand-satchel,
Auntie —glass rolling pin,
Will—silver breakfast cruet,
Ella —satin mantel drape in silk embroidery,
Gertie—satin & plush tidy in silk embroidery,

Minnie—carver's cloth and tray cloth,
Lizzie & Mary Ruby—glass fruit dish set in silver,
Auntie R.—1 doz. solid silver teaspoons,
Auntie C.—teapot, sugar bowl, & cream pitcher in majolica
ware,
Lucy—salt cellar of ruby glass set in silver,
Hugh & Loraine—silver individual cruet & amber glass
pitcher,
Charlie —2 silver napkin rings,
Archie—breakfast cruet,
Albert—silver butter dish,
Cassy—red plush dressing case,
Ida—perfume case,
Miss McLean—set table mats,
Lucy McI.—silver napkin ring

In those more frugal days, wedding gifts were simpler, a handful of treasured items which would always have pride of place in the best parlour. If you had a relation who was well off, you might find your-self receiving a wedding gift of some munificence.

My sister was so kind to them. She gave them a nice parcel, table and fancie chairs (Diary of Jessie Geddes, 12 September 1899)

Matilda Bowers Eby was filled with joyful anticipation as preparations commenced for her brother's wedding.

After dinner we set out for Berlin to make some investment. Mary [the bride] bought a splendid Poplin dress for nine dol-lars. A wedding dress, she also ordered a bonnet with Miss Feik. I had intended to invest in a bonnet but did not find one to suit my taste. We were in every store in town and could not find such articles as we wanted. (Matilda Bowers Eby, 3 De-cember 1863)

This A.M. Mary made her Bridal Wreath. I teased her consid-erably about it but she takes it cool. I pitched into my bonnet, had it done by three o'clock. Mary was kind enough to get dinner. She wanted to see the finishing touch on my bonnet before leaving. I tried to persuade her to stay till tomorrow but all of no avail. She gave us an excuse that she was afraid I would give her a pounding as tomorrow is her twenty-first birthday. After she was gone I went over to Mrs. Tagge and got some ribbons for ties on my bonnet. When I got back Uncle Cowan was in the store. He wanted me to tell him when John is going to get married. He must consider me green if he thought I would give him the desired information. I showed him my bonnet, he said it is magnificent, but several stories too high. (16 December 1863)

Whether or not Uncle Cowan attended John Bowers' wedding is not clear. Matilda did, and wrote about the day.

The long looked for day has come and passed with all its merry gaiety. A little after nine o'clock Joseph and Maria came to fetch us to the church. I went to Mr Turks [the preacher] to meet John, Mary and Daniel Ruby. We went up to the church together. The church was already crowded. I liked the sermon very much. I think it the best I ever heard preached. After the sermon was over the Rev. came down on the platform & Mr Ruby, as he was to act as Groomsman. I for my part did not feel very much flattered by their choosing him for my partner. He is a young man whose company I never cared for, in fact don't like. I think it is very nice to see them married in church. Mr Tuerk's way of marrying is very short it occupies but very little time to get the knot tied. They are a fine looking couple, they made a nice appearance. I sincerely hope they may be as well matched in mind as in outward appearance. May they live a good and happy life and may God's blessings rest upon them evermore. After all was over, those invited all went up to Mr Seiler's to partake of a sumptuous wedding dinner. Father, Mother and Minnie went home so that things might be in order to receive the company at home in the evening. They had a splendid table. I was surprised to see such a beautiful wedding cake. I never saw one that was so nicely finished and that looked so rich. A little after four, all the young folk started for Sweet Briar. [The family home]. Jacob stopped and called for Lizzie as he had promised her. At about seven we had our tea table arranged.

Mary brought the cake with her whole, I was glad she did because it was quite an ornament on the table. We had a very
jolly time over it. Mr Ruby kept the company in a laughing fit
nearly all the time with his witty sayings, while we were par-
taking of the good things. At Eleven o'clock the company separated. John took his bride home with him so my presence is
needed no more and I am not much sorry. This was most a
beautiful day not a cloud dimmed the calm azure vault of
heaven. Sleighing is very good, for so very little snow as there
is. (25 December 1863)

The Bowlby sisters in Port Dover were very excited at the prospect of
their cousin Martha's marriage to a widowed doctor. Any romance in
the family was of the greatest interest, but as they were all dazzled by
the 'fellers' themselves, they wanted to know what Martha had
caught.

I hope we will see the doctor when we go down to Walpole I
expect he will be a sight to be seen for I have heard so much
about him. I expect we will be disappointed in him for I have
imagined how he looks and I suppose he will look different
from what I expect. (Diary of Louisa Bowlby, 9 January 1862)

the Dr and Martha came up Tuesday evening and went to Mr
Pikerson's with us. We spent a very pleasant evening. O! the
Dr how hombly he is. I was never so disapointed in the looks
of a person in my life. You have always some fancy how they
look but I was knocked under when I saw him & so was Dora
disapointed and she said she did not know he was so little,
old, a widower with two children. But I guess hombly folks
are always good. (23 January 1862)

We were all down to uncle Lewis's to dinner saturday last...
we had great fun going down talking and criticising the Dr.
(27 January 1862)

Yesterday we all went to the wedding. We had a glorious time
and saw Martha married for sure. Mr Roy married them. We
had the dinner passed around but we had a splendid dinner.
Let me see if I could tell how the ceremony was done. When

we first went there we were met at the door by Mr. Roy. Then we went to the bedrooms and took off our things. and (fixed a little of course) came out into the parlour. As soon as we got seated Uncle Lewis brought Martha in & Mr. Lacy brought Mima in then the Dr. took Martha and Mr Roy went through with the ceremony. Mima pulled off Martha's kid & Mr. Lacy the Dr.'s they joined hands & the minister pronounced them man & wife. We had a prayer & then we raised up (for we were kneeling) & the Dr. kissed his wife & then we kissed all around. I thought I would not kiss the Dr. but I (some how) had to. We had our dinner then Martha & Mima changed their dresses & the bridesmaid & Groomsman went with them as far as the station...Just think how funny & strange Martha Harrison will sound. (5 March 1862)

Martha married Doctor Harrison, not in the brown silk which her cousins condemned, but in a white dress after all. Louisa's later comments seem to verge on sour grapes.

Martha thinks she lives very happy but I do not think it will last long, for she tries to rule to much (27 May 1862)

Old World customs and traditions were often brought to Ontario, and maintained by those who held them dear. The London Evening Advertiser and Family Newspaper reported on "an odd procession" which passed through the streets of Goderich,

"being composed of two couples in wedding rig, in front, and about fifty persons, male and female, old and young, bringing up the rear. The unusual sight created much interest, especially on the part of the ladies; but a party of men and boys, whose reverence for olden customs was exceeded by their sense of the ludicrous hooted after the processionists in a very uncomplimentary manner. The happy bride and bridegroom in prospective however, marched on as bravely as though they expected nothing short of martyrdom when they arrived at church."[12]

Some brides made a point of picking their own flowers.

Our Wedding Day. Up early down in garden gathered flowers helped mother and Kate to dress Got dressed married in church by Mr Allen—left by 10 then spent day in Port Hope had a drive to ML pulman at 10. (Diary of Lillian de Grassi, 5 September 1883)

Or, friends picked a wedding bouquet for them.

Cab calling for me to go to the grounds, where Daisy, B. Smith & Maggie Hobson joined me & we went to gather thistles as a wedding bouquet for Georgina Osler's wedding, but the Scotch motto accompanying it caused Daisy to desist after gathering several and finding the thorns troublesome. (Diary of Mary Brown, 29 August 1892)

The wedding cake was a very important item.

Commenced making a wedding cake: My mother I mean, we helped to mix [illegible] very hard work, baked it in the bake kettle in the dining room. Mr William Darling & Hamilton called, the former staid dinner. George went shooting with Mr John Steele, dined with him, cake out about dusk, very Tiresome my Mother found it icing it, the almond paste worked beautifully. My mother tired. George home late. (Diary of Sarah Hallen Drinkwater, 6 October 1840)

Today has been very cold and stormy. This morning Jenny washed and I took Ruth over to Norrish's and then drove to Ann Eliza's and got some milk. This afternoon we made and baked my wedding cake. (Diary of Ann Amelia Day, 12 February 1879)

We iced my wedding cake with two coats. (15 February 1879)

Wedding cake was traditionally a rich fruit cake. It was expensive, and therefore "special," and kept well.

after we had eaten our cake and drank their healths there were a number of small pieces put through the ring for all whatever young people to put under their pillows to dream on. (Diary of Eleanora Hallen, 26 February 1844)

A bride's cake was often served at weddings, perhaps in addition to the wedding cake. Several kinds of cake would be served, even at a relatively modest wedding, as people were greater cake eaters then than now.

The wedding outfit was a major concern for the bride to be.

> Today has been cold and somewhat snowy. This morning ma and I went to Guelph and got my hat and shoes and gloves. We got home about 3:30 and found cousin Mary Watson here. We met pa just across the railroad on his way to Farish's mill for flour. He got 200 lbs and Mr John Edwards brought it up home for him. (Diary of Ann Amelia Day, 18 March 1879)

Every wedding present would be acknowledged by a personal note of thanks. It was considered to be quite proper for the bride's mother or sister to assist in writing these, but the bride must sign her name to them.

If you lived in the country, mail was a never ending source of hope. You might have a letter from a friend or faraway family member. Families such as the Campions of Marmora township, who were not rich, depended on those in larger centres to send them newspapers, which were read by everyone. Their importance was such that Victoria Campion noted their arrival in her diary. Sometimes the mail brought even more exciting things.

> Received a paper from Miss Hamilton with some wedding cake in it [her cousins] (Diary of Mary Victoria Campion, 19 September 1861)

Young women were encouraged to take a piece of wedding cake and place it under their pillow at night. They were then said to dream of the man they would marry. Perhaps that is what became of the wedding cake delivered to the Hallen sisters after Tom Hodgetts' wedding.

> The Miss Hodgetts called to ask us to spend the evening there they brought a piece of wedding cake & cards which were enclosed in an envelope with two cupids with a ring tying a true lovers knot (*interesting & pretty*) in ribon. It was

kept quite a secret from C Hodgetts but she found the bonnets under Tom's bed by accident they informed us. (Diary
of Mary Hallen, 1 June 1854)

The mail might simply bring news of a wedding.

a letter from "Flo" telling us she is to be *married* the 1st of
March & wants me to act as bridesmaid very much excited
over it. (Diary of Annie Elizabeth Cragg, 4 February 1888)

For, no matter what one said, there was one simple and universal view
of a marrying couple.

Con's wedding was very pretty—she very rosy, he very white
& solemn. (Diary of Helen Grant Macdonald, 8 October
1891)

The flowerlike freshness of the bride was supposed to make her particularly attractive to other men, hence the traditional jealousy of the
newlywed male.

Mrs. Mewburn is a bride and I cannot understand any Bridegroom as well off as hers selecting lodging where 2 or 3 Bach-
elors "hang out." Doubtless he is of a less jealous disposition
than myself. (Diary of Forbes Geddes, 29 July 1862)

The moment a woman married, she acquired a knowledge and respectability which was impossible for the unmarried to achieve. It was
also supposed to end the social awkwardness of the single state, but
that was not true for all.

It was her first ball since she was married. she was very much
afraid of being a wall flower but the men all knew it & so her
programme was filled to the 7th extra. (Diary of Belle Kittredge, 3 January 1892)

Single women were in a difficult position, characterised by the saying
"You're somebody's daughter until you're somebody's wife." That you
might be somebody in your own right seems not to have been considered. Emma Laflamme pondered over this in her diary.

Yesterday Feb. 8th I was twenty-eight, I am becoming quite ashamed of my age. the only consolation being that it is not any thing to be really ashamed of. Why is it that old-maiden-hood is considered little short of a crime. Well it would not do for me to change my condition. I truly believe that the cares and responsibilities of married life would make me wretchedly unhappy. (9 February 1887)

She would certainly not have felt so self-conscious if other people had not treated unmarried women with such condescension and mockery. An attempt to redress the situation in *The Canadian Gem and Family Visitor* for October 1849 merely underlines the problem.

I love an old maid; I do not speak of an individual but of the species—I use the singular number, as speaking of a singularity in humanity. An old maid is not merely an antiquarian, she is an antiquity; not merely a record of the past, but the very past itself; she has escaped a great change, and sympathises not in the ordinary mutations of morality. She is Miss from the beginning of the chapter to the end. I do not like to hear her called mistress, as is sometimes the practice, for that looks and sounds like the resignation of despair, a voluntary extinction of hope. I do not know whether marriages are made in heaven; some people say they are, but I am almost sure that old maids are. There is a something about them which is not of the earth, earthly. They are spectators of the world, not adventurers nor ramblers; perhaps guardians—we say nothing of tattlers. They are evidently predestinated to be what they are. They owe not the singularity of their condition to any lack of beauty, wisdom, wit or good temper; there is no accounting for it but on the principle of fatality. I have know many old maids, and of them all, not one that has not possessed as many good and amiable qualities as nine out of a hundred of my married acquaintances—Why, then, are they single? Heaven only knows. It is their fate![13]

Those who chose to remain single often had to bite their tongues when it came to coping with interference from scheming relatives. Fortunately, Gertrude and Maud Nicholson seemed to take it all in stride.

Aunt Augusta is a very amusing person she is always anxious to get people married she is very much concerned about us two & keeps recommending nice young gentlemen to us. There is one in particular named Howard Duncan (son of Ino Duncan) he is a lawyer in Woodstock. Aunt A. is also much concerned about Fred & bothers him so that now he says he won't come here any more. (Diary of Gertrude Nicholson, 3 June 1896)

How a single woman came to be so unfortunate was a constant source of conversation to the neighbours.

Then there are the two Miss McVickers Two Old maids—Tradition says they were both in love with the same man & neither would give up to the other & I suppose the poor man was scared to choose between them. However they are unmarried tho' have had *many* offers. (Diary of Belle Kittredge, undated, [late January 1891])

The very first wedding celebrated at St. Alban the Martyr church in Ottawa was that of Clara Reiffenstein and James McPherson. The wedding date was 4 December 1867. It was a bitterly cold and snowy day, which caused many guests, including the Prime Minister and Lady Macdonald, to shiver in their pews. However, summer weddings had the opposite danger.

Very busy all day. Arranging flowers etc and writing letters all morning. Dressing from 12 A.M. Miss Medcalfe came at 2 to do my hair. Mrs. Cannon came at 3 to dress me. The ushers & bridesmaids best man & groom came up about 4 and at 4.30 we were busy getting married. It was frantically hot but otherwise a complete success. Church contained enough guests to fill the main part and the nursery was packed with onlookers. Every one was on time—the bride included. She walked up the aisle to the Lohengrin Bridal Chorus—Gladys first, then Louise & Adelaide, then Daddie & I and lastly Vaux & Will Rae. The Bishop wore his scarlet robes. Everything went off beautifully. James said, "I will," too soon. I said, "Shut up it isn't time yet." I didn't do anything except feel hot…Church was decorated with heaps of daisies tied with white satin ribbons, and a sort of little avenue of palms…(It was about

100)…Dining room where our 227 presents were displayed decorated with pink sweet peas and fern…a big tent in the garden seemed to be quite successful. After the guests left all the relations had a sort of high tea in the tent. (Diary of Marion Chadwick, 30 June 1898)

Several hundred guests came to Marion Chadwick's wedding, most of them invited only to the reception at home. She wore a dress of mousseline de soie and white satin, with a century-old Limerick lace veil, and carried white roses. The honeymoon began in a private railway car to Montreal, on the way to visit the groom's family in England.

Marion was following fashion in having Wagner's *Lohengrin* excerpt to enter the church; the usual recessional was Mendelssohn's celebratory wedding march which is still popular today. Most society weddings had the prescribed white dress. But not all, for Marion's cousin was married in dark blue the following December. For brides of lesser means, the wedding dress would be a sensible frock that could be worn again, many times.

For those leaving on a railway honeymoon, a group of friends would come with them to the station.

Three "cabloads" went to the station, also a bunch of men. Grand old sendoff, terribly noisy. Decorated stateroom door (on Pullman car side) with white flowers off the cake. Rice everywhere—outside & in. As train moved off, Jimmie remarked, "Is this what you call a quiet wedding?" (Diary of Marion Chadwick, 20 December 1898)

The Chadwick family celebrated five of these occasions in one year, 1898, with two of them in Christmas week. With the preparations and the social aftermath (detailed in the chapter on Visiting), Marion thought about little else for eighteen months.

Part of the rowdy pleasure of the happy couple's departure involved throwing rice, a traditional symbol of fertility, and old slippers.

The shoes had several meanings. They, too, meant fertility and also good luck, as the wearer passed on their own good fortune to the new pair. In an older meaning, which came from the middle east, the passing of a shoe completed a contract of sale. Thus, the father of the bride indicated his transfer of authority to the groom.

Then, as now, throwing things created a mess but was enormous fun. Barclay Adams attended his cousin's wedding in Trafalgar in 1894.

> I saw Bessie and her groom going on the same train I was going—of course there were some friends on the station to see them off While we were waiting for the train and while I had handfuls of rice ready to throw at Bessie—and I was speaking to Miss Farr—two ladies from Toronto put handfuls of rice into my collar and shirt but I bent myself down and some rice fell off duly lots remained at the back and all friends were laughing saying that I was the next to be married. Then I threw rice after those two ladies. Then we went aboard the train and Bessie was thrown with a shower of rice. As the train was moving Bessie threw a boot out of the window. I had conversation with them until the train stopped at Burlington and I came back to the villa. Then I retired to bed, I found the rice in my socks, a handful of it.[14]

> There was great rice and slipper throwing, you may be sure when we were leaving the house and Douglas and I had to make a rush through it all to the cab.[15]

For the rich, the honeymoon was a matter of course, and usually involved a visit to Europe, or at least New York. For most people, no trip was possible, but a little festivity could be lent to the occasion by making a brief journey. As weddings were expensive, couples would travel to a nearby community to be married, then quietly return. There may have been a family party, but no more general celebration as such. With the advent of the railway, these short journeys became a little more adventuresome. The tradition of the "railway wedding" remained with us until the Second World War.

For lucky couples romance continued on, long after marriage.

> …I was writing away when all of a sudden somebody's lips kissed my cheek. I was astonished but very well pleased when it proved to be my dear kind friend and husband. (Diary of Catherine Bell Van Norman, 7 February 1850)

One of the more interesting happenings after a wedding was the charivari (pronounced "shivaree"). Perhaps on the wedding night or a few days later, a group of young men would prowl in the dark up to the house where the happy couple slept. Using "tin horns, strings of horse-bells, cow-bells, the horse-fiddle, tin pans, copper kettles, and anything and everything else they could find that would make noise enough,"[16] they would waken the couple and generally cause a fuss. Usually the groom would then invite them in for refreshment, or give them money to go to the local tavern.

These affairs tended to be especially rowdy if the participants thought something was unusual in the wedding, most often if the groom were older and the bride very young.

> Charivari,—Another of these riotous brawls which have "many a time and oft," during the year past, "rendered night hideous," in this town and neighbourhood, took place in the upper town, on Wednesday night. The consequence is, that two individuals have been committed to goal, to take their trial at the next Assizes, on a charge which, we are informed, has assumed the nature of a felony. Justice, common decency, and the reputation of the place, demand, that a check should be given to these outrageous proceedings.[17]

According to *Early Pioneer Life in Upper Canada*, some grooms resented the young men's enthusiasm, and refused entry. There were even violent incidents. Once the rough edges of pioneer days wore away, however, these parties settled into a happier pattern, which included both men and women. The noisy neighbours easily gained entrance, where a regular party (and dance) was held. The newlyweds came to expect the visit and the whole community participated. It was a rite of passage for the young people, showing that they had changed their status with their neighbours, and everyone accepted them in their new roles.

The practice of the charivari was widespread in rural Ontario well into the twentieth century. (One of the present authors attended a charivari in Manvers township in the early 1960s.) The practice of this raffish, but fun, amusement was so common that the name was given to a popular Canadian magazine of the Victorian age.

> The girls went on the Lilian to Huntsville. The new married couple Mr & Mrs. Cadieux arrived at 6 a.m. Edith came in the afternoon & told me about the wedding & seems very happy. In the evening the people (about 125) gave them a chararivi. (Diary of Mary Coldwell Butcher, 6 July 1918)

Once the celebrating ceased, it was time for the newlyweds to begin learning to live happily together. Work was resumed, routines were established, babies arrived, and occasionally there would be the enjoyment of the wedding celebrations of others.

As with the rest of life, there were many rules surrounding courtship. Young women had to be very careful lest their reputations suffer. There was always the possibility that an unscrupulous man would toy with their affections and then abandon them, to the detriment of their future prospects. As protection, there was a law which stated that a woman who had been promised marriage by a man could not be overthrown without penalty. The law was called Breach of Promise of Marriage.

In 1873 a young man named George Washington Ray ran the livery stable in Ayr, and boarded with a family named Hall. He and the daughter of the house, Margaret Hall, had an understanding, but in September of that year he married her first cousin, Catherine Rose. The case caused a breach between the families. Robert Hall, brought an action for Breach of Promise against George Ray.

The reaction of the community can be summed up in the words of Jane Pringle, whose family was connected with the Halls and Roses:

> Young Katy is going to be married to George Ray the mail driver. That is him that Margaret Hall was to get. Her father is going to come on him for breach of promise, but how it will go I cannot tell. That is the talk just now. The Rose girls has been very foolish with men this long time.[18]

At the subsequent trial, George Ray claimed he had promised nothing to Margaret. Two facts told against him. He had taken her out riding in his mail wagon alone on a Sunday afternoon. More importantly, he and Margaret had eaten pie alone together in the Halls' kitchen. The judge found for the plaintiff and awarded her $500.

> It is not considered in good taste for a girl of eighteen to drive out alone with a young man.[19]

Margaret eventually married, and the Rays had a long and happy life together, emigrating not long after to Manitoba, where their troubled past would be unknown.

Protection against Breach of Promise of Marriage extended not only to the young, but to women of every age.

> A few days ago when the Court of Assizes was held in Cayuga, a case was brought up and the issue tried of a most unusual but extraordinary character. The facts of the matter may be briefly stated thus: woman 85 years of age brought an action for breach of promise of marriage against a man 86 years of age. She was a great grandmother and he was a great grandfather. The lady claimed that she ought to be allowed her winter's wood as compensation for the breach of contract. Both parties were about equally matched as to the possession of worldly goods. The jury awarded her $100.[20]

Childbirth

My mother bore me glad and sound and sweet I kiss her feet!
MARGUERITE WILKINSON

PREGNANCY AND CHILDBIRTH were not openly discussed during the Victorian years. It was a time when the body was not only expected to be kept well covered, but its functions were considered to be extremely private. During the early stages of pregnancy, voluminous gowns and layered clothing would help to conceal an expanding waistline; but later on, women in polite society often retired from public view.

In 1846 when Queen Victoria was expecting her fifth child, Princess Helena, she enjoyed opera and concerts only until the seventh month. Later in the century, Emma Laflamme made reference to the practice of withdrawing from society towards the end of a pregnancy.

> We invited Hugh & Loraine up for New Years dinner but in her letter of last night, she says under the circumstances she would feel out of place (She expects an increase of family some time in the near future) (Diary of Emma Laflamme, 1 January 1887)

A new baby was a joyful addition to the family, but the waiting period before its birth was very seldom mentioned. Given this state of affairs it was not surprising that most women had very little to say on the subject while writing their private journals. If it were not for the sudden announcement of baby's arrival, the reader would have no suspicion that a pregnancy had been taking place. Naturally, there were rare exceptions to this rule. Rachel Cormany, who shared her husband's interest in medical matters, frequently made note of her progress during pregnancy.[21]

Frances Tweedie Milne shared one piece of information:

James Lewis Coulter and his wife, Almyra J. Brown, with their children, Alan Benson, Ruth Lillian and Leonard Lewis, 1900. Photo by James Townend, Almonte.

> Courses [menstruation] should have come on, my last 17 Dec. 69. (Diary of Frances Tweedie Milne, 14 January 1870)

Given its rarity, this simple statement is remarkable, for even when referring to the pregnancies of others, most went to great lengths to create acceptable euphemisms.

> Wonder if Mrs Carken has had her condition yet. she had Dr Fulton of Montreal for 14 days at $10 a day. as the little stranger did not arrive in that time he had to leave. (Diary of Emma Laflamme, 26 January 1887)

Such cautious use of words also extended to the official record. In the register of those residing at the Wellington County House of Industry and Refuge during the latter part of the 1800's, pregnant women seeking shelter were classified as "enceinte." Using the French word produced a far more delicate and lady-like sound which would not offend Victorian sensibilities. The media, informing the public of Queen Victoria's activities said "It is now pretty generally known that Her Majesty's accouchement (retirement some of the papers called it) will take place about the middle of the month."[22]

There is no doubt that having babies was still a very precarious business. This reason alone was sufficient to instill reluctance, or even fear, into the minds of women. It was an age when everyone knew somebody who had died in childbirth, and most women faced pregnancy with some degree of anxiety or even dread. Given this state of affairs, it is not surprising that one avoided speaking of the developing fetus, for fear of tempting fate.

A new study of maternal mortality indicates that in the 1850's, an average of nine women died each day in England and Wales during childbirth, or soon after. Rich women fared no better than the poor in this regard. The statistics actually became worse as the century went on, only improving well into this century. Woman had every reason to regard the birth of a child with fear as well as joy.[23]

Upon the birth of Queen Victoria's first child, newspapers reported:

> This happy event, which has given to the British Nation the promise of a continuance of the line of Brunswick on the throne, has elicited one universal sentiment of gratitude and joy throughout the land:—of gratitude to Almighty God, for his preservation of our sovereign, in nature's agony, when a Queen, amidst regal luxury, must alike suffer, with the poorest peasant mother in her empire, the doom pronounced upon the maternal parent of mankind...[24]

"The doom pronounced upon the maternal parent of mankind" was certainly gloomy language, perhaps justifiably, since there were no guarantees that a woman would survive the ordeal. Catharine Merrit, sixty-three years of age, dwelt upon the death of one young mother, daughter of her friends.

Thursday evening—died at 3:00 this morning Catherine Jane Van Devester, only child of Catherine and C. Clark, aged 25. It is a plain short sentence but what does it convey to our comprehension; a bereaved husband, childless, hopeless, comfortless father and mother, motherless infant and sorrowing friends, We know not what a day will bring forth. Little did I imagine the afflictions of my friends when I sat this morning in my bed at 4:00 endeavouring to read to while away the time until our people got up. Oh that I could go and sympathize with the bereaved. Janet kindly offered to go and Mrs Adams always ready to minister to the afflicted. (Diary of Catharine Merritt, 8 May 1856)

For some, the fear of childbearing was so strong that they chose to remain single.

Mrs Ladell died this morning leaving a little baby a week old. the funeral is to be on Wednesday. Lovely day. (Diary of Mary Coldwell Butcher, 21 March 1892)

Father & Mother came to attend Mrs Ladell's funeral. there was quite a crowd there & the little baby was baptized afterwards....(23 March 1892)

In the early Victorian period, the average person knew little about contraception, but by the 1870's a variety of methods were being successfully used by those who understood how. In her book, *The Nature of Their Bodies: Women and Their Doctors in Victorian Canada*, Wendy Mitchinson lists many, including pessaries, herbal concoctions, vaginal sponges, diaphragms, condoms, coitus interruptus and abstinence.[25] However, even after the turn of the century, some people were not enthusiastic about recommending the use of contraceptive devices.

As to prevention of conception, most of the means used are very injurious and especially so to the woman[26]

Abstinence was of course the most foolproof method, but not a very popular one, for obvious reasons. Samuel Cormany wrote:

Wife and I had a long talk on child bearing—we differ on

some points, but sweetly agree to disagree, and avoid any risks by continued abstinence &c, &c. (Diary of Samuel Cormany, 29 December 1860)

Samuel wrote these words when he and his bride, Rachel Bowman, had only been married for one month. Given the unbridled passion enjoyed by most newlyweds, this decision says much about their level of self control and determination.

Some women may have received advice regarding pregnancy from their mothers, grandmothers, sisters or friends. Others might have referred to published material such as *The Ladies' Book of Useful Information*, which offered the following suggestions: "During the whole period of pregnancy every kind of agitating exercise, such as running, jumping, jolting in a carriage, and plunging in cold water, should be carefully avoided, as well as the passions being kept under perfect control." Pregnant women who were generally affected with "heartburn, sickness of a morning, headache, and that troublesome disease, toothache, which accompanies pregnancy" may avoid such "by keeping the bowels gently open with seidlitz powders, caster oil, or pills of rhubarb, which should be taken occasionally, either alone or in combination with colocynth and soap." For morning sickness, two or three teaspoons of the following mixture were to be taken occasionally, or after each meal:

> Calcined magnesia, one dram;
> Distilled water, six ounces,
> Aromatic tincture of whatany, six drams;
> Water of pure ammonia, one dram.[27]

The diarists invariably described their time of labour as being "ill," "sick," or of being "not well." The choice of words is interesting. It was more seemly for the women to use words which indicated a general discomfort rather than to state exactly what the cause of their discomfort was. Even Frances Tweedie Milne, who so candidly informed us that her period had been late, exhibited a reluctance in this respect.

Fine day. Not well all day sent for Mrs Jacques after tea. Wm. got home about 8 p.m. I sent for Mrs. B. & Dr. about 7 p.m. Very sick all night. (Diary of Frances Tweedie Milne, 7 October 1870)

Baby was born this Saturday morning at 1/2 after 6 A.M. We all felt rejoiced when it was over. Dr. didn't go away till 5 p.m. feeling easy. (8 October 1870)

Matilda Bowers Eby, wife of Dr. Aaron Eby also gave no hint when babies were due to arrive.

Today I did not feel very well. Spent most of the time out in the open air being the most congenial to my nature. Susanna white washed the kitchen but it looks shocking. (16 May 1865)

In the following day's entry, we discover the cause of her complaint.

This was the all important day on which our baby was born. Just a little before six o'clock p.m., she was ushered into this world of pain and sorrow. She is very small. I feel quite easy this evening hardly any pains. Had several heavy showers. (17 May 1865)

Once baby had arrived it became quite acceptable to speak of pain and to recount the numerous discomforts and motherly concerns. On the day after her baby was born, Matilda noted that she felt very well after a good night's sleep but gradually got weaker as the day advanced, from the great loss of blood. The following day she reported having very little pain but feeling tired from lying in one position so long. She also noted that she had put the baby to the breast for the first time on that day.

When she was close to delivering her child, Mary Brown of Hamilton wrote:

A most depressed day, sick of waiting, and longing for such comfort as only a dear mother can give. (24 January 1865)

Mary was clearly indicating the importance of a mother's presence at such a time, to provide not only physical comfort, but also much needed security and reassurance. Unfortunately Mary's mother lived in England, so could not be with her. Five days later, the confinement behind her, Mary was able to write:

A sixth son born at 11 a.m., after much suffering, a fat healthy boy. (29 January 1865)

Upon her marriage to widower Adam Brown, Mary had inherited four sons. Eventually she would bear Adam seven children, giving them a total of eleven. To Mary's credit, she made no distinction, nor favoured her own children over her step-children. Her mother, though so far away, took her grandmotherly duties seriously and frequently added words of advice to her letters.

> It is a matter of congratulation that your baby boy is of an equable temperament; nurse him *gently*, but very cheerfully, so as not to induce undue excitability;—much may be done in infancy to make, or to mar, the future man.[28]

Many years later, when Mary was called upon to provide support to her daughter-in-law in childbirth, she may have recalled the longings she experienced for her own mother.

> Went out collecting with Mrs Lucas but had only reached BBNA when Willy called me to go to Emily who was ill; found her in bed, but she got up and when the nurse came I went home to dinner, returned to Jackson St. & remained helping Emily till 8:30 when Dr Mallach administered chloroform. Baby was born almost immediately after midnight a fine boy, both mother & baby doing well. (25 January 1881)

None of these women gave details about the delivery of their children. Presumably, since Matilda Bower's husband, Aaron Eby, was a medical doctor, she would have been given whatever aids were available for pain control. Perhaps chloroform was used, as mentioned by Mary Brown.

Early in the century opium and ether had been popular agents for the pain of childbirth. Generally they were administered in very small amounts, to give some modicum of relief during contractions. One assumes that for most middle class women, providing they had the assistance of a competent physician or midwife, the birthing experience ought to have been made as comfortable as medical knowledge of the day permitted. However, there was no way of completely eliminating pain, unless a woman was to be rendered unconscious.

For some women the childbirth experience was relatively easy, as indicated in correspondence received by Mrs. Joseph Rendall, of Cumnock, Wellington County, from her brother and sister-in-law at Jersey City, who had recently had a child.[29]

I was very glad to get your letter and will try and answer it promptly, for once in my life. I am feeling quite well and getting strong again. Baby is well and has been real good so far. She is quite fair and has blue eyes. In other respects I think very much like Peter and most people say so too who see her. I did not have a hard time at all. The nurse told me that I did not know anything about it as compared with what some do. I hired a nurse for the first ten days…

The husband, too, thought the business of childbirth much overplayed:

Your letter came in due time, found Jean and her Baby both well. Jean is as well as ever long ago she does not owe for her just what people have to make such a noise and a fuss about it for, and as for the Baby why it is not a speck of trouble it only wants two things plenty of time to sleep, and plenty of milk. of course I dont care any thing about it nor yet, any other Baby, but Jean says that she would not trade it for all of the Boys in Canada or in the States either She is just delighted because it is a girl.

The pledge of abstinence agreed upon by Samuel and Rachel Cormany was relatively short lived, for their first child was born on 3 May 1862, just eighteen months after their marriage. Samuel wrote an account of the birth proceedings in his diary, beginning with the onset of labour.[30] His keen interest and knowledge of what to expect is evident.

I found Pet in what seemed labor pains—She had been in bed most of P.M.—Had taken her sitz bath just before I came and the pain came on while in the bath—After I had my supper and had my little chores done I helped her take another sitz bath—Pains kept increasing gradually, at intervals. The Intervals became shorter and the pains lasted longer. At 9 OCK I laid down to take a short nap—We had previously concluded to call no one in until necessity required—I slept very little— say 1 1/2 hours. Pet napped some too, but 15-20-30 minutes a darting pain affected her back, various parts, and awaken her—at midnight pains were pretty severe every 5-10 minutes,

and we concluded—as I was not very well—to call Ma Bowman, and have Pa Bowman call in Mrs Cress from Preston—
all this time Pet would be from lounge to the floor, then
across the bed—and again on her knees to the lounge—with
occasional easing intervals about 2 A.M. Lady Cress came.

"Midwife Gress" or "Mother Gress" as she was usually called, was a
well known figure in the Waterloo County area. Although her fee for
delivery of a baby ranged from produce, such as potatoes, to five dol-
lars, according to her records very few paid more than two dollars.
Elisabeth Gress had come to Preston in 1853 with her husband and
family. She was trained in midwifery in her homeland, Germany. During her career in Ontario she delivered approximately four thousand
babies. Samuel Cormany gives the following account of her at work.

> May 3rd 1862 About 2 A.M.
> Lady Cress came—after examination pronounced all things
> going on satisfactorily—The pains became more and more
> powerful—Too vigorous an effort was made by the Lady to
> have Pet—'Press'—'Pull on the towels fast to the bed-posts'
> 'Beardown'—&c I remonstrated that there was too much hur-
> rying of nature—take time—I urged—give nature a chance—
> so I prevailed—6Ock in the morning—all went to breakfast I
> comforted Darling—she was so glad I stayed by her—
>
> I encouraged her, and assured her all was going on per-
> fectly—according to "The Books"—authority—But she
> needs to press the effort of expulsion as much as possible
> whenever the natural impulse arises—8Ock Pet seemed over-
> come—a little morose—discouraged—and needed much en-
> couragement to impel her to believe that it would soon be
> over—She said several time "Oh! I cannot stand it"—"It will
> kill me" I responded Oh no Darling, soon you will have re-
> lief—Do your utmost at expulsion—and our rejoicing will
> start in—9Ockl! The little pet came—A Daughter!
>
> In less that half an hour Darling was comparitively comfort-
> able—Mrs Cress did her work nicely—but would not consent
> to our wish that she might have a spongebath—said it would
> kill her.

After Mrs. Gress left, Samuel gave Rachel a spongebath. For the next few days he tended mother and baby, bathing them, preparing food, giving Sitz baths and renewing the bed, "all against law of Grannies." When the baby suffered occasional bouts of colic he prescribed warm enemas and a tepid bath.

Not all women were as lucky as Rachel Bowman Cormany. Many did not receive competent medical care. For some, childbirth was to be a lonely and frightening experience. Those living in remote areas often had to rely upon the assistance of untrained friends or relatives. Such helpers, despite trying their best to provide loving care, would have been virtually useless had a complication arisen.

Women who were well trained in midwifery, such as Mother Gress, contributed much to society and were highly valued. Unfortunately tragedies occurred when unskilled practitioners were confronted with difficult deliveries.

Rachel Cormany with her daughter, Cora. Taken from *From the Cormany Diaries: A Northern Family in the Civil War*, edited by James C. Mohr (University of Pittsburgh Press). *Used by permission*

Dr. F. S. Verity, of Hemmingford, presented the following case to "illustrate the difficulties the Country Practitioner sometimes encounters, as well as the cruel treatment to which women are subject, in the hands of rash and ignorant Midwives."[31] This particular incident occurred around 1840 and was Dr Verity's first midwifery case in Canada.

Upon examination I found the right arm protruding through the vulva, wrapped in a piece of cloth "for fear of cold," as the midwife said, and carefully tied to the patient's thighs "for fear it should go back again." On learning the history of the case, I was very angry with the midwife, and asked why she had not sent for assistance sooner; when she cooly told me, that as long as she had *"the smut"* [ergot of rye] she did not expect to require any one's assistance. I asked to see "the smut" when she produced a bag, like a small money bag, from which she took a quantity of the Ergot of Rye, the use of which, she said, she had learned from the Doctors in the States. "So you have been giving her this," I said. "Yes," she replied, "and I *always* give it, when the case is a long one, and I never knew it fail until now." My temper, I confess, was ruffled, and after rating her soundly, for her presumption and rashness in administering such a powerful remedy without a knowledge of its properties and the circumstances under which it was proper to give it, I left her to assist my patient.

In this instance, the mother survived her ordeal. The child, however, was dead when delivered.

Ergot of rye, or "smut," is derived from the dormant stage of a fungus that grows on rye. In the early 1800's it was recommended by some to hasten birth and to control postpartum hemorrhage. Side effects include vomiting, headache, mydriasis, delirium and stupor, as well as fetal death.[32] Once administered it might take several hours for the effect to wear off. In the case of an obstruction in the birth canal, the drug would be ineffective, causing only undue pain and distress to mother and child.

In July, 1865, Dr. J. M. Pemwarden, of Fingal, was called to help a woman who had been in labour for 48 hours. Upon his arrival he examined the woman and soon realized that the attending midwife had made several mistakes.[33]

After a little more search, and a good deal of hard thinking, I felt what I thought was torn muscular fibre; and I then made up my mind that the hand had presented, and that the midwife, by some means or other, had pulled off the arm from the shoulder, and that the bone I felt was the glenoid cavity. I then confronted the midwife, and asked her in no very gentle terms "What she had done to the woman." She answered, "nothing." But, on telling her I would immediately send for a constable and have her arrested, if she did not show me what she had taken from the woman, she produced the *two arms of the child, with the clavicle and scapula attached to one, and the clavicle to the other*; and confessed that by means of a noose, above the elbow of the child, connected to a towel around her shoulders, she had succeeded in extracting, first one arm without much trouble, and then the other after a great deal of difficulty.

The mother in this instance lived until the second night after the delivery.

As dreadful as these incidents were, when it came time to give birth, women felt better knowing that there was someone to help. Unfortunately this was not always possible, as Mary Coldwell Butcher, of Muskoka, discovered.

> I was taken sick at 12 last night and baby was born at about 1:30 before either Mrs Bram or Mrs Forrest who had been sent for had arrived. (Diary of Mary Coldwell Butcher, 21 January 1895)

Happily Mary Coldwell Butcher suffered no complications with the delivery of her child. She was up and about one week later.

For one reason or another, women occasionally found themselves giving birth in the privacy of their rooms, alone, and in secret.

> A servant girl in the employ of Dr. Walker of Dundas, gave birth to a child on Sunday night last, and on Monday morning she got up and attended to the household duties as usual. The doctor, who had been out all night, on coming home, suspected from the appearance of the girl that something had gone wrong. He accordingly repaired to her bedroom, and found the body of a dead child in the bed underneath the clothes. An inquest was held on the body, and the jury, after hearing the evidence, returned a verdict of found dead."[34]

Such stories only emphasize the good fortune of those born into welcoming families. For such children, the nurturing of loving parents provided a sound footing for a happy and productive life. Grandparents too, often played an important role. Those living in close proximity to their grandchildren were often called upon to babysit. One loving grandmother wrote:

> The babe was six months old yesterday, dear little fatty he is so good a child as ever could be with good attendance and has scarcely seen a moment's illness and I hope and pray that

the next one may be as propitious but having the chief will be a trying time. (Diary of Catharine Merritt, 22 December 1855)

...Monday night dear little W.H.(William Hamilton Merritt) waked both M. and me crying, all went up but could do nothing to pacify him, then I went up. I took him, he seemed quite exhausted from crying and went to sleep. I could cry but could do nothing to pacify, it was his maw he wanted. Oh, it is hard to be weaned from the mother. It is the first trial poor human nature has to endure and so young, not one poor year yet and to be cast from the arms when he has always reposed in safety, as the little heart felt to those of strangers, although they might be as kind and as tender, but it is not the bosom on which it revelled. Dear lamb in all the trials of after life may you possess a mind strong to bear them and may you escape some of the trials that are incident to poor human nature. (7 May 1856)

Home

Success in housekeeping adds credit to a woman of intellect,
and lustre to a woman's accomplishments.
The Canadian Home Cook Book, 1877

MOST YOUNG WOMEN were trained from an early age in household skills. Baking, cooking, preserving, cleaning and washing were important; but so were sewing, spinning and a multitude of other tasks. Matilda Bowers Eby developed a keen sense of accomplishment as her level of expertise grew. She wrote the following when she was nineteen years old.

I done the most of the baking today, the bread looks most beautiful. I almost flatter myself that I will become a good baker yet; something not every woman can brag of. I am sorry so many of our Canadian girls don't learn to keep house thoroughly and try to make themselves worthy of the position they all aspire to occupy in the community some day. How often we see that worthless and extravagant wives are the ruin of their husbands. When will women wake up to their duty? It would not be a bad thing if some intelligent woman would write a little work entitled "Woman's duties" and circulate it through our lovely Canadas. (Diary of Matilda Bowers Eby, 20 February 1863)

Not everyone faced the prospect of being a housewife with equanimity:

> I should not like housekeeping, i.e. the sole charge of it for more than three or four weeks at a time. it is astonishing how much time it takes up. (Diary of Emma Laflamme, 14 October 1886)

> I do not think my hands would ever get hard with housework. they become red but not real hard and I have a good bit of work too. what a lot of steps there are about housekeeping. (15 October 1886)

> Now for a dusting tour and dont I wish it were through. (4 March 1887)

Women usually managed to complete many jobs during the course of a day.

> morning work (dusting helping to wash dishes &c.) done. read morning worship. then to sewing made a cape for my drab dress. after which mending shirts for Luther. help'd him to put the 1st young Chickens & hen in the coop. Sometimes chased the hens out of the garden. (Diary of Eliza Bellamy, 17 May 1855)

Maud Nicholson and her sister, Gertrude Nicholson, diarist. *Clair C. Chapman*

Comparing homes, when the opportunity arose, was an interesting pastime.

> Went out in the morning—took tea at Mrs Cunningham's who took us through Alan Gilmore's house, the pictures are very fine, but the house is rather shabby though the furniture is good. (Diary of Janet Hall, 27 July 1876)

> …we went to Mrs Mott's to call. She lives opposite in a nice little house. Her drawing room is quite the prettiest I have

seen here it was so cosy & furnished with such good taste. (Diary of Gertrude Nicholson, 16 May 1896)

A good housekeeper kept a thorough inventory of her household contents. Naturally, for costly items such as silverware, this was particularly important. But linen, too, was regularly counted. Soon after her marriage in 1898, Marion Chadwick did an inventory of the household's possessions. It fills many pages, room by room. Her linens were listed separately, with descriptions, including, for gifts, the names of those who gave. This is what she had:

4 good table cloths	2 kitchen table cloths
12 small table napkins	12 large table napkins
3 tea table cloths	4 carving cloths
4 cake plate doilies	3 tray cloths
5 odd doilies	38 finger bowl doilies (5 sets)
4 pillow chams	16 pillow cases
5 quilts	14 sheets
41 towels	2 comforters
6 blankets	26 kitchen dish towels
3 kitchen roller towels	2 ironing sheets
2 ironing sheets for board	9 centrepieces (large doilies, heavily worked)

SPRING CLEANING

One of the great events in the household year was spring cleaning. Everything in the house was moved, washed, beaten, shaken or otherwise made to seem new again. For Annie Cragg, who took her housework seriously enough to list her accomplishments each day, this was a busy time.

Commenced House cleaning at the Parlor. took down all the Pictures & cleaned & gilded same. Swept the walls. cleaned all the wood work & swept 3 times. Then wiped off the carpet. (Diary of Annie Elizabeth Cragg, 9 April 1888)

It took more than two weeks to finish the house, with help from her sister, her brother, and another woman.

We began house cleaning last Tuesday, have papered Jacks room it looks so nice. (Diary of Avice Watson, 24 April 1887)

The next week was very warm quite like July making house cleaning very hard. (7 May 1887)

The Campion household was also a very busy place during spring time.

All day digging in the garden & ironed the starched clothes in the forenoon. Esther had all the furnishings out of the Parlor when I got done so we were very busy white washing took up the carpet, cleaning woodwork. (Diary of Mary Victoria Campion, 16 May 1861)

Spring was also a good time to decorate the house.

They papered the bedroom over the kitchen. It looks swell. I guess I will take that room this summer it is so nice and cool and it is nice and cool in winter too. (Diary of Hattie Bowlby, 30 April 1874)

Paint was expensive and difficult to use. Whitewash was a cheaper but messier replacement.

whitewashed ceiling mother's room in forenoon papered in afternoon. (Diary of Fanny Goodfellow, 9 June 1891)

McDermot began caleomining 5 rooms, but not the Hall as agreed upon, for fear of finger marks. (Diary of Mary Brown, 23 October 1879)

KITCHENS

The latter half of the century could no longer be called pioneer days in most of Ontario, the exception being the north. The south was settled and most rural people had changed from log cabins to frame houses. The house consisted of a large kitchen, a parlour and another room downstairs, and bedrooms upstairs. The other downstairs room might be a dining room or, more likely, a bedroom. If the kitchen was large enough, the family would use it for sitting in too, and the parlour would be kept for "good."

There were actually two kitchens, one for summer and one for winter. The winter one was indoors, the summer one in an extension of the house, with thin walls. It consisted mostly of a place for the stove and a great deal of workspace. It might have its own stove; if not, the stove would be moved here in the spring and the cooking would be done in a place which would not overheat the house.

> We moved the stove out (Diary of Laura McMurray, 6 June 1899)

> Cooked in the morn. used summer kitchen stove for 1st time since summer (Diary of Frances Gay Simpson, 11 May 1881)

> took down the stove (Diary of Annie Elizabeth Cragg, 9 June 1888)

> Have a great time doing the work & getting the kitchen moved out (Diary of Josephine Anne Ketchum, 21 April 1886)

The workspace provided for all the canning and preserving which was done in the summer months. In winter the stove would come indoors again, to heat the most lived-in room of the house.

Cooking was no longer done on open hearths, but in ranges fuelled by wood. The stove would be banked for the night, most likely going out. The first task of the morning was to light it, both for warmth in the winter and to begin the day's cooking.

> Very cold. Dan didn't come till 10:a.m. and I lit the fires, and the water was all frozen in the kitchen till the fire had been lit an hour. (Diary of Agnes Butler Leacock, 1 January 1898)

The iron range was black, with a reservoir for heating water on one side, and round holes for feeding the fire (with iron lifters for each). The top also lifted, for cleaning or putting in large pieces of wood. The black top had to be cleaned regularly and polished with (appropriately enough) blacking.

Katie & I blackleaded the stove, had an awful time. (Diary of Frances Tweedie Milne, 26 June 1867)

I blackened all the stove and scrubbed the floor (Diary of Laura McMurray, 2 February 1899)

blackning coal stove in forenoon (Diary of Fanny Goodfellow, 28 November 1890)

The mere presence of the stove ensured that there were ash and smoke in the air, no matter how tidy the housekeeping was. This Tennyson described in his line, "The sooty yoke of kitchen vassalage." The result was more work for the cleaners.

Had a good hard days work washed the Ceiling & walls got done about 3 oclock. (Diary of Bertha Harnden, 10 June 1895)

The pipes which took the smoke away were large, made of tin. They might lead through an upstairs bedroom or two, which was a simple way of conveying some of the heat upstairs. Soot accumulated in the pipes, and the regular cleaning that resulted was a messy occasion.

we took down the stove pipes and cleaned them. (Diary of Mary Ann King, 3 February 1893)

In *Harvests Past*, Pat and Frances Patterson mention that stovepipe cleaning was a time that guaranteed bad tempers throughout the house. Those who still remember this activity from their own childhoods confirm this. Velma Taylor says that once the pipes were back in place—always the worst time, fitting the ends together—her father would sing a hymn or two, "Shall We Gather at the River," or "Bringing in the Sheaves." Perhaps it helped him dissipate the sooty feelings.[35]

Cleaned oven and pipes in forenoon (Diary of Fanny Goodfellow, 21 March 1890)

The open fires were dangerous, not only in the kitchen itself but also on the roof, where sparks or an overheated chimney could start a conflagration which could not be stopped. Stovepipes filled with soot held the same dangers.

As well as the stove, there were open flames from the candles used for light in the evenings.

> Every fall a beef had to be killed, not only to supply us with meat for the winter but also to supply us with tallow to make the candles. Enough were made to last the year. They were packed in boxes and put into the root house to keep them cold. Candle moulds were found in every house and calde wick cords made of cotton, was bought in balls.[36]

These were later replaced by oil lamps, whose wicks were still risky. The lamps were especially dangerous when being moved, as they were ungainly, and any fall automatically meant fire. In their advice to female servants in 1867, the authors of *The Finchley Manuals of Industry* cautioned on the proximity of candles and bedclothes. "Never get into bed, placing your candle within reach, that you may extinguish it afterwards. The habit is highly dangerous; the candle may be imperfectly extinguished, a spark may fall upon the bed-clothes, the curtains may take fire, and you and all the family may be burnt to death in your beds. Always put the candle out *before* you get into bed. Do not blow it out, but either snuff it close or use an extinguisher."[37]

Once a small frame house began to flame, it usually burnt to the ground.

> We have indeed had a dreadful experience, last night our house was burned. A spark got into some wood in the chimney and if I had been in bed, would have been killed as a large timber fell on my bed. (Diary of Eleanora Hallen, 7 March 1841)

Even an inexperienced woman such as Victoria Campion knew the real meaning of losing your house.

> Mrs Liggetts house was burnt up took fire at 4 Oclock this morning. (9 January 1862)

> Albert & Robert have gone to help build a house for Liggetts. They lost everything they had to eat. (10 January 1862)

When you had to work constantly to keep a stock of provisions in the house, a fire destroyed everything you had. There was no picking up a few replacements at the store. The winter's slaughter of meat had probably taken place in December, and the resulting pork was in brine in a barrel, the beef hanging. A summer's worth of preserves would be gone in the burnt out cellar, and the supply could not be re-established for six months. It might be possible to hunt game for meat, but vegetables were another matter.

It is likely that, once the communal rebuilding of the house was finished, the neighbours would make donations from their own cellars. Nonetheless, the next few months would be hard times for the Liggetts, as the gifts could not replace a whole cellar full of jars. The need for an ongoing supply of canned fruit and vegetables is obvious; newlywed women often had their cellars "started off" when their neighbours brought a jar or two each to their charivari. From then on, their hard work would ensure that the cellar was never empty.

The Merritt family of St. Catharines lost their home in one of a series of suspicious fires. The incident was a terrific shock to Mrs Merritt, who read of the fire in a newspaper while on holiday in the U.S.A.

> Six weeks yesterday since I wrote in this book, not so long a time as I supposed it was so many occurrences have taken place and changes with us that it appears an age. Then we had a home to write in, now it is in ashes or all but just enough to show what and where it was. Mr Merritt, Jediah and I went up this evening and walked about the grounds and premises. It is a sad sight to see the destruction of property and years of collecting has destroyed in a few hours. It is a sad reflection for one at my time of life to be without a home, but in this affliction we are obliged to submit and be thankful that it is no greater. (Diary of Catharine Merritt, 17 October 1858)

The kitchen would also contain a large wooden table and straight chairs. If there were many children, one side of the table might have a bench instead, to cram in more bodies. The table would be used as a principal working space. There may have been counters as well. A large chest or cabinet would hold some foodstuffs, or a tiny pantry would have shelves for dishes and dry food. Beside the window there would be a rocking chair or armchair with cushions where the old folks could rest. If the room were large enough, there might even be a settee.

The stove took up a great deal of room, being large to begin with, and then having to stand well away from the wall for safety purposes. Behind the stove was a good place to hang wet towels for drying. Shy people often hid there when visitors came. It was both warm and safe. Nearby was the woodbox. It was usually the children's job to keep it filled from the pile outside, where pieces of wood the right size to fit in the stove had been chopped. A smaller box or basket held materials for starting the fire in the morning. In more genteel homes, these baskets were covered by woolwork throws to disguise their unsightliness.

One way of keeping down the dirt in the kitchen was to oil the floor. The bare boards then absorbed the dust.

> we oiled the kitchen floor (Diary of Fanny Goodfellow, 22 June 1891)

The family wash basin would be located here, in the winter at any rate. A pump would bring water directly indoors. In its absence, pails of water were brought from the pump outside. More than one person might wash in the same water, to conserve it. More advanced houses would have a drain leading to the outside; otherwise the used water would be thrown out the door. A pail of drinking water with a common dipper might occupy a quiet corner. There would probably be another dipper near the pump outside.

There were noticeable seasons in the kitchen's year. Things were quieter in the winter, when preserved food was being used frugally and there was more time for non-essential tasks. However, as the first hints of spring came, farm women realized that the inevitable swing of the calendar would determine their activities.

Most preserving was done in the warm weather months. But marmalade was, and still is, made in the winter, when the supply of oranges is at its height.

> Hannah made the orange marmalade. Lena is keeping house for Mrs J. B. Armstrong who is away from home. (Diary of Avice Watson, 25 March 1887)

> Last night I helped Annie cut her marmelade until eleven & to-day I feel as tired & used up as if I had been at a dance all night. (Diary of Belle Kittredge, 7 April 1892)

As the year rolled by, each season brought its particular tasks. When nature provided something valuable, other work was set aside so that advantage could be taken of what was ripe. This was especially true of the parade of berries which began in June and continued into August. In 1861, Victoria Campion dealt with currants, gooseberries, raspberries, strawberries, blackberries and huckleberries; at any rate, those are all she mentioned in her diary.

> Albert & I took tea at Bentleys. had strawberries & shortcake. (Diary of Mary Victoria Campion, 30 June 1861)

> Maggie & Josey picking berries got 16 quarts in the afternoon. (22 July 1861)

> 4 quarts (21 July 1861)

> 5 quarts (23 July 1861)

> Maggie picking berries. (26 July 1861)

> went out to pick berries got the large tin pail full. (30 July 1861)

Once you had the berries home, you had to deal with them quickly before they spoiled.

> making preserves, picking berries (Diary of Mary Victoria Campion, 1 August 1861)

> made pies. (2 August 1861)

> after dinner Josey & I picked 6 quarts of blackberries. (3 August 1861)

The good thing about picking the wild berries was that you could make a kind of holiday out of it, if you went in a group and had an agreeable location.

> We all went down in the woods to eat blackberries. we spent a very pleasant day. (Diary of Mary Victoria Campion, 4 August 1861)

I picked 5 quarts of red berries in the afternoon (5 August 1861)

made 7 pies (10 August 1861)

Esther Albert and I took a walk for blackberries. (11 August 1861)

Finally, it would come to an end,

the raspberries are all gone. (Diary of Mary Victoria Campion, 20 August 1861)

until the following year, when it would happen again:

made currant pies, the first. (7 June 1862)

went to tea at Bentleys had strawberries and Bisct (biscuits?). the first strawberries. (29 June 1862)

finished a tin pail of gooseberries (3 July 1862)

picking raspberries in the forenoon. almost tired out when I got home. (10 July 1862)

It is hardly surprising that Victoria found picking berries so tiring, as it was hot work and you had to find the berries first. The work was difficult, but the pleasures made it worthwhile: the bowls of fresh fruit, the pies and then the preserves during the winter when so little was available.

Almost all women worked hard to preserve the fruits of summer:

Made 32 lbs strawberry jam from fruit Adam sent in Mother's good copper preserve kettle. (Diary of Mary Brown, 25 June 1879)

Gathering red currants, made them into jelly, Normandy. (5 July 1880)

Canned 14 lbs huckleberry jam cut up putting in 4lbs sugar one bottle broke scalding my left wrist rather severely. Prepared gooseberries for cheese to be made tomorrow. (Diary of Mary Brown, 1 August 1892)

Johnson left at 7:30 for Toronto—he gathered a basket of cherries before breakfast which I preserved immediately. (Diary of Frances Gay Simpson, 4 July 1881)

The most common of the fruits for picking and keeping was the apple. While berries required quick work to keep them for winter, apples could be stored in barrels in a cool place without extra effort. They stayed good right through until spring, when the first of the fresh fruit pies might be made. This was, of course, rhubarb, whose season began in May and lasted through into July, or perhaps even August if you were lucky and watched your plants carefully. In some places, the attractions of rhubarb were so strong that it was called the "pie plant."

Drying fruits and vegetables was another way of preserving them:

We spent the evening paring and coring apples for drying. (Diary of Ann Amelia Day, 10 October 1878)

Home made wine was a treat.

Women picking grapes near Grimsby. Photo by R.R. Sallows, Goderich. *National Archives of Canada*

Lena cleaned the drawing room. The grapes are picked & are being made into wine. (Diary of Avice Watson, 17 October 1877)

Cooking bottleing currant wine, makeing rasberry vinegar with many other things. (Diary of Eliza Bellamy, 20 August 1855)

As well as the game which would be available in the autumn, December was a time when hogs and beef were butchered for use throughout the cold months. The pork was often placed in barrels of brine, or smoked, while the beef could hang in an unheated place. It could also be placed in nature's freezer.

In winter, meat is finely kept, if well packed in snow, without salting. [38]

For efficiency, six, eight or ten hogs might be butchered at once, with a team of men working on them together.

killed the pigges (Diary of Jessie Geddes, 27 November 1899)

salted the pork (1 December 1899)

Tonight we chopped sausage meat and rendered lard. (Diary of Ann Amelia Day, 18 December 1878)

Packed Bacon 165 lbs in barrels & dry salted 2 sides weighing 40 lbs. boiled head cheese. (Diary of Frances Julia Davis, 26 November 1888)

The women would be prepared to receive those parts of the pigs which could be converted to sausage and headcheese, and of course the organ meats (liver, heart, brain and kidneys) which did not store well, would provide a feast over the next few days. The fact that the slaughter often came during preparations for Christmas resulted in some odd juxtapositions of work.

We killed pigs to-day (Diary of Fanny Goodfellow, 8 December 1891)

I made Xmas cake and cooked heads (10 December 1891)

The hard work of tapping the maple trees and sugaring off was the task of the whole family, done in the earliest spring when the air was cold, snow still on the ground, and there was plenty of mud.

> I tapped two trees in the afternoon. the sap came fast. (Diary of Mary Victoria Campion, 19 March 1862)

> a rainy day. I spent most of the day in the sugar bush sugaring off. raining quite fast in the evening. We have two hundred-weight of sugar. (16 April 1863)

Although the Campions did buy sugar from time to time—Victoria's brother Albert carried a fifteen-pound bag back from Stirling fair—the maple sugar was part of the store which would be used for cooking throughout the summer. As well, there would be the pleasures of "maple molasses," as maple syrup was sometimes known. It is interesting to reflect that molasses and maple syrup were seen as having the same properties; few people would spread molasses on bread or eat it plain today, as they do maple syrup.

> we made a bowl of maple molasses today. (Diary of Mary Victoria Campion, 26 March 1862)

> the boys sugared off 26 pounds of sugar in the afternoon. (9 April 1862)

Frances Jones of Augusta had high hopes for the sugar season too.

> I began boiling Sap today, I hope I can make a lot of molasses. (9 March 1878)

There was also an element of fun attached to boiling the sap. "Taffy pulls" became all the rage in some parts of Ontario.

> The ladies and gentlemen would take their positions much the same as in an opera reel [a dance]; each couple then seized the taffy in their teeth, and whichever couple could

stretch it the furthest without breaking will be the first to require the services of a minister.[39]

we went with Fred and Annie to taffy pull at Magee's about
forty being present. (Diary of Laura McMurray, 21 April 1899)

Certain kinds of work were better done communally. Someone organized a "bee" in which a crowd of people got together to do a certain
piece of work. We have seen that they held a bee to rebuild the
Liggetts' house after their fire; and everyone has heard of quilting bees
(which were and are, perhaps, more for pleasure than necessity).
There were also apple drying bees (schnitzing bees, as they are known
in Waterloo County).

In the fall we always had a paring bee.[40]

In fact, some bees were much more fun than work.

a rag bee at uncle Jo's party at night good fun a boisterous
time stayed all night (Diary of Annie Boyes, 26 March 1894)

The pig-killing days of December were also bees, if not always called
so. Winter also saw bees to obtain wood for those hungry stoves.

Had a fine wood bee (Diary of Jessie Geddes, 29 April 1899)

James has gone to James Irelands wood bee. (11 April 1900)

Had our wood bee Got 14 cords cut (14 April 1900)

Although Mrs Geddes would not have been expected to help cut the
wood, the bee would have given her a hard day's work, feeding the
men who did the cutting. This would have been comparable to the
threshing days of summer, when crowds of men worked hard in the
sun, and it required several women working fulltime in the kitchen to
give them their three or four good meals.

We were busy baking all day. we baked 13 loaves of bread, 190
buns, 6 sponge cakes and 10 railroad cakes for the raising.
(Diary of Ann Amelia Day, 21 June 1878)

As the men moved from farm to farm, they had a chance to compare the fare of different cooks. There was inevitable competition.

They complained that Ethel or Mary had served just too many desserts or meats and vowed that they would not compete with them.[41]

Rosie wasn't known for her heavily laden table.[42]

PARLOURS

Parlours or sitting rooms might be used on a regular basis; or they might be kept for more formal occasions, if the principal life of the family revolved around the kitchen. Upholstered chairs and couches with wooden side tables were grouped around the fireplace or small heater.

prepared dining room stove for use. (Diary of Frances Gay Simpson, 7 October 1881)

A picture or two hung on the walls, often religious or sentimental in nature. There might very well be a portrait of the Queen. In more affluent families, there would be knick-knacks, framed wreaths of wax flowers or human hair, as well as the coffin-plate mementoes described in our chapter on Funerals. The makers of the human hair wreaths could name the donors of each colour of hair used in the weaving. These were usually family members whose hair would remain as a reminder long after they had died or left the area.

Ann Amelia Day, diarist, in old age. *Wellington County Museum and Archives*

The many kinds of handwork done by women of leisure were often of a practical nature. The style was to fill the parlour to bursting with decorative touches. Handpainted cloth was one form of self-expression which was popular in Port Arthur in the 1890's.

One room was filled with it. painted sofa cushions, pictures &
ornaments...there was a mantlepiece, & from that mantlepiece
hung a drape. A painted drape. The drape I think was plush of
some dark color but I couldn't tell for the flowers & sprays almost covered it. (Diary of Belle Kittredge, 31 March 1892)

The coldness of the floors, which were usually of bare boards, made
carpets a necessity. There were many inexpensive woven imitations of
Brussels and Turkey carpets available. They might be put down with
straw underneath, to make them softer and warmer, or some other
lining. The edges would be tacked to ensure they would not curl. The
following excerpt, taken from a diary written in the United States,
shows how universal this practice was.

When I was four years old I remember my mother wove many
yards of carpet on her mother's loom 3´ wide and sewing
these widths together to make a one piece covering for the entire room. Then we would go to the strawstack and carry in a
sheet enough straw to cover floor 4 to 6 in. deep, over which
the carpet was spread and after a thorough stretching was
nailed fast to floor along outside walls. How I enjoyed rolling
over this straw covered floor. About every two years the straw
was replace with new, and what a difference it made in keeping the house warm.[43]

There might also have been small homemade rag rugs.

We finished my mat today. (Diary of Ann Amelia Day, 15 October 1878)

Larger rugs were made by saving up rags to send to the weavers.

I forgot to say that the carpet rags for Jacks new carpet were
taken to the weavers last Friday. (Diary of Avice Watson, 19
April 1887)

Jacks new carpet came home. (24 April 1887)

Modern eyes admire the patchwork effect of rag rugs made from mul-
ticoloured scraps of cloth; but more colour coordination was ensured

by dyeing the scraps using natural dyes or those bought from a travelling peddler. Nineteenth century cookbooks include recipes for dyeing, with rag rugs in mind.

> Dove and Slate Colors of all Shades: boil in iron vessel a teacup of black tea with teaspoon of copperas and sufficient water.[44]

> coloured rags for rug (Diary of Laura McMurray, 24 February 1899)

During spring cleaning, carpets were taken outside and beaten.

> I took up spare room carpet. (Dairy of Frances Gay Simpson, 26 April 1881)

For more ordinary cleaning, they were sprinkled with wet tea leaves and swept. Chopped potato was another sweeping agent. A good housekeeper also

> sponges the carpet with ox gall, and dusts it with a damp cloth, and keeps a door mat on the porch, and sends the boys back every time to use it till they get the habit of keeping clean.[45]

Often mentioned in the diaries are 'druggets', a smallish carpet made of woven coarse wool and silk.

> very busy all the morning cooking & putting down clean drugget in dining room (Diary of Frances Gay Simpson, 3 August 1881)

The housekeeper of a century ago was much more frugal than today. She had considerably fewer things, and what she had she cherished. Replacing even the smallest items might cause expense, so she was careful.

> After floors were swept, the contents of the wooden or metal dustpan were sorted through so that nothing as precious as a needle or a hairpin was thrown away.[46]

There might also be a dining room, and certainly would be one in larger houses. A heavy dining table and chairs with sideboard and china cabinet gave this room a substantial air. Perhaps nowhere exemplifies the Victorian love of gadgetry more than the dining room, where there were so many little items with but a single function. We do not think much of them today, the fish knives, salt cellars, sugar tongs and little silver crumb pans with brush.

> One can sympathize with the hostess of that day in trying to be sure that croquettes were not served with a patty server, or cucumbers with a tomato server.[47]

The Brown family of Hamilton seemed to have a mania about spoons, giving sets of very specialized ones to friends and relations at every opportunity. Mary Brown recorded in her accounts a transaction with the Meriden Britannia Company of Hamilton which itemised

> 1/2 doz. sterling Dessert Spoons 16.14
> 1/2 doz. sterling Tete a tete spoons 3.95 (13 April 1888)

the function of the latter being totally unknown to us, but sounding very friendly.

Among the ferns and geraniums which we associate with 19th century parlours, there might even be some forced plants blooming in the winter. In the busy days of summer, Victoria Campion took time to prepare for a winter pleasure.

> I planted out some Pink roots. They look beautiful. (10 September 1861)

> I have some lovely Pinks in bloom now. (12 March 1862)

One of the difficulties facing the indoor gardener was maintaining a suitable climate for plants during the cold weather months.

> When we got home & before we were out of the cutter we were greeted by Ann [the servant] saying "all your flowers are frozen Miss" we rushed into the sitting room & found they really had been but Edgar with his usual good nature had been watering them which had almost restored them though not

quite. We had taken such pains with them & were so proud of them they looked so well & green even the ivy which nearly reached the top of the room had all the young leaves frozen, it was most strange their freezing in the day time but fire had been left very low though not out. (Diary of Mary Hallen, 25 February 1853)

BEDROOMS

The bedrooms were plain and small in farmhouses. There was a double bed where two or three might snuggle together, a washstand and perhaps a chair. In larger houses there might be a desk or bookstand. Clothes could hang on hooks on the wall if there were no closet. A chest in the corner could store out of season clothing or extra garments, although most people had few enough of them.

Beds had high tops and bottoms, to protect the sleepers from drafts, and the mattresses (or ticks) lay on ropes which were woven from side to side. Later the ropes were replaced by boards, but this made the bed harder.

Mr Clark came here to hire & was harrowing all day. G & I went over to Mrs Hays & filled a straw tick....(Diary of Mary Coldwell Butcher, 5 June 1892)

The ticks were filled with straw, which would gradually become damped down and lumpy. On a famous day once a year, all the ticks would be taken outdoors, emptied and refilled. The result was a very fat and fragrant place to lie, at least for a while. Barley and rye straw were uncomfortable but were said to discourage mice, and wheat straw was considered less dusty that oat straw.[48] In winter, feather ticks, more yielding and warmer, were placed on top of the straw ones, making beds high and soft. In this downy comfort, with a handmade quilt or two on top and a brother or sister to snuggle with, children were able to stay warm despite the fact that the bedroom was unheated.

It is, of course, unlucky to put pigeons' feathers in a bed, And there is a rider to this axiom to the effect that no one can die comfortably with his head lying on a pillow to the filling of which pigeons' feathers contribute.[49]

Mrs Keating informed us a large flock of geese had their departure from the Garrison 30 in number she supposes they must have been blown away in the late high wind & will not return. She said poor Mrs Campbell had reconed on 16 good dinners besides the feathers. (Diary of Mary Hallen, 5 November 1848)

The washstand held a china basin and ewer. These were in a matching set, proudly bought and used. Fancier sets might include a soap dish, brush holder or other smaller pieces. Also matching, but not so prominently displayed, was the chamber pot. It was kept underneath the bed or in a special section of the washstand with the door closed. One rather unusual piece of handwork made by some nineteenth century women was a sewn muffler. It fitted the rim of the chamber pot, just large enough to ensure that the lid did not clank when being removed or replaced.

Many washstands also had a rail for the towel, and some even had a mirror. Their drawers held toilet articles and smaller pieces of clothing.

The water in the ewer remained chilly most of the year round. It might very well freeze overnight in the winter. It was unusual to bring hot water to the bedroom, so warm washes would take place communally in the kitchen, or outside. Perhaps not surprisingly, these mundane occurrences are not much discussed by the diarists.

To modern eyes, nineteenth century bedrooms, spare of furniture and bare of floor, are uninviting places. In fact people did not spend much time there. They were too busy working elsewhere. Other rooms, particularly the kitchen, had greater attractions.

CLOTHING

Most people had few clothes. It has even been suggested that two suits of clothes were all they had, one for every day and one for good. In the earlier period, people had to make all their own clothing, often spinning the yarn and weaving the cloth first.

This week made a pair of full cloth trousers for Father. (Diary of Eliza Bellamy, 2 December 1854)

Andrew paid $2.40cts for cloth for a pair of pants. (Diary of Frances Jones, 31 January 1871)

As towns grew, the stores there began carrying ready made clothing. It may not have fit well, but it was serviceable. Nevertheless people made do with only a little clothing, caring for what they had.
Making and altering clothes was also important.

Today we made some more on the quilt—I had to fix my dress, so that I did not get much done, but every little helps. There is nothing more disagreeable to me, than a tight dress. I have often been surprised at some girls, for wearing such very tight clothes, in fact lacing themselves so tight that it is almost impossible for them to breath. It must be injurious to health, it cannot be otherwise, still, they will not abandon the detrimental practice. I hope the day may not be far distant, when Mothers and Daughters will learn to be wise. (Diary of Matilda Bowers Eby, 16 February 1863)

Even a well-off family such as the Browns in Hamilton had their clothes mended. Mrs. Brown frequently unpicked a dress to have it re-sewn, renewing its life.

Mrs Holmes for remaking Lily's frock 1.50 (Diary of Mary Brown, 29 May 1888}

Mrs Holmes for turning Lily's sailor's suit 1.50 (24 October 1888)

At the same time, Mrs. Brown had her best frocks made in England. She sent to Miss Hephzibah Squirrel on a regular basis, and also in 1890 to a smart dressmaker in Bond Street, London, for the wedding dress of her daughter Daisy. She does not give us the cost of the dress in her accounts, but the customs duty alone was $15.00.
At the other end of the scale from those with only two suits of clothes were those whose dresses had only one function. Such women changed three or four times a day.
On an undated note slipped into her diary for 1889, Mrs. Brown planned her new wardrobe:

Miss Dalgleish: Travelling dress $25.00 Receiving dress $35.00 Serge dress for present wear $30

Miss Squirrel: Evening dress $35 Calling dress to suit also for spring $40

Whether in the city or the country, one of the joys of young women was new clothes:

This morning and yesterday ditto prepared black lace ball dress, wore it this evening to Mr Stephen Jarvis's first dance of season—very jolly. (Diary of Helen Grant Macdonald, 23 September 1891)

I guess I will wear my muslin dress to church tomorrow just for a passtime. (Diary of Hattie Bowlby, 7 June 1874)

However, then as now, parents and children did not necessarily see eye to eye about fashion:

Had on a new very close fitting dress. Mater calls the shirt a pillow case, Rose remarked that it made me look "underfed" (Diary of Helen Grant Macdonald, 6 October 1891)

Little Gwyn being sent up to put on a clean petticoat, dons it underneath her already worn one & explains to her mother: "The underneather you go, the cleaner you should be." (23 August 1891)

Mothers had to spend a great deal of time thinking about clothing for their teenage daughters.

The Misses West made Daisy's dresses fit for Toronto. Daisy's new brown net dress was very becoming. (Diary of Mary Brown, 20 January 1888)

Lace for trimming Daisy' combinations, $1.40. (12 January 1888)

Made flannel petticoat for Daisy. (23 January 1888)

Send Daisy new flannel petticoat & 2 pairs Combinations, canton flannel & lawn, with eider down jacket. (27 January 1888)

The practice of tightly laced corsets made movement awkward. Ladies having tea or paying calls did not mind so much. But as we have seen, even as a young single woman, Matilda Bowers Eby did not approve of those who tried lacing too much, in the style of Scarlett O'Hara. Working women probably left off lacing on an everyday basis, saving it for special occasions.

Some young women however longed for corsets:

Pa is going to order me a pair of corsets, because I have been longing for a pair made to order for years. (Diary of Emma Laflamme, 27 March 1887)

Not everybody appreciated the grace of a corsetted figure:

They done their best in playing, singing and looking foine but I guess she did not look so very foine for she looked as though she had a poker put through her she was laced so tight. (Diary of Louisa Bowlby, 3 February 1862)

Sewing sufficiently well to make clothing for herself and her family was a skill learned at a young age. It could be painful.

I did a little hem stitching on some flannel until tea & I found afterwards I had worked on the wrong piece & all my work was useless. (Diary of Belle Kittredge, 9 December 1892)

A young woman making clothes for her first baby might have her grandmother watching her every move. After an hour or two's labour, the older woman might pick up the piece, look it over and pronounce: "Rip it out. The stiches aren't even." The advent of the sewing machine made such a difference.

cut out new blinds & Bessie machined them. (Diary of Frances Gay Simpson, 16 June 1881)

For many women there was not the time for a great deal of sewing.

Bessie Simpson (1853-1886), daughter of diarist Frances Gay Simpson. Photo by Atelier Patté Fils. *National Archives of Canada*

In the afternoon she had to go out so I kept baby & did some sewing. It was quite a boon to me for I have been out so much in the evenings my sewing has gotten very much behind. (Diary of Belle Kittredge, 20 January 1892)

The itinerant seamstress made life easier. The need for professional sewing also provided work for single or widowed women, whose only alternative might have been the poorhouse or refuge with grudging relations. These women stayed for a few days with the family. For their board plus a small fee they sewed clothing or linens. Miss Hawthorne, the visiting seamstress of Toronto, makes regular appearances in Marion Chadwick's diary. The work of Isabella Johnston of Galt in the first decade of this century was remembered eighty years later. Another factor which made these women welcome visitors was their store of newsy gossip, picked up at the many houses they visited.

Fanny Goodfellow of Innisfil Township was a trained seamstress. She both did handwork and had a Singer sewing machine. Her work was various.

I was sewing I made my linen apron. (Diary of Fanny Goodfellow, 27 January 1890)

I was sewing at my quilt (28 January 1890)

I was sewing at my lace (12 February 1890)

I made an apron and mending vests (17 February 1890)

I went to Nessie's Sewing bee today (28 February 1890)

I put in a rug (3 March 1890)

finished Jamima's dress (12 March 1890)

made Button Holes in my Jacket (28 March 1890)

patching pants (29 March 1890)

I made Will a shirt today (8 April 1890)

churning in morning knitting and cro-cheting in afternoon.(14 April 1890)

I cut Annie's Gray Basque in afternoon (16 April 1890)

I finished A's dress and cut Will's pants (24 April 1890)

I made a tick in afternoon. (24 February 1891)

Sometimes Fanny would make a visit to someone's house for the purpose of sewing, just as the professional travelling seamstress' did. Before Christmas 1891 she visited her sister-in-law.

I went up to Stroud to sew (14 December 1891)

Elizabeth Haggarty (formerly Carey), dressmaker and milliner of Smith's Falls, ca. 1890. *Author's collection*

I was sewing at Jane's dress. I went to school concert in evening (15 December 1891)

I was sewing at Jane's dress. (16 December 1891)

I finished Jane's dress and came home. (17 December 1891)

Hats were also important, as women did not go outside without one. Around the farm, or garden, simple bonnets or old straw coverings would do. Hats for town were trimmed by the wearer, and so could be changed to renew them. A new one was a matter of some excitement, as happened each Easter by tradition.

An invoice showing Elizabeth Haggarty's purchases for her business from a supplier in Perth, dated 5 August 1898. *Author's collection*

finished trimming her bonnet & trims her cream hat with pink very pretty (Diary of Annie Elizabeth Cragg, 7 June 1888)

Veils were also useful.

> From the Sun on the Snow I decided to get a Veil as they are cheaper than Glass & may keep off some freckles too. Still it is very hard for me to wear one I have a stifled kind of a feeling with one on because I can't see [illegible] (Diary of Belle Kittredge, Wednesday undated (late January) 1892)

One diversion during Lent was the unveiling of the new spring hats at local millinery shops, in preparation for Easter.

> went to Murray's opening—*such* hats! *very* pretty & odd summer styles. (Diary of Bessie Mabel Scott, 17 March 1891)

Shoes were thin, and kept out neither the cold nor wet. One welcome invention was the rubber shoe. These proved to be indispensable items, once discovered. Eleanora and Mary Hallen, who both had a great passion for scrambling outdoors year round, viewed them with great favour.

> In the evening Mary and I walked out going up a little path we had used to go when we lived here before we find the great advantage of our Indian rubber shoes. (Diary of Eleanora Hallen, 7 November 1845)

OUTDOORS

Whenever they could, women took their tasks outdoors. Naturally this was impossible in the winter. But from May to October, a great deal of food peeling, chicken plucking and handwork could take place on the porch. The communal washbasin might be moved out there too, as it was easier to empty when you could simply fling the water over the nearest flowering bush.

The messy business of the weekly laundry naturally took place outside. Helen Wismer recorded her "grandmother's washday receet" from The Twenty in the Niagara Peninsula.

Grandmother's Washday Receet recorded by Helen Wismer

1. Build a fire in backyard to heet kettle of rainwater
2. Set tubs so smoke wont blow in eyes if wind is pert
3. Shave one hole cake of lye soap in bilin' water
4. Sort things. Make 3 piles. One pile white. One pile cullard. One pile work britches and rags.
5. Stir flour in cold water to smooth, then thin down with bilin' water.
6. Rub dirty sports on board. Scrub hard, then bile, rub cullard but dont bile. Just rench and starch.
7. Take white things out of bilin' water with broomstick handle.
8. Spread tee towels on grass, hang old rags on fence.
9. Pore rench water on flower beds.
10. Scrub porch with hot soapy water.
11. Turn tubs upside down.
12. Go put on cleen dress, smooth hair with side combs, brew cup of tee, set and rest and rock a spell and count your blessins.[50]

Although it was a novelty when a young woman first began to help mother with the wash, the joy quickly faded once it became a necessary chore.

> In the morning we commenced the washing. Father went to town. We were very busy amusing ourselves at the wash-tub, if we can call it amusement. I always like to wash. I think it just as healthy an amusement, as any girl can be engaged in. (Diary of Matilda Bowers Eby, 14 January 1863)

> This morning the weather turned out very beautiful, so I prepared myself for washing. There was nothing I could have enjoyed more than washing this forenoon, it always makes me feel well and active when I take wash-tub exercise. (13 May 1863)

> Today I commenced my weekly routine with a very large wash. Am extremely tired tonight in consequence. The poor wretched women have the same course of work to pass

through week, after week, no wonder if they would get tired of it. (12 September 1865)

Once they were washed, the clothes were hung outside on a line, very chilly work on a cold day.

had to wash and it stormed all forenoon but got them dry by night. very tired. (Diary of Annie Elizabeth Cragg, 31 January 1889)

There was nothing worse than having wet clothes hanging around for days.

We washed but I don't know when the clothes will dry. (Diary of Mary Coldwell Butcher, 13 September 1892)

Women who first encountered a machine to help with the laundry were very grateful. The men in their lives might be somewhat more re-sistant.

Washing machines were unknown for many years. The first we ever heard of was through an agent who called. He met fa-ther at the gate and asked if he could sell him a machine. Fa-ther said, "he had two very good ones in the house." He wanted to know what make they were and father said "he had better come in and see." So he brought him in to where sister Sara and I were busy with tubs and boards.[51]

Once they were brought inside, most of the clothes had to be ironed, a painful process involving heating the irons on the stove and using a board stretched across two chairs or the kitchen table as a flat surface. Many items which no modern woman would think to iron were still painstakingly cared for in this way, including dish towels and sheets.

Ironed table cloths and sheets. (Diary of Frances Gay Simp-son, 11 March 1881)

Ironing the weekly wash often took the best part of a day. With two working days of the week devoted to laundry, it is obvious why women welcomed the arrival of their daughters at an age when they could help, and why houses short of hands needed to hire someone. The outside laundress was someone even the most modest home could welcome.

> Hired girl wash'd early and left here for her Aunt's wedding. (Diary of Eliza Bellamy, 17 January 1855)

> Mrs Carl came to wash. (Diary of Frances Gay Simpson, 27 June 1881)

> 6 weeks washing $5.25 (Diary of Mary Brown, 2 April 1881)

The vegetable garden was largely the woman's province too. The men would probably do the cultivation, but the whole family contributed to the planting and maintenance of the growing plants. Once things were ready for picking, eating and preserving, the women would be solely responsible, with the children urged to help with simple tasks.

> the boys were busy pulling carrots. (Diary of Ann Amelia Day, 15 October 1878)

Sometimes there were pressing tasks connected with the barnyard too.

> went out to barn and helped with three load of oats (Diary of Fanny Goodfellow, 26 September 1891)

> Set out about 50 cabbage plants and some tomatoes in evening. (Diary of Sophia Adams, 18 May 1880)

> Just came in (9 o'clock) from hunting the red heifer. She did not come up tonight. (2 May 1883)

Despite the fact that there was rigourous division of labour between the sexes, some tasks were done by both. When Ellen Adams, who had moved from farm to city, returned to visit her parents in Trafalgar, she was keen that her son learn some farm skills. He turned the table on her.

> Barclay is learning to milk. I was anxious that I should see how well he could do it so this evening I went with him & he

really does very well but imagine his surprise when he found I could milk. I evidently rose several steps in his estimation.[52]

To store vegetables through the winter, a pit was often dug in the garden. This was before the days of a more organized fruit cellar. Tusie Zurbrigg of New Hamburg remembered the one behind their house:

> My dad put a pit in the garden. He dug quite a hole in the garden, quite near the house so it would be easy to get at, so that the snow wouldn't bother them too much. Away in the bottom he'd lay boards. In would go the cabbage, the carrots, the beets, the turnips, whatever we had—beans, carrots, peas, then the boards were sloped like a roof, so that the snow would slide off. And then for the end he'd have boards that he could pull out. Sometimes it was quite a task, they were frozen pretty solid. Then he'd take out a basketful for us and a basketful for the neighbours that didn't have a pit. Oh my, that cabbage, I can still hear it crackle & the celery was so good![53]

The pit had to be carefully constructed or the vegetables would freeze.

> Mr Loree came over for the pick and George went back with him to help get turnips out of the pit. (Diary of Ann Amelia Day, 27 December 1878)

Later the pit would become larger. It took on more permanent characteristics, such as doors, before moving indoors as the fruit cellar beneath the house. The latter would have shelves for preserves and baskets full of vegetables, and often a direct hole leading outdoors to let in the cold.

Flowers were of great importance for many women:

> The tulips are gone and the red peonies, nearly. The yellow daffs, my dear Ma admired because they were so early. The white and pink peonies are in bud. I prize my flowers for the friends who gave them to me. Aunt Baker sent me the tulips, observing that there was a greater variety among them than most persons had. She gave me a great many others—Some or most are dead. Colchichum, Persian iris, Mrs Crafts, Ragged

Robin, a very showy red flower, spirea, pink and white, rose multiflora, York and Lancaster. Of Ma the white peonies, red, daffies. (Diary of Catharine Merritt, 5 June 1859)

Many country women sold eggs and dairy products to supplement their housekeeping money.

Rosalia Al and Ina went in in the cutter. Rosalia took 10 lbs of butter. She got 28 cents for it. Al got his face frozen. (Diary of Thomas Adams, 23 February 1889)

As well as feeding the chickens, caring for them required putting them inside at night, letting them out in the morning, collecting the eggs, and occasionally cleaning out the henhouse. Many of these tasks were ones which children could do, especially collecting the eggs. William Rusk of Pontypool remembered an 1890's visit to an uncle one Sunday afternoon.

I went out to help my cousin Maggie Jane Lunn collect eggs. I put some in my vest pockets. She had the longest arms! she started to chase me and I ran but she threw her arms around me and broke all those eggs.[54]

Other surplus produce could be used for ready cash as well.

Picking plums. Sent 5 baskets to sell with Mr Blanchard. $1.35 a bus[hel] (Diary of Mary Coldwell Butcher, 17 September 1892)

HANDWORK

Aside from the pressing tasks of everyday—cooking, cleaning, laundry—most women spent a great deal of time doing handwork. Susanna Whaley, when still a teenager, had already developed a number of skills.

It is a midling nice day. I was baking and ironing this forenoon and made a chemise this afternoon, we finished spinning for cloth to day. (Diary of Susanna Whaley, 23 September 1864)

Besides spinning wool for weaving into cloth, knitting yarn was also produced. Susanna Whaley spent a great deal of time at this occupation, often spinning several skeins a day. However, before Susanna reached the spinning stage, she would have spent many hours preparing the fleece. Usually the fleece was washed. When dry it was carded, a process which helped to remove foreign matter and separate the fibres, giving the wool a light fluffy appearance. The wool was then ready for spinning. In order to create the desired thickness of yarn, several strands of spun wool would be twisted together. After spinning, the wool might be dyed. Once these jobs were completed, it was time to begin knitting.

> It is a midling nice day I finished coloring black today I colored 98 scanes....(Diary of Susanna Whaley, 1 October 1864)

> It is raining and it rained all day Eliza and I washed the yarn to day and then we knit some (9 November 1864)

> It is a nice but midling cold day I finished twisting the stocking yarn to day Eliza was helping pull turnips this afternoon and was doubling yarn in the forenoon. (10 November 1864)

Susanna sold some of her handwork, thereby adding to the family coffers.

> It was a very nice day. I sold four pair of socks and a pair of stockings to Tomas Halls, we repaired a pair of stockings for Ma then started to knit mittens Mrs Holinger was here for tea this afternoon they were picking Potatoes but did not get quite done. (22 November 1864)

The amount of handwork completed by Susanna Whaley would make most women dizzy. Not only did she knit and spin like fury, but also she sewed pants, shirts, dresses, and quilted petticoats to keep the womenfolk warm during cold weather. For many women though, handwork projects were done on a more leisurely basis.

> I have made three pairs of mitts and two pairs of socks this fall. (Diary of Jessie Geddes, 26 October 1898)

Began knitting white rug. (Diary of Frances Gay Simpson, 3
May 1881)

Knitting seal silk stockings for Daisy. (Diary of Mary Brown, 1
February 1881)

As well as the knitting of useful things, many decorative items could
also be made using crochet or lacemaking. Some things, such as the
woolwork throw covering the woodbox in the kitchen, were a combination of beauty and function.

Young women higher on the social scale were taught that it was
always wise to have something to occupy oneself, since "idle hands
were the devil's playground." They would work on embroidery or
lace. For farm women, handwork had a more pressing quality, making
items which were necessary for use at home.

Emma Laflamme thought of the handwork as a pleasure, but if
some girls rebelled, it might have been because of the view that it was
"good for them." In the religious magazine for youth, *The Cottager's
Friend*, published in Toronto, Mrs. L.H. Sigourney lectured on its ad-
vantages:

> Needle-work in all its countless forms of use, elegance and or-
> nament, has been the appropriate occupation of women....
> The numerous modifications of mending are not beneath the
> notice of the most refined young lady. A very sensible, ratio-
> nal self-complacency arises from the power of making "auld
> claiths look amaist as well as new." And here permit me to ad-
> vert to that almost forgotten utensil, the large spinning wheel.
> From the universal yet gentle exercise it affords the limbs, the
> chest & the whole frame, it is altogether the best mode of do-
> mestic calisthenics which has hitherto been devised.[55]

At a time when everyone depended on natural light and women had
so much needlework to do, the seat by the window was of great importance. It was necessary to have a good clear window for adequate
light, and a comfortable chair (though not an easy chair by any
means).

On the upper floor of the house the rooms were ranged along either side of a hall which left a space at the end, often with a window.
This large space was sometimes enclosed as a separate room, but al-

most always was used for sewing, large enough for two or three to sit together in the good light, working and chatting together. Here the girls could learn a great deal from their elders, and form bonds which would last a lifetime.

The good window seat often faced the lane, so that visitors gave fair warning of their arrival as they turned in. Fresh aprons could be put on, hair arranged and the kettle put on the stove.

> I spent the greater part of the day at my embroidery. But I really don't believe it is good for any one to be stooping over embroidery a whole day. It must be injurious to the eyes, to look so sharp, I know a little by experience. (Diary of Matilda Bowers Eby, 12 February 1863)

It was too bad that handwork was easier to do in the winter, when the light was not so good, than in the brilliant days of summer:

> I do not intend to work any next summer. it is not pleasant work in summer. It needs such constant attention & a cool hand, which becomes very difficult in the hot, close, sultry days. (Diary of Emma Laflamme, 6 February 1887)

It was also important to keep the home supplied with bedding and linen.

> Today, Maria and I commenced her quilt. It is a "double star" patern. I like it very much, it looks most beautiful and very showy. I think it looks much better than if it was three colors. We made two and a half patches. I think we done well for a beginning. There are fifty-six pieces in a patch and it takes twelve patches—consequently there are six hundred and seventy two pieces in a quilt without the border. I like to make patchwork very well. (Diary of Matilda Bowers Eby, 2 February 1868)

Lace making kept many a young woman occupied.

> I gave Katie a lace collar last week. Must try & work at lace today. Yesterday was busy copying receipts and doing some marking. day before it was too dark in the afternoon for any-

thing like lace work. (Diary of Emma Laflamme, 1 September 1886)

I have a very good mind to start some knitting, I cannot work at lace except in a good light—when my weeks mending is out of the road I have no pick up work now. (16 February 1887)

PESTS

Even the best regulated homes were plagued with pests of the kinds we know today—mice, ants, beetles—but people also had to put up with some of the more unsavoury bugs.

a brute of a flea has been at me where could it have come from! (Diary of Emma Laflamme, 15 August 1887)

In the absence of today's chemical products, people were always on the lookout for useful ways to do away with these unwelcome visitors. Some methods were healthy and natural, such as the suggestion that flies would not enter a room which had a window box of geraniums and calceolarias, "which is always a source of pleasure and which now proves also to be a source of comfort."[56]
However they had their own chemical concoctions:

To Prevent Red Ants: Put one pint of tar in an earthen vessel, pour on it two quarts of boiling hot water, and place it in your closet.[57]

Bedrooms were especially liable to bedbugs and moths, which were attracted to woollen clothing and rugs in the warm weather.

To destroy bed bugs, moths and other vermin: dissolve alum in hot water, making a very strong solution; apply to furniture or crevices in the walls with paint brush. This is sure destruction to those noxious vermin and invaluable because easily obtained, is perfectly safe to use, and leaves no unpleasant traces behind. When you suspect moths have lodged in the borders of carpets, wet the edges of the carpets with a strong solution; whenever it reaches them it is certain death.[58]

Not only the house but also the body might be invaded by pests. Here is a remedy, the reading of which might make the modern person wish to head for the shower:

> To expel nameless intruders from children's heads: Steep larkspur seed in water, rub the liquor a few times into the child's hair, and the business of destruction is done. This is an effectual remedy. Does it not make your head itch?[59]

While housekeeping required a great deal more energy before the age of automation, life maintained a less hurried tone than we know today. The weeks and years passed, following long established traditions, such as washday on Monday and berry-picking in June. It might have been while reviewing the endless tasks which filled the days of a housekeeper that the following popular mid-nineteenth century rhyme was created.

I'm sure if I were free again,
I'd live a single life;
And not be such a simpleton
As to become a wife.

Cooking

I had such a good appetite and we lived off the fat of the land.
DIARY OF CATHARINE MERRITT, 24 SEPTEMBER 1855

THE VICTORIAN HOUSEWIFE did not have anything ready-made for her, nor a restaurant to turn to if she did not feel like cooking. The rules of her kitchen were simple: everything made from scratch, fresh and hearty, three or more times a day—every day. Although the farmwife had her root cellar for keeping things cool, there was no refrigeration for longterm storage. As early as April 1884, The Ladies' Journal was carrying a plan for a "cheap ice box." The iceman was soon a common sight on town streets, but even the icebox had a limited use. It was, anyway, not available to those in the country.

The meals which she produced were similar to the ones we grew up with thirty or forty years ago. The last twenty years have seen a revolution in our cookery. But before that there was a simple sameness about the daily dinner.

> we had a leg of mutton, potatoes, carrots, bread pudding and custard. (Diary of Eleanora Hallen, 19 July 1841)

There was a strong emphasis on meat.

...dinner, at which we had tomato soup, Round of Beef very delicious, & Calves head with bit of bacon. Apple tart & bread pudding. no dessert, but delicious coffee & cake. (Diary of Mary Brown, 20 February 1893)

The term 'dessert' meant fruit and nuts, not sweets, as it does to us. From the evidence of Mrs. Brown's diary, there were plenty of sweets! She does not mention vegetables, although there surely would have been some. From her household accounts, it is clear that vegetables were very expensive, especially in the winter (if they were available at all). So people doubtless ate many fewer of them than we would.

Catharine Merritt was on holiday in Buffalo when she wrote the words at the head of this chapter. She continued:

sweet potatoes, green corn and tomatoes every day, for dinner. Peaches always for tea. Fowl, roasted and boiled, beefsteak and lamb, pumpkin and apple pie and apple pudding, rice cakes, muffins, gingerbread, corn muffins, melon, pears, blackberries. These are things I particularly like, not to mention soup and maccaroni, baked potatoes, Windsor beans, rich cakes, etc. (Diary of Catharine Merritt, 25 September 1855)

With so much cooking to be done, everything had to be accomplished efficiently, and many hands made the work lighter. In the country, daughters learned quickly that they had a role to play.

My mother was a wonderful cook. Their habit in that day was, a daughter learned to cook and a son had to learn how to farm. That was my mother's way and she had me learn to bake bread before I was ten years old. I can see myself. There was a wooden bake trough—four feet long and about two feet high and sides. I'd be standing there kneading the dough.[60]

The day began early, with the lighting of the stove. Then, while the farm animals were being seen to, breakfast would be prepared. The animals always came first. Sometimes chores needed doing, and the cooking had to take care of itself.

They would put the cream of wheat pot on the back of the stove and then go out to the barn. When they got back, it was ready.[61]

The breakfast would be a large one, setting everybody up for a day's hard work. There would be meat and potatoes, or porridge, bread and jam, pie and tea. The rule was very clear: pie three times a day.

After a long morning's work, the men would return from the fields for their dinner. This was the principal meal of the day, heavy with potatoes and bread, meat and vegetables, and plenty of sweets for dessert.

The habit might be different in town, where the day's big meal would wait for evening. This was especially true in fashionable families, where the arrangements for meals had taken another turn.

For those who needed a large meal at midday to fuel their working hours, dinner came earlier. Office and factory workers often returned home for dinner, if they lived close enough, and farm workers came in from the fields. Since many had no clock to guide them, some houses had a belfry. The pealing brought the workers in. Those without this luxury were known to hang a sheet out an upper window. It acted as a welcome flag to those working far from the house.[62]

Those whose days were more relaxed fixed their dinner hour in the evening, when they could formalize it, make it more of a party. They laid out a pattern for the courses, complicated the table settings and insisted that everyone dress up for the occasion. For these people, 'luncheon', the midday meal, was an informal, scarcely noticeable time. It was not until this century that the lunch party filled the festive void at noon.

Those who had their dinner at midday often called the evening meal 'tea'. It was a simple meal, perhaps of soup, leftovers and preserved fruit. It should not be confused with afternoon tea, the social occasion discussed later, in Chapter 9

> Sunday. Had breakfast and dinner at Will Vails went to Mr Saxons for tea. Started for home at 7 p.m. (Diary of Thomas Adams, 29 August 1886)

The nibbling between meals which we know was not as common then. For one thing, there was less food, and the kinds of food eaten were not of a nibbling sort. That is not to say that food treats did not exist.

My grandmother told me that eating contests were very popular in the family and that her brothers, all six feet tall, could eat their length in cobs of corn. A very common thing for her sister to do in an evening in the winter was to bring into the kitchen a big wooden bowl of apples and they would spend the evening eating the apples and cracking hickory nuts by the fire. Mother remembers her Aunt filling a "milk tin" with apples to eat. This "milk tin" was placed on the kitchen table and everyone sat around. The "milk tin" was used for separating the cream from the milk.[63]

A characteristic of gentle society, one that increased as the century wore on, was the dislike of being seen or heard eating. The Victorians loved dinner parties, but preferred to pretend that they spent all their time talking, not eating. This was part of the general dislike of all bodily functions, which became an inhibiting fetish.

Mary and Mis M we laughed at afterwards for not taking apples as although they liked them, they did not like making a noise eating them. (Diary of Eleanora Hallen, 17 January 1846)

Tea was the common drink at meals, although the more expensive coffee also had some currency. Everyone drank water which came fresh and clear from the pump and was kept in a bucket in the kitchen. Lemonade was possible for special occasions, hand squeezed, made with brown sugar, and very pale and delicious in flavour. In autumn when the apples were plentiful, there was the pleasure of cider.

Mrs Loree sent over a pailful of cider. (Diary of Ann Amelia Day, 14 December 1878)

the boys went skating this afternoon and we girls ate apples and drank cider and talked nonsense. (25 December 1878)

Cookbooks offered recipes for root beer, ginger beer and cream soda, but they were a lot of work for a small return.

Much of the housewife's day would be taken up with concerns about the coming meals. This was especially true in the morning, with the big meal at noon. The afternoon would not require as much immediate care, although preparations for the next day and the next week might be necessary.

Because the early winter was a good time to butcher, meals during the cold months contained more beef or pork. The summer was a little leaner, but the availability of so many fresh foods at that time was a compensation. Anything that could be preserved during the summer for eating during the winter was "done down," and stored. Fruits were stored in sugar syrup, much sweeter than we like today. Some were dried. Vegetables were kept in the pit or root cellar, or preserved in brine.

The town housewife did not have the extensive stores of the farmwife but did have more access to the butcher and greengrocer. She probably shopped daily, particularly for meat.

9 lbs Beef $1.35 (Diary of Mary Brown, 28 June 1888)

Fish was rare in the country, although there were fisheries in the Great Lakes in those days. Belle Kittredge met a fisherman in the street in Port Arthur.

I passed a dog team of fish…a box sleigh about as long as a cutter runner but low, about the height of a dog. It was filled with frozen fish. Around the sides they were standing up like palisades around the "fort" at Toronto and in the centre the fish were piled one on another, the pickets of palisades keeping them from falling out. The sleigh was drawn by four dogs all different kinds of mongrel but nearly one size and one was harnessed ahead of the other tandem fashion. The man said he had from Seven to Eight hundred fish in the sleigh. (Diary of Belle Kittredge, 29 January 1892)

Inland from the lakes, it was possible that a travelling fishmonger would call at the farm.

At noon a boy called with fresh herrings. (Diary of Ann Amelia Day, 24 September 1878)

For Frances Gay Simpson in Hamilton, there was a greater choice.

Went to the butchers and bought a fish (Diary of Frances Gay Simpson, 13 July 1881)

Pickled fish. (23 July 1881)

Sometimes there would be an exotic surprise available.

Mrs Allan Geddes sends us a present of some lobsters which we enjoy at dinner. (Diary of Forbes Geddes, 8 April 1862)

One of the few foods which seem unusual to us but was everyday fare to the Victorians was the oyster, sold by the barrel in the grocer's.

Oyster supper at Siffang's expence—Had them *cold* at Tea—a mistake—only good with Beer or Half-&-Half. (Diary of Forbes Geddes, 13 December 1862)

Frank had a Gentleman's Whist party so when we got home we went up to the kitchen. Annie was getting their supper ready I never tasted oyster salad before & never will again. (Diary of Belle Kittredge, 6 January 1892)

Cookbooks of the time often suggested stuffing poultry with oysters or adding them to the gravy. Other shellfish are rarely mentioned.

A woman fishing on Georgian Bay, 1890s. Fresh fish was a rare commodity.
Breithaupt-Hewetson-Clark Collection, University of Waterloo

The cooking of meat was similar to our own. Large pieces were roasted in the oven, smaller ones were fried. For the working man, the usual thing was to fry the meat in a large metal pan on top of the stove, take it out and make pan gravy with the remains, pouring it over the meat and potatoes. Boiled meats, generally regarded now as tough and tasteless, were very popular. Even whole fowl, including turkeys, were boiled in huge pots. Since much of the pork was salted for preservation, it had to be soaked in cold water or milk before cooking. Nonetheless it was more salty and fatty than we are used to. This was regarded with equanimity.

Certain parts of the meat which we might regard as being without interest were used regularly, as frugality was a virtue of every good housekeeper.

> Sheep's trotters are sold ready cleaned and very cheap...cook them, by way of a treat, for supper or otherwise...[64]

As well as the usual organ meats (heart, liver, kidney and brains), there was tongue (which required long cooking and paring), heads and feet. One cookbook gave a recipe for a stewlike soup made from lamb's head, heart and lights (lungs). Headcheese was the ground meat from the pig's head. A calf's head could be boiled, the meat picked off carefully and put in a mould with the juice in which it had been boiled. With a little salt and pepper, and a layer of hardboiled eggs, it was a tasty meal for lunch or evening tea, served under the at-tractive name 'jellied veal'. Pig's trotters could be done the same way, and served without mentioning the origin of the meat.

> My dad would always have to have—it was a delicacy for him. He loved them. He always got the fried pig's brains for sup-per. Just fried in butter.[65]

Simple roasting or frying, and particularly boiling, meant the meat tasted very plain. A wide range of pickles and prepared sauces were available, which would enliven the meat. They would also help dis-guise the taste of any meat on the verge of turning.

Leftover meats for use at evening tea or lunch could be made into soup, pie, a loaf or croquettes. Soups were especially handy for using up bits of vegetables, potato and meat. They were easy, economical and welcomed by the family.

Fowl was a pleasing change from meat. Even in town, many people could keep their own chickens. The meat was fresh, and available when you wanted it, providing you had time to pluck and draw the hen. If you did not keep your own, you were dependent on the market.

Could not get any spring chickens. (Diary of Mary Brown, 11 June 1888)

Turkeys and geese were usual fare for special occasions, including the still traditional Thanksgiving and Christmas.

Turkey 1.25 (Diary of Mary Brown, 17 November 1888)

Goose 75 cents (10 November 1888)

Not so very long ago, the sky over parts of Ontario occasionally turned black, as huge flocks of pigeons arrived. The farmers may not have welcomed this event, for fear of losing crops and seed. But the frugal housekeeper was filled with joy at the thought of providing nutritious meals for very little cost.

The boys went off this morning to Johnny Talbot's with Dunbar's gun, Alfred having told them there were a lot of pigeons up that way. They got our gun from Johnny but they did not find the game until afternoon. They came home at dark with 5 pigeons.(Diary of Ann Amelia Day, 5 September 1878)

Vegetables were usually boiled, although some were fried or baked. Most recipes of the time call for long cooking of vegetables, making them very soft. *The Canadian Home Cook Book* (1877) suggests boiling cobs of corn for thirty minutes and beets for several hours. Both salads and the eating of raw vegetables were rarer than now. The most common salad was of cold cooked vegetables with mayonnaise, although cabbage with boiled dressing was also a possibility. Rice was primarily eaten as a pudding. Mushrooms were scarcely known at all, except as a pickle, although most farmers probably had some growing wild on their property. The poisonous qualities of some of them may have put people off.

Cookbooks of the time used much more of their space discussing the sweeter parts of the meal than they did the primary courses. They knew that there would be meat, potatoes and vegetables, whose basic appearances would not vary much. If a cook wanted to be creative, then she had the opportunities provided by the various pies, puddings, and especially cakes.

Baking might seem problematic to us. The heat of the woodburning range could not be as easily adjusted as on our stoves. For cooking pastry and cakes, the temperature is of great importance.

> One thing the learning baker was shown was how to judge an oven's heat. There were no thermometers; instead, the baker put her hand into the centre of the oven and held it there for a short time. Through experience, she could tell if the oven was the correct temperature for whatever she was preparing—"slow," "medium" or "quick" were the terms used. In a variation of this technique, sometimes the hand was dampened with water. The time it took to evaporate was an indication of the temperature.[66]

A more scientific method was suggested.

> When about to bake try an oven every ten minutes or so with a piece of white paper. If this blazes or blackens directly it is put in, the oven is too fierce for anything; if at the end of a minute or two the paper becomes of a dark, almost chocolate, brown, the oven is fit for small pastry, such as patties, etc., if it turns a lightish brown (the tint of a cigar), you may put in fruit pies and tarts; if it turns a darkish yellow (about the shade of deal), the oven is fit for game or meat pies, pound or other rich substantial cakes or bread; but for sponge cakes, meringues etc., the paper should only just become of a pale yellow—in fact, should but just discolour. This is a most excellent way of testing an oven, and may be thoroughly relied on.[67]

It was necessary to know your range well, because the housewife did not bake a single pie or a dozen rolls. Instead she spent a whole day baking.

Made 3 big cakes, 18 little ones 2 pies 2 pans of buns—bread

& currant bread. (Diary of Annie Elizabeth Cragg, 27 January 1888)

did Saturdays work & a big baking 13 doz. buns (5 April 1889)

The baking of cakes was difficult at the best of times. As Edna Stae-bler has said, even the best cook can make a disastrous cake. The secret is to turn it into something else, perhaps a pudding (if you can); and bake a better one next time.

I made 2 cakes one good the other miserable. (Diary of Annie Elizabeth Cragg, 2 March 1889)

The quantities of the ingredients in some nineteenth century recipes are astonishing, indicating a huge result. Here is a list for a traditional wedding fruitcake:

Eighteen pounds of flour, twelve of butter, twelve of sugar, six of raisins, six of currants, three of citron [peel], twelve dozen eggs, half pound of cloves, one quart of brandy and as much other spice as you like.[68]

A recipe for mincemeat in *Mother Hubbard's Cupboard* (1881) made three gallons!

Fruit pies were popular, following the season through the summer: rhubarb, currant, strawberry, raspberry, gooseberry, cherry, huckleberry, peach, plum, apple, pumpkin. Apples provided fruit for pies through the winter, and dried fruit could do the same.

This A.M. I made some fancy pies for the Pic-Nic such as raisins, Lemons and Apples. I was well pleased with my success (Diary of Matilda Bowers Eby, 14 August 1863)

Mincemeat pie, which really did contain meat in those days, was good for a winter meal as well, not only at Christmas. What we call cream pies came in one flavour only (vanilla), and were known as custard pie; cream pie was a cake with a custard filling. With a chocolate topping, it was later known as Boston Cream Pie. The pieplates of the time were somewhat shallower than our deep ones.

Puddings were very popular because they "stuck to the ribs". Cookbooks offered many variations. They involved a lot of flour, sugar, raisins or currants. They were steamed for hours in a pudding basin or cloth. The result was somewhat heavy, but it was relished by our ancestors.

Custards were also popular and made in many flavours, as was jelly. There were no mixes, but gelatine did come in packages easy for flavouring.

One interesting pudding-cum-cake was made from cornmeal. Corn had been introduced to North American settlers by the native peoples. it had never caught on in Britain, where it was regarded as appropriate for animal feed. Pioneers came to realize its usefulness. In the southern United States, cornmeal was put to many uses; in Ontario it was used in bread, pancakes and the very popular dessert, johnny cake.

> We are going to have a good supper tonight. We are going to have a johnny cake which Margaret is making. It is very healthy. (Diary of Catherine Bell Van Norman, 25 January 1850

> Rain last night which was much wanting—everything looks lovely this morning. a calf was killed had veal for dinner. cook'd made pies & jony cake for supper (Diary of Eliza Bellamy, 14 May 1855)

The following recipe was given to Viola MacKenzie Parrott of Oshawa in 1909 by her great-aunt, Edwina (Doddridge) Burton of New Richmond, Quebec.

Johnny Cake

Preheat oven to 400. Grease an 8 inch square baking dish. When the oven is heated, place the greased dish in the oven for five minutes just before filling with the batter. Cream one tablespoon butter with 1/2 cup sugar. Add one egg and beat well. Mix together one cup corn meal, 1 cup flour, 2 teaspoons baking powder, one teaspoon salt. Add the dry mixture to the butter alternately with one cup milk. Pour batter into heated pan (this gives you a crispy outside). Bake for 30 minutes & test for done. Serve hot in squares with butter and maple syrup.

One reason for the popularity of this cornmeal cake was that it kept well, and was frequently packed by travellers. Its popularity was universal in Canada and the United States.

There were some nuts available, if you could find them in the woods and gather them yourself, but most baking did not include them.

I went to gather beech-nuts in Burchills bush got about one quart and a half. (Diary of Laura McMurray, 24 October 1899)

Raisins and currants were used instead. They required a great deal of work, because raisins still included the pips from their time as grapes, and currants had stems. Each raisin or currant had to be worked over before baking could begin.

Stoned nearly 10 lbs raisins—an easy way to clean them, which Gert told me, is to pour boiling water over them, leave in three or four minutes, then drain—it loosened the stones & they slip right out. (Diary of Emma Laflamme, 12 December 1886)

Figs were much more popular than they are today. They were made into a steamed pudding, cake and pie, and combined with strawberries or rhubarb to make a flavourful jam.

Although we do not find cookies mentioned as often as we might expect in cookbooks of the time, they were still popular. Even in 1891, however, cookies were not as tasty as 'the good old days.'

Sometimes we chose a cooky instead, a cooky 'as was a cooky' not a thin wafer-like, dry cooky, like the cookies of this generation, but a full inch thick and almost as large as a saucer—a cooky to delight the heart and still more the stomach of a hungry boy.[69]

Small pastries which were referred to as 'cakes' were universal. They came in many forms, and were closer to scones than buns. They were not as sweet as the big proper cakes, and were not iced. They had seeds or currants inside. They and the huge cookies like saucers were kept in stone crocks in the cool pantry, covered by a lid or simply a cloth over the top.

> It is long since some of us have seen any of the crullers of which we were so fond when grandmother made them. She used to make, also, a toothsome little seed-cake, fragrant with carraway and anise seeds, with sugar on top, the like of which we have not seen since we used to slip into her pantry, and help ourselves out of the old blue stone jar in which they were always kept.[70]

As the nostalgic writer notes, Grandma used to make doughnuts too; these were raised cake doughnuts, fried and rolled in sugar.

Bread might be bought. Even a village as small as Kendal had a baker: Susan Armstrong was famous for her delicious buns. She simply baked at home and sold to her neighbours. Of course the towns had bakeries. Most people would have to make their own bread however. One difficulty was keeping the yeast going, from one baking to the next.

> I had to walk to Rockwood for some yeast cakes to set yeast and that made me late with my part of the washing. (Diary of Ann Amelia Day, 14 October 1878)

> I went and took the shawl home that I borrowed the other night and took a pitcher for yeast but they had just made new yeast and it had not risen enough then so I left the pitcher (28 May 1879)

Those lucky enough to have a bakery at hand found a limited selection. Brown bread had a countrified or old fashioned quality; everyone wanted the new, better white bread.

Town bakeries would offer fruit pies throughout the summer; apple pies all year; mincemeat at Christmas; fruit and butter tarts; bread. There were no frosted cakes, as they did not travel well. Instead fruitcake and pound cake were available, cooked in large pans, and cut off, in half or one pound slices, as the customer wanted. Pound cake was much more popular then.[71]

The making of candy was very much for special occasions. As we have seen, taffy-pulling was part of the maple syrup process. Other types of candy might appear at Christmas, but every young woman knew how to make fudge.

we have been saving up our coppers for some time & as we have 12 we bought a pound & a half of brown sugar, after try-ing for it in three different stores and are going down soon (9.45 P.M.) to make some candy. (Diary of Bessie Mabel Scott, 28 November 1889)

Bessie's sweet tooth led her to frequent bouts of fudge-making during her two years at the University of Toronto. The other students soon began expecting sugary treats as her contribution to their meetings!

When so many weddings were held at home, the supper after-wards would have to be provided for the guests. *The Ladies' Journal* for October 1890 proposed the following as the menu following an af-ternoon wedding.

Scalloped potatoes	Cocoanut cake
Pressed chicken	Kisses
Boiled Ham	Lady's fingers
Salmon Salad	Bride's cake

Kisses are small meringues. This simple meal would be easily pre-pared ahead; only the potatoes are hot, and they could be made ready for the oven in the morning and heated as soon as the service was over. Essentially the meal consists of cold meat, hot potatoes, two cakes and two kinds of cookie. The dressing for the salmon (with let-tuce and hardboiled eggs) is a creamy vinaigrette. All of the sweets are white in colour, appropriate for the wedding theme. The menu is typ-ical of those proposed for similar parties at the time. Coconut cake was often suggested as party fare. Its soft icing decorated with flaked coconut looks very festive. Bride's cake, which was naturally widely served at weddings, is a plain white cake frosted with a boiled and whipped white icing. There was also a groom's cake.

A more complex, but still similar, cold collation for an afternoon wedding is given in Emma Laflamme's account in the chapter on Courting. It has in common with this one the pressed chicken and cold ham, coconut cake and bride's cake. But the Laflammes added an assortment of pickles to spice up the cold meats, and both fresh and preserved fruit.

The number of pickles made would probably surprise us, as modern hostesses seem to confine themselves to olives and dills, and make very few themselves. In the past, almost anything might be pickled. As well as simple pickles in brine, there were sauces (quite a few kinds of catsup, both grape and mushroom being popular), and varieties of ground pickles, both sweet and sour. In her *Food That Really Schmecks*, Edna Staebler points out this basic dichotomy in pickling, but sweet pickles are not as popular as they once were.

Basic to pickling is vinegar, probably needed in large amounts. While you might buy it, making your own was cheaper and quite simple, a winter job.

> Vinegar for pickling: Put two pounds of coarsest brown sugar to one gallon of fresh cold water, mix well, then put a little yeast on to a piece of toast, and lay on the liquid; stir well for a week, then cover the vessel with brown paper, in which holes have been made with a pin. Keep in a warm place, and in about four months' time you will have good strong vinegar.[72]

An even stronger vinegar is made with cider.

The housewife could start early in the season and pickle asparagus, then small onions, cucumbers of course, cauliflower, grapes, cherries, sliced peppers, butternuts, pears, peaches, plums, crabapples, watermelon rind, mushrooms and oysters. Capers could be made using not only the traditional nasturtium seeds, but also marsh marigold buds and unripened elderberries.

Some of these pickles were very simple to make. Cherries required nothing more than choosing the best candidates for preserving, putting them in a jar with a little salt and vinegar, filling with cold water and putting them away for a few weeks.[73] The result provided extra zip at the winter table.

At the same time as pickling, she would be making preserves, fruit done in sugar syrup. The heaviness of the syrup depended on one's taste; the Victorians liked theirs much sweeter and stronger than we do now, but experimentation doubtless took place.

> Cathie and I peeled the pears and she canned them during the day. Cathie roasted lamb. Cathie put 1/4 lb. of sugar to

each bottle of pears. (Diary of Frances Gay Simpson, 9 September 1881)

The first preserves of the season (not counting the winter-made marmalades) were jars of rhubarb, followed by currants, strawberries, raspberries, cherries, pears, peaches, plums, quince, citron, pineapples, gooseberries, blackberries. All of these could also be made into jam, a necessity of the breakfast table, along with more experimental things such as vegetable marrow marmalade. This invention of a poverty-stricken prairie farmer's wife is surprisingly tasty.

The Victorians' preference for strongly flavoured fruit preserves may be indicated by the Damson Preserve recipe in the first Canadian cookbook, *The Cook Not Mad; or Rational Cookery*, published in Kingston in 1831. It starts with a strong sugar syrup and combines it with the damsons, whole oranges and a pint of brandy. The result will still knock your socks off (if you can find the damsons to start with). The rational cook suggests that cherries and grapes are also good when done this way.[74]

There would then be preserved vegetables, especially tomatoes, which are so versatile with other foods.

Relishes and other chopped pickles were common. Green tomato relish, consisting only of the chopped tomatoes, onion and apple in a sweet brine, was very popular. Variations of these pickles added curry or hot peppers or mustard for a piquant flavour. The basic pickles, which any house could be expected to have, would include catsup, cucumber pickles, horse radish, and a relish or two, such as chow-chow or chili sauce.

Eggs were plentiful in the warm months if you had your own chickens, but the hens did not lay so well in the winter. People learned to preserve eggs in a lime and salt solution, which kept them fresh. As a result, "Families in towns and cities by this plan can have eggs for winter use at summer prices."[75]

By the end of the century, towns were more likely to have a restaurant or hotel dining room. Certain people, businessmen and those who were travelling, would patronize these establishments. But ordinary folks did not consider having an evening out to eat. The food in the restaurants was not so different from the food you would get at home.

met Dr R down King & went with him to dinner at the Walker

House—quite fine! my first dinner at a hotel (Diary of Bessie
Mabel Scott, 27 March 1890)[76]

The *Berlin News Record* for 18 February 1907 carried an advertisement from the Clarendon Restaurant. Dinners there were 25 cents
each or $1 for five. Diners had a choice:

SOUP
Vegetable, Rice, Tomato

FISH
Baked, White

ROASTS
Roast Turkey with dressing
Sirloin of Beef
Spring Lamb—Mint sauce

ENTREES
Boiled Sirloin—mushrooms

VEGETABLES
Potatoes—boiled, mashed
Green peas, Stewed carrots

RELISHES
Pickles, Celery

DESSERT
Pie—Apple, Lemon
Pudding—Tapioca, Chocolate
Tea, Coffee, Milk
Fruit

Servants

Do not rashly give credence to a wife complaining of servants.
CATO

I T WAS NOT ONLY WEALTHY FAMILIES that enjoyed the luxury of servants, for many families of moderate income also had them. In addition, especially during times of ill health or pregnancy, many families hired help to assist with heavy work such as washing.

> Annie Goodall came and washed. We gave her 1 dollar. She will just have to get 50 cents next time. (Diary of Jessie Geddes, 1 February 1900)

In rural areas, hired girls were often enlisted to help farm women with dairy and household chores, while others, who could afford to do so, hired "dailies" to come whenever necessary. However there was often a fast changeover in servants and this points to the fact that things were not always smooth sailing.

> This morning I hired a little girl. She can do little errands for me and take care of the baby so that I am not bothered so much. (Diary of Matilda Bowers Eby, 24 March 1866)

I am very much disappointed in the girl I got. She told me today that she intends leaving next week. I am not sorry at all. (Diary of Matilda Bowers Eby, 4 September 1866)

Some people became so used to leaving all work to the servants that the possibility of having to do it themselves was very distressing.

very very cold & what made me feel it more getting up early as we have parted with our servant & another is not yet come (Diary of Mary Hallen, 16 January 1853)

Cook gave notice to leave. All the children except Harry and Harley dining at grandmammas. (Diary of Mary Brown, 26 December 1864)

Oh! dear, in the midst of Xmas preparations Mary's mother takes her home for Xmas and this produces general consternation of course we all have to set to work! Mary promises to home Friday but then the worst of the work is over. (Diary of Bessie Mabel Scott, 22 December 1901)

For the newly married woman, the hiring of a servant might pose her first wedded difficulty.

Had no regular maid for our house so hired Kate Wood temporarily (Diary of Marion Chadwick, 21 September 1898)

Kates cooking is hopelessly doubtful (24 September 1898)

Engaged Florence Cook to be cook, housemaid, parlourmaid & laundress (28 September 1898)

Well trained servants were not easy to find, and those who had them were greatly envied by friends and acquaintances. But, no matter how thorough the servants, the lady of the house invariably thought that things did not go well unless she was directly supervising activities.

Still mild but colder—the walking very difficult. Reading & Housekeeping in the morning after being late for breakfast. I must take myself to task for this. Everything goes wrong down stairs among the servants when I yield to temptation & breakfast in my dressing-room. (Diary of Lady Macdonald, 3 January 1868)

The household was only run as well as the master and mistress allowed. It was therefore incumbent upon them to maintain an atmosphere of calm supervision.

The household machinery, oiled by her tact is never heard to creak, neither directions nor reproof are given to a servant before a third person. If there are disappointments, griefs or surprises, the visitor does not know it. Family affairs are kept strictly within the family.[77]

Agnes, Lady Macdonald, diarist, May 1868, Ottawa. She realized her diary was an important historical document. Photo by William James Topley. *National Archives of Canada*

Servants might misbehave in a variety of ways, but one of the most distressing was drunkenness, as there seemed to be no easy way to handle it. In a society where many middle class women had been caught up in the temperance movement, a servant's drinking would probably lead to a parting of the ways.

I was obliged to lock the lower door & take off the key to prevent Ann Danger [the cook] getting more of the mountain dew which had completely stupefied her. no doubt she wished to drown the sorrow she felt at the sudden death of her niece in confinement. *that* excuse will or may be accepted for a day or so but not after. (Diary of Mary Brown, 11 February 1890)

Ann Danger still indulging. (12 February 1890)

Ann Danger much better & trying to do some work but after lunch she persisted in going out quite against my wishes leaving us without a servant of any kind. [Mrs Brown then received callers] 14 in all, we could have no tea, but the arrivals came opportunely. (13 February 1890)

Ann not back, her room in a disgraceful state. Mrs James [the charwoman] and I put her things which were hanging about into a basket & covered them for her, put the mattresses into the corridor. (14 February 1890)

Engaged an old servant Hester McGee who came Saturday. (15 February 1890)

Cooks were coming and going all the time. Three years later, Mrs. Brown re-engaged Ann Danger for her kitchen.

Servants, too, had their share of problems. In some households, children of servants were not welcome which meant that somewhere had to be found for the child to stay.

Went away up north today to see the Boy's housekeeper's baby. She has boarded it out at $6.00 a month, let a friend of her own have it 1st Friend taken ill 2 nights after following morning baby deposited at front door by man. Then she took it to a woman who was highly recommended. After 2 days went down to see how it was, found it lying naked on bed woman drunk on floor. A neighbour promising to look after it for that night she left it. Next evening found same state of affairs so took baby away, drunken woman threatening her with broom-handle all the time. She had to borrow some clothes next door to bring the child home in, as the broomstick would not allow her to approach either its clothes or the carriage which she had been obliged to buy for baby before the second woman would take her. Since then the housekeeper has been making at least tri-weekly visits to her child's late aboad & has arranged with the ex-nurses husband that he shall have the carriage mended & returned to shop it was bought at, the woman having broken it. she has also recovered a few of baby's garments in very mildewed condition from shed. The woman has never yet been found sober. The baby is now with a woman recommended by G. Gillespie & doing well, charge $6.00 a month. Mother earns $10.00. The mother's own winter clothing was sent in summer from Homoeopathic Hospital by mistake to another woman, who instead of returning it sent word of the error, securing her own property at same time. When Mrs C's things were at last demanded she reported having put them out in shed, whence they had vanished. They have never since turned up. (Diary of Helen Grant Macdonald, 2 October 1891)

For the wealthy it was often considered appropriate to engage a governess to help with the children. As a young woman Mary Brown had worked as a governess for the Rothschild family in Germany, so it was quite natural that she should think about hiring one to assist in looking after her own children. She discussed the possibility of doing so in correspondence with her mother who lived in England. In the following excerpt, Mary gets some advice from her mother on this matter.

…She has a young lady who comes for nine hours daily. At 9 a.m. till 6 p.m. leaving after she has taken tea with the children in the schoolroom. She dines with them at 1 so that if morning visitors come, Mrs Sprott leaves her to care and while she goes to her friends in the drawingroom some part of the day the governess walks out with her charge. Thus leaving Mrs Sprott free to make calls or ought else without fear of the child being a servant's associate during her absence. I am not in favour of experienced old governesses for young children. I like youthful minds; and moderate you may think—good temper & good health, one who herself has been trained to early obedience, and has been brought up to be useful, rather than a lady in the absurd sense in which it is understood and acted upon by some, who, fear being classed with the servants in a family if they stooped to take off their own goloshes—much more if they buttoned a child's boot.[78]

A housemaid, drawn by Mary Cowes Clarke for *The Hostess of Today*, by Linda Hull Larned (Scribner 1899). *Author's collection*

The Browns did hire a governess who was addressed by the family as "Fräulein."

When household chores were so labour intensive, ill health, particularly on the part of the woman of the house, often required additional assistance from servants.

I am getting on with the house-cleaning, but have to be cautious. I cannot hurry it through as well as when we have fine warm weather, or when I am quite well. I was afraid on Friday that I had taken cold from the draughts through the house, and the dampness together, but I am pretty well today again, and shall have the woman at work tomorrow to finish as soon as she can now. I fully intended writing to you yesterday but could not sit steadily enough. We are anxious to begin the garden, and hope to do so on Thursday or Monday. The day-laborers ask such wages, it makes a serious matter of it, and William threatens to set to work himself with the boy by way of shewing he can be independent of them but I rather think we shall have to come to their terms. They ask 3/6 per day and fine themselves.[79]

Often the correct religious affiliation of a servant was of prime concern. It was considered to be important for harmony and smooth running of the household. This requirement could make the task of finding a new servant difficult, as in the case of Ann and Reverend William Macaulay of Picton.

> Today Jane McEwen our servant woman got a letter that alarms her about her other sister and she goes down in the boat (Sunday) tomorrow leaving us in destitution, not to return, for Susan is sick at home, and may not return. We have a woman at Kingston engaged but she cannot come before 7th Sept. and Ann is very weak if not sick. Can you learn for us whether the servant (Mary I believe her name is) who lived first at Revd. Job Deacon's, is still at Mrs Macpherson's or if she is disengaged. She would just suit Ann as housemaid as she is a church woman and accustomed to a country house. We will have none but church servants. It is both a duty and with us a convenience. Our Jane has been a good and honest one.[80]

The phrase, "We will have none but church servants" refers to members of the Church of England as opposed to any other denomination. Religion is a theme which dominates when hiring servants for the Macaulay household. Reverend William Macaulay wrote the following to his mother, Mrs. Ann Macaulay at Kingston:

> Our new servant woman answers well. She is a good washer and baker. In cooking she has something to learn. She is strong and active. Our old servant, Jane McEwan, went we understand for a week to Mr Miller's of the Montreal bank, which she left, and is now at Mrs Harper's. The girl that would answer you well is named Mary, was at Rev. Mr Deacon's. She is a church girl and when she leaves Dr Sampson's you will do well to get her. Strangers are to be avoided, as having the fever, or the seeds of it, in them, which is a great pity....(17 September 1847)

> Ann does not know of any servant girl here that would at all answer you. In this part, the Quaker and dissenting manners soon spoil them. The best also have been married off and this year's emigration has brought no further supply. but I shall be on the lookout, and think I shall be able in a few weeks to find you a thorough one. (20 November 1847)

The courtship and marriage of servants was resented by employers, as it caused them so much inconvenience. They did what they could to keep the process at bay:

> Miss Dewar…tells me the maid Elsie they had in Muskoka went out one Wedns. evening professedly to a ball thereby "skipping" Mrs Watson's Bible class for servants. When she returned she had a wedding ring on her hand. it transpired later that there had been no ball, but she & Harris (settler of the blue canoe) had paddled down to Port Sanfield where they were quietly married. They have taken a house for winter at Port Carling. He has land in Muskoka but has not begun to work it yet. (Diary of Helen Grant Macdonald, 8 October 1891)

> The young couple had many little jokes with our hostess re: the days when she aided and abetted their courtship which Mrs C's employer, a chaperone, greatly disapproved. (1 September 1892)

When the servants did marry, however, their mistress might attend the wedding and would certainly send a handsome present.

> Putting ADG on six silver spoons a wedding present from Harley, Hilly & me for Annie Dean [their maid] 1.00 (Diary of Mary Brown, 12 October 1888)

Though such scenarios were greatly discouraged, romance did occasionally flourish between servants and members of the higher classes. Such was the case when John Steele of Penetanguishene ran away with his Father's servant girl in December 1845. To accomplish this, a careful plan was devised. The girl requested leave to go home. John Steele arranged to borrow the Hallen family cutter, on the pretext that he wished to pay a social call. Just as the pair hoped, John was assigned the task of driving the girl part way home. Everything worked perfectly. Off they went, stopping near Newmarket to get married. Naturally the Hallens were rather annoyed when their cutter was not returned in time for them to visit relatives.[81]

It goes without saying that this exciting and shocking event contributed immensely to the gossip enjoyed around the tea-tables of

Penetanguishene; gossip further fuelled by the fact that Steele had been engaged to another woman for more than a year. Naturally, deepest sympathies were directed towards Steele's mother who was ill and not expected to rise from her sick-bed. Several weeks later, as the condition of Mrs. Steele Sr. deteriorated, Steele and his bride returned to the parental home. Unfortunately their home-coming was not a happy event:

> the Scotts and Mrs. St John drove up they stayed the evening with us. The latter has been staying with Mrs. Steele who is worse than she has been having violent convulsions she says it is really wretched up at Purbrook. John Steele and his wife are there which only makes it worse as all the servants in the kitchen are in a state of mutiny on account of the latter being in the parlour and giving orders which as it is so short a time since she was with them they do not feel inclined to obey. (Diary of Eleanora Hallen on 3 February 1846)

Mrs. Steele died about ten days later. Whether or not the servants reconciled themselves to working for the new Mrs. Steele is not clear.

Servants were occasionally dismissed for one reason or another. But generally, because of the difficulty of finding replacements, people tended to put up with them for as long as possible. Matilda Bowers Eby was fortunate when her younger sister came to stay, allowing her to dismiss an unsatisfactory servant.

> At last they succeded in getting Minnie transported to Sebringville. She came with the 11 o'clock train. Oh I am so glad she will stay all winter so that I can send the girl away. She is an eye sore. (Diary of Matilda Bowers Eby, 7 November 1868)

> This evening I made over Minnie's old hat, no one would dream it to be anything but new just imported. Dismissed my servant girl today and glad when she is gone as she proves only a nuisance. (21 November 1868)

Servants sometimes left of their own volition, causing no end of upset for the families left to cope on their own.

William spent the eve with Jediah and me. We took a cup of tea, read, tried to get a nap on the sofa. Laughed at J's condemning the English railroad contractors etc. He drove the children and me out in the carriage this afternoon, after I went a visit to Frances. Poor F. was lying on the sofa resting, the three children playing about the floor. Her two girls left her this week. (Diary of Catharine Merritt, 22 October 1857)

General dissatisfaction seems to have been the norm in most households when it came to dealing with servants. However, blessings were counted when things went well.

....I have to be constantly on the watch lest my woman should spoil things by trying to cook them without asking how it should be done. However, she is very useful in many ways, and is steady and stays at home, and is always busy so that I may consider myself very well off.[82]

We have a young woman here, by the name of Miss Margaret Campbell, to work. She had been here some time and is a very good girl. (Diary of Catherine Bell Van Norman, 9 January 1850)

Margaret became such an integral part of the family that, when Mr. Van Norman's brother lay dying, the maid was as assiduous in her visiting the sick man as the rest, even sitting up all night with him during the crisis of the illness.

Sometimes supervising the servants created more work for the mistress:

...I have had a girl, lame, Irish, better than two weeks, to help sew and mend. It kept me busy fixing, pulling and ripping her work. It tried my patience not a little. However, I have let her go which is a great relief. (Diary of Catharine Merritt, 25 October 1856)

For most people it was rather comforting to know that elderly relatives had trusty servants to aid them.

Aunt Augusta is very grey & rather haggard looking. She has

small eyes & wears spectacles. She was very pleasant & asked us to tea next Thursday. They keep a big strong servant so she can't have much to do. (Diary of Gertrude Nicholson 16 May 1896)

Even a quite simple household such as the Campions' in Marmora township needed extra hands.

The Queens birthday. Very bad pain between my shoulders tonight. Work too hard I suppose. it can't be helped we can't get a girl to help. (Diary of Mary Victoria Campion, 24 May 1861)

But when someone came and offered her services, she might not be the sort you would want to have in the house.

Biddy Green came to hire. Mother would not have her. (Diary of Mary Victoria Campion, 29 April 1863)

this morning a girl came to hire. she as a fact does not know anything. (Diary of Mary Victoria Campion, 6 August 1862)

The responsibilities of the parents of very young servants would be taken by the master and mistress of the house. "Discipline," in the sense of harsh treatment, would be of the greatest importance. This treatment might be termed abusive today, physically and emotionally. Sexual abuse was not spoken about. For the young servant whose family no longer made him or her welcome, the situation must have often been desperate indeed, for society's attitudes would not be sympathetic.

On Monday evening the 29th ult. [29 Dec 1885] Jane Hawley of Bath, a domestic in the employ of David Preston Esq. & Ed Roberts, a lad of about 12 years, in the employment of the said gentleman ran away from their employer carrying off all their effects & a purse belonging to Mrs Preston containing some two or three dollars.[83]

These children, fleeing who knows what, tried to reach the mainland across the ice from Amherst Island. They fell in and were both drowned. The newspaper account expressed no sadness at the death but thought of the unhappy employers: "No reason can be assigned for their departure from their employer."

The servant's day was long, often starting hours before the family stirred. In grand houses there would be a multitude of tasks to accomplish, even before breakfast was prepared. The very first job was to light the kitchen stove. Water was then heated and delivered to bedrooms so that the family could take their morning wash. Then the breakfast room was made ready. This involved lighting the fire or stove, shaking the hearth-rug, cleaning the fire irons, dusting the furniture, sweeping the carpet and shaking the curtains. Next the hall and stairway were cleaned, not forgetting to remove and shake the door-mat and to sweep the street-door steps. Dirt had to be removed from the boot scrapers and splashes of mud from the door. Then the door handle, door-plate, bell-handle and knocker was rubbed. This work accomplished, the servant would put on a clean apron and proceed to ready the breakfast table. Next the servant would return to the kitchen and prepare and eat (as quickly as possible) her own breakfast. Breakfast for the family was then cooked and served. While

For some classes of society, outdoor meals required tables and chairs brought from inside, and servants to wait on table. L.J. Breithaupt's Sunday School class from the Berlin Evangelical Church. *Breithaupt-Hewetson-Clark Collection, University of Waterloo*

it was being eaten, the servant would commence cleaning the upstairs rooms. And so the day would continue, with never a minute to spare.

> We awoke early. We heard the servant hard at work a long time before breakfast & as the walls are thin you can hear every sound....At breakfast we had hashed ham & mutton & Mr R. was very scornful about it... (Diary of Gertrude Nicholson, 8 July 1896)

There was not much distinction made between a servant and an apprentice. Popular sentiment sided with the master when things went wrong.

> Preston stayed all night & went off in the stage to Barrie to bring James Horamee his apprentice boy back who ran away last *Sunday* week. Yesterday my Father had a letter from old Scott saying he was there & some nonsense about his not being treated well & not having enough to eat which is the fashionable complaint when servants are discontented. (Diary of Mary Hallen, 24 May 1854)

Though written tongue in cheek, the popularity of the following verse perhaps indicates a callous attitude of some masters (or mistresses) towards servants.

> "There's been an accident!" they said
> "Your servant's cut in half; he's dead!"
> "Indeed!" said Mr Jones, "and please
> Send me the half that's got my keys."[84]

Poverty

I envy the poor: it must be so delightful
not to have to think about appearances
A VICTORIAN WOMAN[85]

POVERTY WAS A NORMAL STATE OF AFFAIRS for many people in Victorian Ontario. Since there were no social welfare programmes, it was essential that those who had established themselves should maintain a benevolent attitude towards the less fortunate. As a means of accomplishing this, most municipalities established Houses of Industry and Refuge, where the homeless and destitute would be looked after. Some inmates at these institutions would only stay for a few days. Others might stay for several years. While there, they received food, clothing and shelter. In return, those who were able were assigned certain chores, thereby contributing to the running of the institution.

For many, the prospect of going to the House of Refuge was a dire one. It was the dreaded "poorhouse" or "workhouse" (even, in places like North Bay, called the "pesthouse"). Simple and low paying work was preferable to the comforts of the House of Refuge.

> Her husband was killed by a tree falling on him and then the old lady kept herself by washing for the neighbors. (Diary of Catherine Bell Van Norman, 15 January 1850)

Unfortunately, not everyone who deserved assistance received it. There were still many people who, for one reason or another, had to rely upon their own wits in order to eke out an existence. Some of these people took to begging, moving from place to place in order to avoid being apprehended as "vagrants"; others became tramps.

The life of tramping or begging was certainly not restricted to men, for diarists have left numerous accounts of women living in this fashion. Some were able-bodied and willing to work for their bread, but a good proportion suffered physical or mental disorders, making their plight exceedingly desperate.

> This morning we had an old beggar woman here for her breakfast but she proved so saucy that she left without it. (Diary of Ann Amelia Day, 5 September 1878)

For most rural dwellers, it became a matter of course that they should receive several calls per week from such people. Most attempts at charity perhaps were met with a more graceful response than that of Ann Amelia Day's "saucy" beggar woman. Nevertheless, the prevailing Victorian attitude, which in most part grew out of strong religious values, created a deep feeling of obligation towards the needy.

Many homes in the Waterloo County area kept a special room, called the "Tramp Room." The Joseph Zinger house located in the village of Maryhill had such a room. Holy Marks often stayed there. Irish Mary, who was always followed by her cat, was another tramp who came to the Zinger house. She was not a seamstress, but she helped with basics such as darning socks and cleaning. The Zinger tramp room was last used in the early 1920's.[86]

It is unfortunate that we do not know the correct names for these two individuals. Holy Marks, so nick-named because of his beautiful writing, made his way in the world by entering the births, deaths and marriages into family bibles in exchange for bed and food. Irish Mary, it seems, would turn her hand to whatever needed doing, staying only for a day or two, before moving on to another farm.

For those who were able-bodied, there was always the hope of finding a little work in order to earn their keep. However, for the elderly and the physically infirm, things were rather different. They were totally reliant upon the generosity of others.

> An old beggar woman came here this evening we kept her all
> night. This was a splendid day not so warm as usual. (Diary of
> Matilda Bowers Eby, 24 June 1861)

From the matter-of-fact way in which Matilda wrote about it, one can
assume that this was not an isolated event at the Bowers' home.
Matilda's parents had succeeded in making a comfortable life for the
family. They welcomed strangers into their home, near Berlin (Kitchener) without a second thought.

Larger towns and cities also contained poor people who relied
upon assistance from the wealthy. In St. Catharines, the Merritt family
obviously earned a reputation for benevolence. Consequently, they
were inundated with large numbers of people.

> A poor woman gave us a fright last night. She came for some
> milk for her child and fell from her chair to the floor, in a fit.
> She recovered in about half an hour and we sent her home in
> the sleigh. She was very ill through the night. There is a great
> deal of suffering in this place, about fourteen were relieved
> here today. (Diary of Catharine Merritt, 3 February 1856)

Homeless women in towns and cities often ended up in a court of law.
At Sandwich (Windsor), Margaret and Kate Hoffman, charged with
vagrancy on 3 October 1861, were fortunate enough to be discharged.
But the court ordered them to leave the place. Presumably by order-
ing vagrants to leave, the community hoped to rid itself of the problem. What often happened was that vagrants left but then reappeared
in the community, only to end up in court again. After several such incidents, they would be committed to jail. After serving their sentence,
they would be out on the streets again, thereby establishing an endless
cycle. The plight of the mentally ill was dealt with in a more decisive
fashion. On 17 January 1862, Sarah Ellsworth was charged with being
a dangerous lunatic, and was committed to gaol for safe keeping. One
of the most pitiful cases was that of a vagrancy charge brought against
"An Old Woman, (unknown)" on 14 August 1862, who was discharged on promise to leave the county. One cannot help but wonder
about her pitiful existence. Perhaps she was senile and no longer
knew her own name.[87]

Prostitution was a common occurrence in urban areas. Magistrate
records point to the same women coming back to court time and time

again. Upon conviction, fines were imposed. In the event of the prisoner being unable to pay the fine, the convicted faced a jail sentence, sometimes with hard labour. After several convictions the court would order the individual to leave the district, which some did, only to reappear within a few months. The frequency with which many women appeared in court increased with the onset of the cold weather months.

It is difficult to say how many tramps and beggars were roaming around rural Ontario during the 19th century. But it is safe to say that there were occasionally incidents that gave some people pause for thought.

> Tramps were numerous. Some were old, some were young, some on crutches while begging, but when out of site, the crutches went under the arm, the legs miraculously strengthened. One at least had his arm tied to his side and empty sleeve dangled; some were inoffensive some ugly tempers if food were not forth coming immediately; some were pitiful and needed help, both food and clothing. One night one came in father's absence and stated that we couldn't put him out. When father came and showed him the door, he beat a hasty retreat. Father thought best to follow him away down over the hill. Often they slept undisturbed in the barn. One night mother went in to get some barley to boil for her chickens, and the first thing she got hold of was a man's leg. One farmer whose name I could disclose, and who was blind, started out with his little girl, a pretty curly headed child of perhaps twelve years old and begged so successfully that he ultimately bought a farm. These callers averaged one to five a day, all expecting food. Few asked for clothing, the farmer was expected to see that that was needed.[88]

Mary Hutchinson was born in 1850. She lived with her family in Wellington County. As a young child she developed her own strategy for dealing with tramps.

> Many times I ran all the way to Fergus and back except up the "Big Hill." There were no wild animals in the woods at that time—not even deer, so I had nothing to fear except for tramps and these I could outrun.[89]

However, winter sometimes brought dreadful consequences:

> Jack saved the life of a tramp from being frozen to death one
> stormy night. (Diary of Avice Watson, 13 January 1891)

Tramps in the cities may have caused greater fear for the inhabitants.
They would not have been familiar faces, as many were in from the
country. To those around them, the urban poor often seem to be a
threat.

> Were invited to dine at Mrs John Cawthra's tonight & go St
> George's Society concert with them. Owing to visit of tramp
> night before I did not like to leave Mater. (Diary of Helen
> Grant Macdonald, 5 November 1891)

Tramps and beggars were the visible poor. Everyone became accustomed to them as they roamed through towns and countryside looking for handouts. However, other needy folk were not so visible.
Neighbours living in hardship, desperately trying to keep body and
soul together, often needed assistance. The Hutchinson family of
Wellington County were fortunate enough to be in a position to help.

> As today, there were both well to do and poor, only the poor
> were poorer. There were some who had practically nothing.
> Farmers who were in good circumstances were more charita-
> ble than the average person of today. I know of one family
> whose children are still in our midst, who lived all one winter
> on boiled peas. The husband was away chopping wood. The
> baby was rocked in a sap trough. Another family who had no
> cow, spread their scones with tallow from a tallow candle.
> This woman was above work. She told us on several occasions
> she had gone to school with the Queen. On one occasion
> mother was called to nurse a woman with a new baby. She
> went to make her a cup of tea and found there was absolutely
> nothing to eat in the house. Mother hastened home and re-
> turned with a laden basket. The woman asked Mother if she
> would be good enough to make some biscuits. She had to mix
> them in the top of the flour bag as there was nothing else large
> enough in the house. The dishes were washed in the frying
> pan. In the meantime the other children were in the woods

looking for cow cabbages before they could get any dinner.
These were perhaps the worst cases but there were many others who were very little better off.[90]

As reported by the *The London Evening Advertiser and Family Newspaper*, gypsy camps were not an unusual feature of Victorian Ontario:

> We noticed a number of gypsies in the city today. They seem
> to be the same party who visited us during last summer, and
> number thirty or forty in all. They have some fine horses.[91]

The gypsies' unconventional way of life was often viewed with great
suspicion. Out of ignorance, rumours often circulated of supposed il-
licit activities on the part of the gypsies, such as chicken theft and
baby stealing. The Gypsies, who made their money by making and
selling useful items, always maintained that their way of life was an
honourable one. One of the old rhymes taught to children, warning
them about associating with gypsies, goes as follows:

> My Mother said that I never should
> Play with the Gypsies in the woods.
> If I did, she would say
> You naughty girl to disobey.

As for the elderly, if they were without means and their family did not
take care of them, they would be completely at the mercy of the street
or a charity—providing that their case came to the attention of someone powerful enough to care. In the summer of 1888, Mary Brown of
Hamilton had one such case arrive on her doorstep.

> Mrs Weston arrived from Toronto, sent by her son William
> who was breaking up house & sending his wife & children to
> her Father's at Weston. The maids kindly made up bed in
> their room for her to sleep. I have written her brother Mr
> Cox, manager of *Commercial Bulletin* Boston asking for En-
> trance Fee to Aged Women's Home for Mrs Weston. (Diary
> of Mary Brown, 12 July 1888)

> Mrs Weston's Admission Fee into the Home from Mr Cox
> Boston. Have written to Mr James Cox. (19 July 1888)

Rev. C.R. Miller and some wards of the Berlin (now Kitchener) orphanage. *National Archives of Canada*

Telegraphed Miss Law, Matron, Well's Hill, Bathurst Street, Toronto asking her to let Annie Weston know about her Mother's death. (6 January 1889)

Mrs Weston buried. funeral from Orphans Asylum Board Room filled to overflowing. Ladies Fuller, Ewing, McLaren, A R Kerr, A Brown with others present. Annie & Willie Weston both came up from Toronto to attend. Mr Boville's assistant minister read the service. (7 January 1889)

Paid Annie Weston $1.00 (8 January 1889)

Annie Weston $1.00 Poor woman 25 cents (9 January 1889)

The threat of losing one's home and belongings was always a worry for the poor. When the Bailiff appeared on the door-step, a desperate situation existed.

> Lent Miss Corridi Three Dollars toward releasing her & her furniture from Miss Iredale, who had a Bailiff in the house, to be returned soon. (Diary of Mary Brown, 26 July 1888)

> Poor man 25 cents (9 June 1888)

The plight of orphans was often grim. Food, shelter and clothing were provided for those taken into care. Nevertheless, the children were not always happy.

> Johnnie Foster & Willie Brown are spending tonight in the cells for running away from Orphan Asylum. 3 other boys ran away yesterday but Miss Denby brought them in from Dundas & put them to bed after having a bath. they were to work hard today (Diary of Mary Brown, 8 June 1888)

A difficult situation was that of the wife who had to cope with a drunken husband, and the consequent monetary hardship.

> Heard Mrs Pounden instructing her pupils who are—Allan's Rose, Edith, Fred, Gamble's Georgie, Captain Kinder's little girl and Mrs Doctor O'Reilly's 2 girls. The Poundens (whom I live with) were once in very good circumstances in Montreal. They are Irish people, well born, but like all Irish refuse to let their modesty stand in their way—Since his misfortunes Mr. P. has been little better than an idle vagabond, a dweller almost in saloons, supported by his wife, a highly educated and Christian lady who can hardly make both ends meet. Her husband's dissapation and brutal conduct prevent her having a good school. (Diary of Forbes Geddes, 17 March 1862)

After Mr. Pounden's situation deteriorated further, he left for Toronto, abandoning his wife, who then tried once more to set up a small school. With Mr. Pounden gone, it was no longer respectable for Forbes Geddes to live in the house with Mrs. Pounden, so he moved away, although he remained friendly with her and tried to interest himself in her welfare.

Another possibility for raising money was the pot luck supper, including cash donations to the worthy cause. This novel idea was used in Burlington in mid-century.

> There is a donation party tonight for the benefit of Rev. Mr Webster for his services. This is a new thing, lately got up. Every generous one can give just what she thinks best. They have a supper or tea and whatever they choose is placed upon the table and they all stand up and partake. (Diary of Catherine Bell Van Norman, 22 January 1850)

One of the pleasantest ways for the better-off to deal with their obligations to the poor was the charity event. It is still popular today for fundraising. Bazaars, teas, balls, and fairs were all held for good works.

An interesting idea for providing clothing to the impoverished was for rich women to make themselves a dress of calico—the material of choice among the populace in those days (one might say the acrylic knit of the time)—which they would wear to a ball and then give to charity:

> A "calico" ball on a large scale is to come off in Quebec shortly, for the benefit of the local charities. The dresses worn by the ladies to be given up to the Ball Committee for the benefit of the Poor—Good idea. (Diary of Forbes Geddes, 4 February 1862)

> Mr. Forbes Geddes felt very strongly about poverty in Hamilton. Meeting…of the Bible Society. Sheriff Thomas addressed the meeting—and spoke of the good accomplished in distant countries.—but forgot to tell the audience that "charity begins at Home"—that only a day or two ago, at their very door in Hamilton a woman was starved to death—and that there is destitution enough among us to call for sympathy and charity quite as loudly as the wants of distant heathen. (17 January 1862)

When Mr. Tysson, a friend of the Hallen family, returned to England from Penetanguishene, he left a few garments with one of the needy people of that community.

The old French-man who we often give things to as he is very badly off came he had with him a coat leggins & some socks which Mr Tysson left for him. Mr T has been so kind in remembering all the poor people about here. (Diary of Mary Hallen 11 November 1848)

Christmas-time benevolence was a way of life for the Hallen family. On 25 December 1845, Eleanora's brother, Preston:

drove to Gosses with a piece of beef and a plum pudding for them as we thought it would be a treat to them as they are not well off but very respectable people. (Diary of Eleanora Hallen, 25 December 1845)

Within the Quaker community, benevolence was a way of life. Gertrude Nicholson wrote the following account of one unfortunate woman, whom she encountered while visiting relatives near Rockwood.

The meeting house is a little shanty quite nice & comfortable inside but very insignificant externally. The grass all round it is quite brown & eaten off by grasshoppers, there are no trees. The meeting house stands quite alone except for a very rickety old shed close to for people to tie up their horses in—There

Friends Meeting House, Rockwood, a watercolour from the diary of Gertrude Nicholson. *Collection of Clair C. Chapman*

were about a dozen people there 6 or 7 of them being Harris's. Mary Ann Mingie a quaint little old woman (whom we used to know well) was there & spoke & prayed in a very high squeaky voice. She has very sore eyes & squints terribly & wears a very short dress. She is very poor (her husband having been in the asylum many years & she is so blind she can't see to do anything for a living. The Harris's are being very kind & help her a good deal. (Diary of Gertrude Nicholson, 16 July 1896)

A little while before dinner Mary Ann Mingie turned up. She generally comes twice a week either here or to see Mrs John Richard Harris's & has a good dinner & gets something to take home. She is the most comical object I ever saw & she laughed once quite hysterically in dinner & set us all off too. To look at her is enough. When her pie was handed her she put it close up to her eyes & squinted most horribly right into it. (17 July 1896)

Mary Ann Mingie had been spending the day there & she came in & told us some of her remarkable stories & made us quite ill with laughing. She seems to gather up all the latest news & then goes from house to house spending the day & imparting what she has learned. (13 August 1896)

Even the most benevolent had prejudices about the poor. When Rose Eby, daughter of Matilda Bowers and Aaron Eby, wrote the following, she was fourteen years old, and already picking up signals from her parents:

Mama went to see a poor family named Rose and she said when she came back that they had a fearfully dirty shanty how is it that dirt almost always goes with poverty. (Diary of Rose Eby, 4 January 1879)

As the cities grew, the conditions of the urban poor became more difficult. Sanitary conditions were bad, factories made the air yellow, and the simple matter of having clean clothes was beyond many. One means of alleviating the situation was to provide outings for clean air in the summer. Many of the wealthy families left Toronto to live on its

Island for the summer. The Hospital for Sick Children had a house on the Island, where chronic care patients could be sent for a week at a time. The Fresh Air Fund was set up to provide holidays in the country for children whose only playground was the city street.

Went to Cricket Club meeting. settled up affairs in grand style. paid all expenses—gave $25.00 to the Fresh Air Fund & had some 90 odd dollars left.... (Diary of Marion Chadwick, 12 June 1893)

Toronto's Fresh Air Fund gave these children free admission and lunch at the Canadian National Exhibition in Toronto, 1892.
National Archives of Canada

For many, there was little extra cash in the house for giving. So the ways and means of raising money were confined to activities involving organizations, such as the Bible Society in Hamilton and Toronto's Cricket Club.

we then discussed what work we would take up. we decided on the talent system. We are each to have a quarter given us & we are to use it for materials for making something to sell & then buy some more with the proceeds…I've got the names of some people who would like to have some one come to see them. (Diary of Belle Kittredge, 6 January 1892)

Many people were unfamiliar with the ways of aboriginal people. Consequently, stories and gossip regarding their activities were often fed by suspicion and ignorance. While Sarah Hallen's concern for an abandoned woman reflect her charitable inclination, one wonders whether she questioned the authenticity of this story:

Heard of a poor Squaw who has lost the use of her legs, and in consequence all her relations have left her with only a bag of Indian corn; they say she never will die until someone kills her, which they want to do, but the Indians will not as she will call the thunder down upon them. Poor creature, my Father wants someone to go to her, but its a day and a half's journey. (Diary of Sarah Hallen Drinkwater, 2 January 1841)

Whether this tale is accurate or not, Sarah's reaction to it serves to confirm that charity was extended to those in need, wherever and whenever possible. A strong sense of Christian duty towards others did play a significant role, but so did goodness, compassion and generosity. The realization that hardship and crisis might afflict any family ensured that most maintained a benevolent attitude. "There, but for the grace of God, go I," was perhaps kept foremost in mind.

Visiting

The business of her life was to get her daughters married;
Its solace was visiting and news.
JANE AUSTEN, *Pride and Prejudice*

INDUSTRIALISATION AND THE GROWTH OF THE TOWNS created a new class of people, who had more leisure time and were more sophisticated in their social outlook. At the same time, society in general became more complicated, with a proliferation of rules for behaviour, many of them obscure and hard to understand. To make it easier for people to know how to behave, etiquette books were published, giving details for every kind of social outing concerning what people should say and do. It could be quite confusing. Even the most socially adept sometimes had trouble.

> I am having everything to myself now-a-days. Nobody condescends to call on me. That is our village ladies. It appears, it is not the fashion with them to call first. (Diary of Matilda Bowers Eby, 6 May 1863)

Naturally there was some variation in the way the rules were applied. Women living in large cities, with busy and important social lives, were more inclined towards a formal approach in visiting etiquette. For this class of women, any divergence from the acceptable way of doing things would be unthinkable. Everyone knew that the consequence of such would cause irreparable damage to a person's reputation. For women living in smaller communities, or the countryside, things were often done on a less formal basis. Nevertheless, most people abided strictly by the convention appropriate to their community.

In most urban areas, women usually had one or more particular days of the week when they would remain at home to receive visitors. A woman would leave or send cards to her associates announcing the day upon which she would be "at home." In addition, information regarding who would be "at home", and when, often appeared in newspapers, as well as other publications aimed at those in society. A glance at these listings kept the public apprised of which days women of their community were "receiving." Should a woman decide not to have a special day upon which to receive visitors, she was expected to be prepared to see them at any time, unless occupied with a special task. In such cases, a servant would be directed to inform the visitors that his/her mistress was engaged. The visitor would then leave a card.

Those without servants were often caught off guard.

> I was very busy in the forenoon. Afternoon Mrs Murray and Miss Dobbin paid me a visit, and hindered me not only a little but a great deal from doing so much as I had intended to do. Having so much company I am getting quite tired of it. It is

Gertrude Nicholson included many watercolour sketches to illustrate her diary. This shows the home of S. Walker, Norwich. Collection of *Clair C. Chapman*

misterious to me, how women can contend themselves by going about visiting, gossiping and doing nothing useful. I don't intend to commence to run about it is a very disagreeable practice. (Diary of Matilda Bowers Eby, 1 June 1863)

On 31 March 1863, when age 19, Matilda was sent to assist her unmarried brother, John, post-master and general store owner at the village of Bridgeport. Her duties were to run the house and help in the store whenever necessary. Bridgeport provided Matilda with her first experience of village life. It also brought a visiting ettiquette different to what she was accustomed. She often regarded visits from village woman as a definite intrusion upon her time, and frequently expressed distaste for the whole business.

I have done a little sewing besides my housework. I have been kept very busy ever since I am in this miserable place. It is quite surprising to me how some of our village women manage to go about visiting and doing nothing I should like to know very much how and when they do their work. (Diary of Matilda Bowers Eby, 12 May 1863)

This sort of attitude was not typical, however. For most women, visiting brought a great deal of satisfaction and fulfillment. Perhaps because of repression and constraints put upon them, particularly in terms of career opportunities, visiting became a necessary component of life. Eventually it developed into an institution whereby women gained a sense of their own place in society. The associated etiquette defined the boundaries within which they could maneuver, in attempting to climb the social scale.

For a woman such as Belle Kittredge, who worked all day earning her living, the paying of calls was still a duty.

I got a half holiday to return some calls. Birdie & I started out early but did not finish them all as we were very fortunate(?) in finding every one at home. We are returning some first calls & the drawing rooms are all new to us. There was "art" in all. (Diary of Belle Kittredge, 31 March 1892)

There were, of course, various kinds of visits, and specific times at which those visits were to be made. Morning visits, made between the hours of twelve and five, were of a short duration. Generally one was expected to stay about fifteen minutes, and to leave when another visitor arrived. Refreshments were not necessarily served at this time. There was also strict protocol regarding what clothing to wear when visiting. An outfit was devised for every possible occasion; for example, one had a walking dress, carriage dress, tea dress, house dress, day dress, morning dress, afternoon dress, visiting dress, receiving dress, dinner dress, evening dress, and a ball dress. All of this was enough to make even the most fashion conscious creature befuddled at times.

> Miss Hawthorne was here all day to make me a 5 o'clock tea dress. (Diary of Marion Chadwick, 2 January 1894)

Etiquette books of the day kept women informed about what to wear. For making morning calls, a woman was advised to wear either a walking or a carriage dress. Carriage dresses, however, were only permissible if one actually arrived via carriage. A hat or bonnet, gloves and suitable jewellery (diamonds were not considered appropriate for morning visits) completed the outfit.

> Sat with Emily to receive visitors but sloppy & few came. (Diary of Mary Brown, 3 November 1879)

The weather greatly affected the activities of women, and consequently they paid much attention to it. It was deemed advisable to avoid exposure to the elements so as not to run the risk of taking a chill. Therefore on inclement days, visiting was at a minimum. However, given fine weather, a woman might make several calls in one day. At each place, she would leave her card so that the hostess would not forget the visit had been paid. The hostess would then be obliged to make a return visit. Generally, a morning visit required a morning visit in return; an afternoon visit paid required an afternoon visit; and so on.

> …Daisy & I took sleigh & called on Mrs Ewing, Jas Turner & Hobson, attended "At Home" at Mrs Baucher's where Mrs Stuart & Mrs Scott, poured out tea & coffee. (Diary of Mary Brown, 5 January 1893)

The Macdonalds of Toronto moved among the top people in the city and knew everyone there. But when they paid a visit to Boston, things were a little different. Their daughter, Helen, records in her diary visits to Julia Ward Howe, author of "The Battle Hymn of the Republic," and to Quaker poet John Greenleaf Whittier. But it was possible to meet too many people:

> Mrs L gave an afternoon reception for us—wore dinner dress—position end of drawing room, madame centre, Mater right, HSM left. A few of the New England Women's Club ladies present, otherwise a long series of new names emphasised by hand shakes—a little music—Everybody "very happy to meet us" after 1st shake & "so pleased to have met us" at the last. We shall have to keep a lookout on the streets hereafter for people who look as if they are going to bow. (Diary of Helen Grant Macdonald, 18 December 1890)

Since visiting was such an important matter, it was given much priority, even at very busy times.

> Very hot again. Went to Dr George MacKelcan's to get some medicine for Fanny, she has had an attack of diarrhea. Busy in kitchen. Mary bought pail of raspberries. Cathie, Bessie & I called on Mrs Minty, Mrs Partridge, Mrs Robertson, and Mrs Robinson. Yates [the handyman] came to pull the white heart cherries. (Diary of Frances Gay Simpson, 11 July 1881)

A very special occasion called for an "At Home." These daytime or evening affairs were often given in honour of a particular person, a birthday, anniversary, engagement; or sometimes simply to repay social obligations. Sometimes also they were given on behalf of organizations or clubs. Whichever category the "At Home" fell into, it was incumbent upon the hostess to ensure that things were very well organized. On 19 April 1890, Frances Gay Simpson of Hamilton gave details of such an affair in a letter to her son, Philip, the youngest of her 12 children. He was a lawyer in St Paul, Minnesota.

> My dear Philip,
>   ...Since I last wrote to you our long talked of "At Home" has taken place. I sent out about 120 invitation and 68 ladies

Frances Gay Simpson, diarist. Photo by Eckerson and Millman, Hamilton. *National Archives of Canada*

came. Miss Grant poured out tea, Martha the coffee and Fanny escorted the ladies from the drawing room to the dining room, where a long table was prepared. We made jellies, custards and trifle at home, and I ordered six very pretty cakes from Pattisson's. The two Miss Oultons, Miss Pringle, and Miss Dempsey, handed the things about. Ellen kept washing up what was necessary and supplying fresh coffee from the lift and looked a very imposing personage. I engaged Mrs Fring for the kitchen and her little girl who kept at the hall door to open it as the bell rang. The invitation was from 4 to 6 o'clock (as usual) so it was soon all over. I confess I dreaded the whole affair very much. I wished to give an "At Home" and I am very thankful it is over. It passed off very well and nothing was broken or lost. We had a beautiful day and did not require a fire in the drawing room....[92]

The Watson family of Wellington County were relieved when a new girl arrived just in time to assist at their "At Home."

Jessie Green our new girl came. We are very thankful to have one at last. That day also was our "At Home Day" & a load came from town Charlie & Guy amongst them. Guy bringing me such nice presents from Papa a lovely book & a lot of writing materials. Snow enough for pretty good sleighing. (Diary of Avice Watson, 15 January 1891)

Perhaps the most significant "At Home" of a woman's life was the one she gave for the first time after her marriage. Once she was settled, she gave a very large reception for virtually everyone she knew. She often wore her wedding dress, especially if the ceremony had been "quiet" (that is, attended by only a few), or in another town. If most of those attending had seen the dress, something new could be shown off. The bridesmaids attended and did wear their wedding attire. They were expected to pour the tea and coffee. The bride's mother, or in her absence, mother-in-law, would support her.

> Mrs Grayson Smith will receive on Monday and Tuesday next, October 10 and 11, at her new home, 280 Huron street. This should be one of the most popular of the many post-nuptials of the season, and no bride has more admirers and friends than clever Mrs Grayson Smith (nee Chadwick).[93]

For her first reception, Marion Chadwick wore pink satin. She had 76 people representing 60 families on the first day. But it rained badly the next, and only 22 neighbours came. That was still almost a hundred people. Marion would have to return all their calls within a reasonable time. She announced her visiting day as Tuesday; the following week 102 people called on her that day. It took her until past the New Year to repay all her callers.

After several weeks she found she could not be at home on her own visiting day, but people did leave their cards.

> Paid 24 calls in the afternoon. Missed 18 visitors here. (17 January 1899)

At the post-nuptial of her cousin, Mamie Bain,

> Cards fell like drifts of snow into her card-tray and flowed over the table and floor. (25 January 1899)

Parties at home were still the principal amusement.

> Large "congregational" party at the rectory. There were 136 invitations about 80 present. They were entertained by music, bagatelle, stereoscopic views, and last tho' not least the supper an interesting feature in the entertainment—did not break up till 1.30. (Diary of Forbes Geddes, 24 April 1862)

> A small party at Dunstan's where I reside—Mr & Mrs MacKenzie (parson), Revd Mr Walshe Garrison Chaplain, Mr and Mrs Mewburn, Miss Arnold—sit down tea, Bagatelle, euchre, and conversation. A pleasant evening enough. (2 September 1862)

The danger of house parties was that there would be too many people for the space available. It could become hot and the rooms crowded.

> the ceilings are low and the men are big. The house seemed full. (Diary of Belle Kittredge, 11 December 1891)

Whatever the games and refreshments, conversation was the primary reason for the parties. Some people were better at it than others, whose social footing was uncertain.

> He talks all the time or rather makes terrible efforts to keep a running conversation. It is so evidently a determination to keep talking that one is inclined to let him do it & not attempt to help him. He is so ugly but they say he is a very nice man. (Diary of Belle Kittredge, 4 December 1891)

> I am sorry I wrote as I did of Mr Evans. He is a very nice man. I liked his sermons so much…(9 December 1891)

Invitations were usually received with great joy, but one was not always able to attend the function.

> Mrs Tate tells me she received a letter from his mother last winter in answer to invitation to Mill ball as follows:

> *Mrs Tate*
> *Dear Madam*
>
> *Mr & Mrs Amos and likewise Fred Amos regrets being unable to accept your kind invitation to the ball*
>
> *Yours sincerely*
>
> *Lilly Amos*
>
> PLEASE TURN OVER
>
> (reverse side)

You can have all the cream and skim milk you want if you call for it

the young man is now familiarly known in Lakefield as "Likewise" (Diary of Helen Grant Macdonald, 25 August 1891)

For the young women who lived in the country, days were filled with housework, sewing and the work of the farm. Many of them lived in large households. But they still longed for the visits of friends or even strangers, who would add variety to the day and bring news of the world beyond.

I do wish somebody would come. I feel so lonely (had a very singular *dream* last night. I dreamed about a ring. I thought I got it in a letter & it was a very pretty one with a cubic in it & such a long letter. I did not get it all read before I woke up. too bad) (Diary of Mary Victoria Campion, 14 May 1861)

Oh, what a beautiful day but I do feel so lonesome I don't know what to do with myself. I ought to be ashamed to say so when the woods & fields look so lovely & green. If there was only someone here to enjoy it with me. (20 June 1861)

I do wish somebody would come for a short time. (18 December 1861)

The conversation was mostly about local happenings. For some, who yearned for the lights of the big city and higher education, it was not enough.

how it would take one out of the narrowing process of a life in which one never hears anything discussed beyond ones neighbors. (Diary of Belle Kittredge, undated [late January 1892])

Sixteen year old Edith Elizabeth van der Smissen, the daughter of a professor at the University of Toronto, had no shortage of stimulating conversation and social commitments.

Fine day—Got invite from Mrs Matthews for Monday answered it. Went to Church. To Nana's to dinner—got
dressed—went to Arlington to receive. had 18 visitors. (Diary
of Edith Elizabeth van der Smissen, 1 January 1896)

Mr Bazet called. I entertained him. He was quite charming—
invited him to Tea on Sunday. (16 January 1896)

Mr Bazet here in evening—discussed subject of higher math-
ematics for women. (5 March 1896)

Eleanora Hallen was an astute observer of the social activities of her
associates. No details were spared when she wrote her diary.

We were late in getting up. Soon after breakfast George and I
set out to Orillia. We drove first to Mona cottage; where we
found the Sibbalds and Mrs P. already seated with bonnets
off...Mrs St John immediately asked me to take off my bonnet
which I did and we spent a few hours very pleasantly. After
dinner Mrs Scott played and sang one very pretty song. "A life
on the ocean waves." It certainly makes a "great difference"
now Sarah and Arabella are both gone: The former being
married to a Mr Todd who resides in Montreal and the latter
being now on a visit there. Mrs P had seen them both lately
and of course Mrs St John was very anxious to hear all the
particulars as to how they were going on. I quite pity poor
Mrs Sibbald who complains that everything in their house
freezes and she without a servant and three small children...I
was quite amused at the conversation after being exactly what
ladies were laughed at for, consisting of the matches (weddings) now likely to take place about the country and the
beauty of such and such young ladies. (9 December 1845)

In fact visitors were many. After the day's work was done, people
might travel a distance to visit friends, spending the evening and staying overnight. They would leave quickly after breakfast to return
home to their own duties, leaving their friends to theirs. Since there
was no way of telling people of an impending visit, everyone had to be
prepared for unexpected visitors. There was always food at hand and
a bed was quickly prepared.

After dinner Agnes & I went to town for more thread when we were at Mr Thompsons the stage crowded with people passed. Mr T said it was the Moberley's but we said it could not be as we did not expect them but to our horror we heard at Mr Hamiltons that it really was them. We felt very angry when we got home we found My poor Mother really in surprise. Seven people had actually arrived besides George who had returned from Northbrook there was not one room in the house but was in the greatest confusion. My mother's bed had just been moved into the dining room which will be their bed room in future a door has been cut in the corner of their old bed room to conect it with the new part of the house. The Barrie party had all walked out & by the time they returned we had the old sitting room looking quite comfortable with the tea on the table....Walter & Mr Bennet slept in a room without a window which was rather an advantage as they did not get up until a candle was taken them at nine o'clock....(Diary of Mary Hallen, 23 September 1851)

We were quietly seated by the window after dinner we heard the side gate go. On looking we discovered cousin Sam's familiar face. We laughted at him for carrying a large pail of apple sauce up from the station. (Diary of Matilda Bowers Eby, 14 November 1868)

Norman Wilcox felt he was paying the highest compliment to his grandmother, Sarah Woodward of Orono, when he said

she had a meal and a bed for anyone who called[94]

One of the dangers of making an impromptu visit was the risk of finding nobody home to receive. Whether in town or country, such an occurrence would be most inconvenient, particularly if one had travelled some distance. However, when a knock at the door was deliberately left unanswered, it was positively annoying.

Sleighing good yesterday & to day. Agnes & I called at the FitzGerald's after an imence deal of knocking we at last gained admitance we think the next time we go there it would be a good plan to take Skeeler's rifel hamer as there is some danger of breaking our knuckles some times we think it is a convenient deafness that sceases them for when we went in the cloth was laid for dinner. (Diary of Mary Hallen, 12 November 1848)

The welcome accorded one class of visitors might seem strange to us today. The travelling pedlar called to sell all manner of things—or to buy such things as rags. These widely travelled beings retailed exciting stories along with their goods.

> ...A rag pedlar came I sold 24 cts worth of rags. I paid out 10 cts for lamp chimney. (Diary of Frances Jones, 19 February 1878)

> A butcher called to see if we had anything to sell. (Diary of Ann Amelia Day, 14 March 1879)

> There was a man here to dinner. his name was Dean selling Doctor Brooks. He was a great talker. (Diary of Mary Victoria Campion, 12 December 1861)

As in the old and disreputable joke, these travelling salesmen sometimes stayed overnight.

> Mr Deorthman that sells medicine Books stopped here all night. (Diary of Mary Victoria Campion, 7 February 1862)

Naturally, the Campions bought one of the books.

In some areas, it was customary for the native people to sell articles door to door.

> ...the Squaws was here and we got three baskets. there was a pedlar here and he gave me a tract (Diary of Susanna Whaley, 27 April 1865)

Unmarried farm women in their late teens or early twenties often went on extended visits to relations to help out. When Victoria Campion's sister-in-law Emily died in June 1861, her sister Esther went to help brother Thomas take care of his four small children. The births of babies also meant that someone needed to help.

Maria's baby was born on the 13th, a Thursday. (Diary of Mary
Victoria Campion, 15 March 1862)

Maggie went back with William for to stay a week with Maria.
(16 March 1862)

Came home from Stirling with Albert. he drove down for me.
have been away almost three weeks. spent a very pleasant time
altogether. Annie has got a little baby. (28 February 1863)

These visits meant work, but also a change of scene, the chance to
meet new people and have different experiences.

Among the Amish, it was common for a young woman to go on
one of these extended visits, often quite far from home. She would
learn as well as help, and have the chance to meet new young men.
This arrangement, which has the nature of a short-term apprentice-
ship, is still practised among the Old Order Mennonites in Ontario
today.

Once the railway was in universal use, the chances for old settlers
to see their farflung relations grew. This was especially true for those
whose children had grown, and who might have a little leisure to
make a long journey. If the two parties who met had only memories of
one another when young, they might find it a little shocking.

Mary my Sister was here too years ago and I never saw her for
25 years and I was very glad to see her and She looked very
old.[95]

Catherine Miller counted her own blessings during a visit to her husband's sister:

How tired she looks and how poor they are. My heart over-
flows with thanksgiving to my Father for his gifts and mercies
to me and mine and for a good Husband and home. Simon is
not pleased because I went to T. Brandon's last night. [i.e., instead of staying with Simon & Elizabeth Van Norman] but if
he wants company why don't he be prepared for them. (Diary
of Catherine Miller, 5 August 1890)

One of the saddest events in the life of parents was the prospect of saying goodbye to grown children when they moved to other parts of the country.

> With a troubled mind, I write my dear children are about to be separated from me in this world. they are packing their things to go to Goderich. how shall I part them. last Thursday I went with Father to the soiree My heart was heavy when I thought I must so soon part with my children all pass'd off well. (Diary of Eliza Bellamy, 15 October 1855)

And when Eliza Bellamy's son left to be married she was equally despondent.

> This morning my son left here at 8 Oclock on his way to St Andrews to be married on Wednesday. I shall say nothing of my feelings at parting with him. I may never see him more on earth. none can tell what a Mother feels when oblig'd to part with her children. (10 September 1855)

Sometimes when you said a farewell to one of your children, it was redeemed by their return.

> Daniel left for the North West (Diary of Jessie Geddes, 15 August 1898)

> We have got two letters from him he does not think much of the country there (14 September 1898)

> We expect Dan home in two or three weeks (15 October 1898)

> Daniel came home today we are so delighted to see him (11 November 1898)

Visits from family members from afar were eagerly awaited, but sometimes had unfortunate results:

> Addie, my brother Charles' eldest daughter arrived from Chippewa on a visit to the rectory she is a tall blue-eyed girl—

but quite unsophisticated—and quite deaf ever since an attack of scarlet fever. She speaks her mind very freely, told the rectory girls that they were not in the least like clergyman's daughters—and she was quite disappointed with them. I doubt if she continues her visit long. (Diary of Forbes Geddes, 19 March 1862)

Addie is tired of Hamilton and will leave for Toronto tomorrow. (Diary of Forbes Geddes, 23 March 1862)

One of the pleasures of visiting, especially in the country, was riding in the open air. For people who travelled less than we do, and at slower speeds, the exhilaration must have been tremendous.

I just came from the shop where my Dear is painting his buggy. It is almost finished. I think it will be quite fine and I anticipate the pleasure of taking, some fine rides next summer if the Lord spares my health. (Diary of Catherine Bell Van Norman, 15 January 1850)

Wintertime visiting was often precarious due to weather problems, but year round, one had to be prepared to cope with unruly horses.

Went calling in a sleigh. Mother & the kids. Horse got crazy & tried to run away—Took us into a brick wall. All pitched out & waited around St Alban's Street for a new horse which arrived during the afternoon & we still had our drive.... (Diary of Marion Chadwick, 13 March 1893)

Later in the century, the advent of the motor car and the electric railway caused horses and their drivers even more distress.

The driver of the [electric railway] car saw Tony was frightened he stopped it till we past. Tony backed & plunged a little from side to side but finally past & how he did go after we were past it. He shewed his paces then. (Diary of Belle Kittredge, 7 April 1892)

Providing there were no disasters, part of the fun of visiting was getting there. Whether one travelled on foot or on horseback, whether one arrived by sleigh or by fancy carriage, it fortified one, upon arrival, to sit back and enjoy catching up on news. Especially for those who lived in relative isolation, it was a time when spirits were replenished and energies renewed. Then they were ready to get on with the business of life.

TEA

It must be nearly tea time
so must attend to tea table.
DIARY OF EMMA LAFLAMME, 4 MARCH 1887

A FTERNOON TEA was one of the more pleasurable pastimes. Even so, it took the Victorian age, when everything was done with great flourish and on as elaborate a scale as possible, to provide the perfect setting for entertaining with tea.

Rich Victorians liked to show off their wealth with things, stuffing their houses with furniture and accoutrements, creating new household implements, each with its own, single use. This was in particular true with respect to the ceremony of afternoon tea. Eventually, a fully-staffed household would need the following for a tea-party:

Teapot Fancy	Kettle for boiling water
Caddie Caddie	Spoon
Small Spoons	Cups and Saucers
Cream Jug	Slop Dish
Sugar Dish	Sugar Tongs
StrainerMuffin	Dish
Plates	Jam Dish & Spoon
Muffineer	Toasting Fork
Tea Tray	Tea Table

Thus, in formal circumstances (such as receiving morning calls, which were always paid after lunch), the table was small, big enough only for the tray holding all the rest of the things. The lady of the house presided and her eldest daughter, companion, or maid handed round.

The tea itself would be Indian, Ceylon or China tea. Everyone had a preference, also between green and black. Smoky Oolong was never quite as popular as Darjeeling, and it took a real connoisseur (or bohemian) to favour Earl Grey, with its exotic flavour of bergamot. There was no doubt about Catherine Miller's preference in this direction. For when the time came for her to depart, after visiting her husband's sister, Mary Ann (Polly) Pearens at Clinton, she made the following note:

A cosy tea party: Rosina Eliza Crosweller and a companion, ca. 1890.
Collection of Lenore Law

Dear old Pollie is dreading the time for us to leave…And now comes the parting cup of tea. By the bye I have learnt Pollie to drink Black Tea. (Diary of Catherine Miller, 12 August 1890)

Once purchased, the tea was kept in a caddy, probably wooden. The best had three compartments, one for black tea, one for green, and a centre spot for mixing them. The caddy spoon was short-handled and often shaped like a shell. It was used only for taking tea from the caddy and mixing it. The lady would prepare the pot, put in the tea and then add water from the kettle. The strainer would ensure that no unsightly leaves ended up in the cups. The slop dish would hold any small amounts of tea in the bottom of cups at refill time, as well as the drips from the strainer.

The lady would often add the cream or lemon; later, the cream jug and sugar dish would come on a small tray of their own, so that people could put in their own additions. Tea experts would question the use of cream, too, saying milk was better. There has also been an ongoing debate as to whether the cream should go into the cup before or after the tea.

The practice of putting cream in first started because people feared the hot tea might crack the delicate china cups. (In fact, bone china is quite resistent to this kind of problem.) After a time, it became fashionable to have a preference, and to insist on "milk in first" or not.

The muffin dish had a lid and held warm muffins (the kind we call English muffins) or toast. In less formal circumstances, the toasting fork could be used on the fire right there. The muffineer was similar to a very large salt shaker or castor, from which one could sprinkle sugar or cinnamon on the muffins.

In some circles, afternoon tea came to be known as "The 5 o'-clock Function." This was a rather elegant affair, popular in the late Victorian period. A woman attending such an event naturally wore her hat and gloves, which often remained on during tea. It therefore became incumbent upon the hostess to provide dainties that could be eaten without causing too much damage, particularly to the gloves.

> I intended to have a five o'clock tea 30 asked—lovely preparations—storm came everything was blown to bits—nobody dared venture out. Parsons & we ate food. (Diary of Marion Chadwick, 18 August 1893)

There would be plates of sandwiches—cucumber are the most famous—but if they were not to be had, one could think of many other kinds, meat or fish paste, egg or some savoury jelly. Finally there would be cakes, one of several kinds of unfrosted substantial confections so popular then, such as fruitcake, pound cake, seed or nut cake. Currants were a staple addition. These rather firm pastries went well with the tea, and could be held in the hand to eat.

Afternoon tea was the most informal of all social entertainments, giving the hostess opportunity to provide refreshments on as simple or as elaborate a scale as she chose. She might just have one or two close friends in for a chat and a cosy cup of tea, or two hundred people to whom she wished to give social recognition.

> After the match we went down the Main St [of Guelph] two
> & two & then to Mrs Rennels for high tea & it *was high*.
> (Diary of Marion Chadwick, 1 October 1892)

Most people were not able to entertain on such an elaborate scale, nor did they have much in the way of back-up personnel. For less grand functions, it was simply a matter of providing a setting in which women could come together to give and receive mutual support, as well as to enjoy the warmth of friendship. As today, a smaller, more intimate group may have been more conducive to relaxation. But whichever type of tea one attended, it was a time for keeping up with the happenings in the community; a time of sharing news; and yes, in some cases, a time to gossip.

> Amy Riordan had a "Lent tea"—Just a few girls and lots of
> gossip. (Diary of Marion Chadwick, 8 February 1894)

For less formal occasions, or in less grand households, the teatray would hold the teapot, cups, saucers, cream jug and sugar dish, with a plate of cakes or sandwiches. There would be considerable less ceremony attending the tea-drinking. But doubtless the drinkers found the same comforts from the warm beverage, the food and the conversation.

> The Miss Marsh's brought Lena home. Papa put up the storm
> windows. Last Tuesday Mr Christies & Miss Wright spent the
> day here. In the afternoon Mrs Alick Hewat Mary & little
> Alice, now Mrs George Richardson came. So we had a large
> tea party. I will be glad when this run of visitors ceases there
> is hardly a day without someone. (Diary of Avice Watson, 11
> November 1886)

Afternoon tea was certainly the most popular social tea. But there were other types as well. The Kettledrum tea party became quite popular in the 1800's. This was an event to which men were also invited. *The Ladies' Journal*, of June 1884 suggests that it was called such because it is made up of a great deal of noise and very little to eat. Another was called a "thimble tea." At this event, guests would either bring their own hand-work or work on communal projects, before settling down to dainty refreshments and tea. It seems that almost any occasion, or any cause, might justify the planning of a tea party.

> It is a beautiful day I was to a temperance tea party to day at Reynolds Woods. (Diary of Susanna Whaley, 14 May 1864)

For those in society, there was rather an important component of social etiquette woven into the business of afternoon tea. Firstly, it was not considered proper to give a tea if one owed any social calls. Therefore, a good hostess would be sure that she had done all the visiting required before she organised her tea. Once the tea had taken place, she would then owe a visit to everyone who had attended. To simplify the business of trying to remember who had attended her tea, all of the guests would have left their calling cards. This way, one was able to check exactly who had attended and to whom one owed a call.

The type of teacups used at an afternoon tea would depend very much upon the wealth of the hostess and upon the fashions created by the manufacturers. Teacups have an interesting history. When tea, coffee and chocolate first came on the scene in the seventeenth century, they were all expensive and novel, and all were drunk from the same large handleless cups, called "cans." Gradually each developed their own shape. Coffee cans grew large and tall; chocolate cans had lids; and tea cans became smaller with a shallow saucer.

The saucer grew larger and deeper, and it was usual to pour a little tea into the saucer, blow on it gently to cool it, and drink it. About 1840, the can had a handle added, and genteel people started drinking straight from the cup, as it was now called. Really "nice" people no longer drank from the saucer, although the habit of doing so continued well into our century, especially in areas where fashion was less an influence than tradition. As the teacup became more important, the saucer got smaller and was used mainly as a platform on which the cup rested, along with the tiny teaspoon.

The greatest of the English potteries made tea sets (teapot, cream and sugar, cups, saucers and plates, perhaps even the muffin dish) in the most popular designs, which are highly collectible today. People who have inherited their grandmother's Derby, Worcester or Wedgwood teasets have a treasure in both senses of the word. Less rich families could have bought sets from the potteries which made for them—Derby, Johnson or Mason Brothers. These often portrayed designs showing exotic locales, using the customary inexpensive dyes (mostly blue and turquoise, although there was also a pale pink). These sets have been less likely to survive, but are equally prized.[96]

Mary Hallen enjoyed an early evening tea at the home of Mr. Tysson, a gentleman who captured her heart, and who left her feeling quite melancholy when he returned to live in England.

> At seven o'clock my Father my Mother Agnes George and I went to Mr Tyssen's….Mr Tyssen has his room very comfortable the silver tea pot coffy pot & candle sticks added much to the comfort of the tea table. I poured out the tea & Agnes the coffy. George played a great deal on the melodian and he sang several new songs which we have not heard before. (Diary of Mary Hallen, 21 October 1848)

Often the pleasure of the moment included memories evoked by old and precious teacups.

> Four o'clock tea set brought me by dear Father (Diary of Mary Brown, 6 October 1880)

Although the following note was written from a nephew to his aunt several years after the Victorian period, we include it because it expresses sentiments which are timeless.

> Doris gave me a tea party yesterday—there were just the two of us present—and we had your beautiful silver tea set for the first time and you have no idea how useful and ornamental it is, nor how much better the tea tasted out of it.[97]

During the late Victorian period only the elderly would recall early rules of etiquette surrounding the business of tea.

> Certain customs may be remembered in this country among us who had grandmothers trained in the ceremonies of a later day. One of them consisted in putting the spoon in the cup to show that no more tea was desired; another was that of turning over the cup in the saucer for the same purpose. Etiquette

also demanded that the tea should be tasted from the spoon, and that the hostess should then inquire "Is your tea agreeable?" Certain scrupulous old ladies ask that now, and the question savors of a more sedate and gentle day than this.[98]

Regardless of the age, the whole business of afternoon tea has always been one of enchantment. Whether a summertime garden tea-party suffused with the fragrance of blossoms, or a cold weather tea-party where guests hugged the fireside, it has always been a special event, when memories are made and friendships cemented. This wonderful institution has been enjoyed by many generations, each adding to the tradition.

Illness

Two thin soles make one cold:
two colds one attack of bronchitis,
two attacks of bronchitis, one elm coffin.
Spirit of the Age, 15 JUNE 1859

ILLNESS WAS AN EVER CONSTANT THREAT during the Victorian age. Unfortunately it was a time when very little could be done to cure many afflictions. The young and the elderly were particularly vulnerable. Patients of all ages were often overwhelmed by conditions which would be regarded as relatively minor today. Care-givers worked with whatever they had, often relying upon home remedies passed down from mother to daughter. At such times, the sick-room became the most important room in the house. Some sat by the bedside providing whatever comfort they could, while others fussed in the kitchen, preparing foods for the invalid. However, through it all, those involved were filled with uncertainty and fear.

Avice Watson of Wellington County had suffered off and on with chest problems. Despite doctoring with emulsion of cod liver oil, as well as an array of other medications, she worsened. She wrote the following words a few weeks before her death on 29 January 1892:

> Cleaned the Drawing room. Aunt Maria died very suddenly from heart trouble. So many of our relations & friends have gone this year & so unexpectedly. It shows what a slight hold

we have on life here. God grant that we may all lay hold of life Eternal through Christ then death can have no sorrow for us. (Diary of Avice Watson, 14 November 1891)

Sometimes hope for recovery was pretty futile right from the beginning.

Mary rested pretty well last night. Temp. 100 1/2° this morning 103° in the evening. the Drs. seem puzzled as to what may be the matter. While consulting with Dave, Dr. B. refused to give an opinion. He wanted to make out it is a severe case of "dissentary" Dave refutes that & still believes it to be Typhoid fever. Went away however saying "I can give no opinion on the case." (Diary of L. H. Wagner, 7 May 1887)

Mary Wagner had no shortage of medics tending her. David Merner Staebler was her brother and a newly graduated doctor. It is apparent from L.H. Wagner's diary that the doctors were in disagreement about the cause of her illness. Possibly Dr. B.'s insistence that Mary was not suffering from typhoid fever, as diagnosed by her brother, was partly due to stubbornness. Mary did in fact have typhoid fever.

Some lucky patients at the Hospital for Sick Children in Toronto were able to spend time at the Lakeside Home for Little Children, where they would benefit from the fresh air. These children are en route for their holiday. *National Archives of Canada*

Illness in children was always a tremendous worry to parents. Not only were treatments often "hit and miss," but patients often lay around for weeks, unsure of the cause of their malady, and without confidence that a cure would be found.

> Was 14 years old today. Taken sick the night before and had to take a pill. Pa went to see W. Woodruff, M.D. Gave me some brown powder for pain. Liver all wrong from eating too much pot-pie the sunday before (awful good though) but have been bilious all along. Pa gave me an Album for a present. Edith came down and we made her stay to tea. Gave me birthday card. Ma tried recipe for making cake; my birthday cake, but I can't eat any. Makes my mouth water to hear them eating rosebud and to know I can't have any. Too sick to want any though. Nice day I guess, can't see outdoors. (Diary of Mary Frances Cleveland, 12 September 1882)

During the course of Mary Frances' illness, she went through the standard routine of pills, powders, medicine, mustard plasters and greased cloths, none of which seemed to relieve her symptoms. Eventually her father, perhaps in desperation, set about brewing a herbal concoction.

> Pa gets all up now. Goes up to our David's to get some beef's gall to have an injection. Mrs Nichols tells him her brother had had the inflamation on the bowels two or three times and has been cured with Smartweed cloths. Gets everybody going. Pa comes home and puts over a great big kettle full of smartweed and none of it is used. Township fair today. Doctor Routledge comes in today. Got the malaria fever and a little inflamation on the bowels. Get out of my head every little while. Some folks up to Bangharts today from away off. Doc gave me some powders for the pain and some fever medicine (Woodruff's fever stuff was not right, I know) Patience is getting pretty well done out. Got to hold on though. Feed on milk now-a-days. Have not had anything to eat since Monday the 11th but milk. Pa got me some peaches the other day but I can't eat them. Liza Dale came over this evening and so did Mrs Banghart and Edith. Now come the linseed poltices and hot water cloths are dropped

off. Was throwing up green bile tonight. Awful sick at stomach today. Yelling with pain. So ends today. (15 September
1882)

It is quite amazing that Mary Frances had the energy to continue writing her diary. Not only was she suffering a great deal of physical pain,
but she was not sleeping much at night. However, she managed to
maintain an interest in what was happening outside of her sick room,
and continued to document her illness.

Put in an awful night last night. Ma was sitting up with me
giving me medicine every hour-and-a-half. I was fairly wild in
the night. Don't feel today like speaking. Haven't all along.
Rest better every other night. Suppose I'll rest pretty well tonight if not, I'll have a powder. Not Woodruff's brown powder but Routledges pain powder. Wind blew terrible some
time along near this time but as my brain is so upsidedown,
don't know when it was. Margaret Ann Caldwell was down
some time today but I was not allowed to see her which was
according to the doctor's orders. Mrs Cole was down one day
last week but don't know which day it was. Doctor Dale and
his wife were over to see me this evening. They were admitted
into my room because he's a doctor. Pulse ran 100 today.
Came down a peg. It ran 100 and 4 or 5 Friday. Oh, I guess
I'll be around in a few weeks. Hope so anyway. Doctor intended to come yesterday but was called away and so came
this morning....(17 September 1882)

One sort of remedy, which was heavily used and has disappeared, was
the poultice. It was more or less a hot, wet bag which was placed on
the location of the illness (often an inflammation), and was intended
to "draw out the poison." The inside of the poultice seems as often as
not to have been something in the food line: bread, mustard, flaxseed,
cornmeal, onions—cooked to boiling, sewn into a piece of muslin and
then applied "as hot as the patient can stand." No one who has experienced a poultice remembers them with pleasure. It seems clear that
Mary Frances Cleveland was not very fond of them.

Feel better today. Getting along first rate...Have no linseed
poltices on now, quit them and went to rubbing lineament on

my side and a hot flannel. (Diary of Mary Frances Cleveland, 26 September 1882)

Philip not very well on account of a gathering—applied poultices in the eve'g of linseed which gave him great relief. (Diary of Frances Gay Simpson, 9 August 1891)

Since Saturday p.m. Mary has been complaining chills. Took foot bath Saturday eve. Today we laid a mustard plaster across her kidneys & took pain in back away. Went to her head & had very severe neuralgia. Put mustard plaster on back of her neck & slept then. (Diary of L. H. Wagner, 7 March 1887)

The mustard plaster was a very popular stand-by, and is sometimes still used today. It is made by mixing equal amounts of flour and mustard. To this a couple of spoons of goose oil or lard has been added, which helps to prevent the skin from blistering. Its use was not confined to rural areas but was universal.

On the sofa in the sitting room all day long with mustard plasters—quinine—& an ulcerated throat. (Diary of Marion Chadwick, 6 January 1899)

One rather unusual commodity was purchased by the Hallen family, possibly to be used in preparing a salve, or as an ingredient for making a poultice.

An Indian brought a half pint bottle of bears grease which we bought for a quarter of a dollar we were glad of the opportunity of getting it. (Diary of Mary Hallen, 18 November 1848)

An illness which showed up with clockwork regularity was "summer complaint." This polite and descriptively named condition produced symptoms of diarrhea and dysentery. It may have been caused, at least in part, by ingesting food that had begun to spoil in warm weather. Other contributors may have been sudden changes in diet with the arrival of fresh fruits and vegetables, or perhaps drinking or washing food in unclean water. Whatever the cause, almost every diarist suffered from it at one time or another.

Cure for Summer Complaint: Two ounces tincture of rhubarb, one of paregoric, one-half of essence of peppermint, one-half of essence of annis, one-half of prepared chalk. dose for adult, one teaspoon in a little water; take as often as needed.—Mrs L. Bradley[99]

Mary Brown gave an account of this, as well as other illnesses experienced by her family during the summer of 1864.

Little James Harley cut sixteen teeth before he was fourteen months old. Had diarhea in July, recovered at Beach returned after a fortnight's stay then Dysentry came on severely for ten days, so was sent back to Beach, and came back with ague. Jack came home from Galt 26th August, Saturday night ill with the ague worse with Diptheria and completely shaken with the blow of a bat on his mouth. Port wine quinine and iron were the remedies, the throat was very sore uvula & right side covered, and the breath in consequence very offensive. The first week very slow progress then sudden change for better the throat greatly improved and spirits cheerful again. Poor Harry laid by on the sofa suffering from his hip again. (Diary of Mary Brown, [undated] early September 1864)

Although Mary Brown had a difficult summer, she was fortunate to have assistance in the house, making her task of nursing sickly children far easier than it would have been otherwise. Of course she was not the only mother who struggled through summers of illness.

Mrs Ingersoll is looking poorly and the youngest boy has been more or less ill all Summer, first measles, chicken pox and lastly the summer complaint. (Diary of Catharine Merritt, 27 July 1858)

One constant difficulty all housewives faced was food spoilage. Without refrigeration and other modern methods of food preparation, there was always the danger that edibles would "go off" without the family noticing. For the Wyllie family of Ayr, the worst happened in 1876, and John Wyllie wrote to his brother-in-law about the results.

The wife made a meat pie yesterday. And on Sabbath eve eat

it up; well that pie was a mystery to all of us. It did not seem to lie well on the stomach and kicked up a fearful racket. The wife kept piling over the bed and disturbing me in my regular sleep while Jean & Bob kept the air musical with the Ohs and Ahs. That ere pie gripped hard. Yes it did. I just got one grip and started for the Seat of War. And staid there. Moral: don't eat meat pie. It was tough and the stomach threw it up and made Bob throw. Look out for meat pies they are a horrid thing.[100]

Certain beliefs sprang up around food which clearly came from the spoilage issue. For example, it was considered bad luck to pour the cream from the jug back into the pitcher. Cream that had sat out in the little jug for a time might well be on the turn, and would contaminate the greater amount in the pitcher if put back in, hence the "bad luck."

Doctors were expensive and people often treated themselves. Every newspaper contained advertisements for patent medicines making extravagant claims about which ailments they cured. These were followed by testimonials from persons in faraway towns showing that they had been at death's door before rescue by this tonic or that pill. Certain items—liver pills, Lydia Pinkham's, electric oil—would have been in every household. One popular item, Burdock's Blood Bitters, emphasized the popular idea of purifying the blood. There were so many of these popular remedies that Sears, Roebuck had a section of their catalogue devoted to patent medicines, including a couple which are still available today (Castoria and Murine). Occasionally they would issue that section separately from the rest of the catalogue, a sure sign that it was in heavy demand.

Home remedies were of tremendous importance to most families. Many were based on formulas involving ingredients which had some healing properties; others were traditional folklore. A.W. Chase, a medical doctor, took advantage of this interest in making medicines at home by publishing *Dr. Chase's Remedies* (1867), with 800 practical recipes. His book was hugely popular. Almanacs, which were found in every home, were also common sources for both advertisements and recipes.

It was not uncommon for people with livestock to use medications upon themselves which had been prescribed by the veterinary surgeon for animals. This was especially so of liniment. Perhaps the basic premise, "if it's good enough for animals it's good enough for me," was sufficient to encourage experimentation. Medications purchased from the vet were generally cheaper than those obtained from a doctor, a fact which added incentive to use them.

Because diagnostic skills were not well developed, the job of the doctor was often difficult. This occasionally caused disharmony between care-givers and doctors.

> Mary seems rather worse this a.m. I gave her 3 drops of Laudinum & Digitalis in a teaspoonful of glycerene & reported to the Dr. He was very indignant at me interfering with his patient, called it a "terrible blunder," but I believe what I gave her, did her good for it relieved her. He pronounced her a "very sick woman." Coming up about 11:30 a.m. he found her abt 130 & temperature abt. 103° Inquired whether there were any fevers in Hespeler. We know of none. She took (inhaled) a strong dose of poison somewhere. Katie Lepp is doing the housework today. She is very good to the baby. The Dr also drew her urine. (Diary of L. H. Wagner, 2 May 1887)

Mary Wagner (formerly Staebler), taken in February 1887, three months before her death. Photo by Smith, Galt. *Breithaupt-Hewetson-Clark Collection, University of Waterloo*

During Mary's illness, L.H. Wagner became highly frustrated by Dr. Brown and his lack of making a firm diagnosis.

> ...Dr Brown called at 4:30 p.m. Mary has been prespiring ever since yesterday. Her hands are cold & clammy. there are quite a number of callers in today. We allowed no one in to see her but her cousin Mrs John Fry. Mary did not see her. We sent the baby with Katie to her house. It is too noisy for Mary. About 8:15 p.m. Dr Whiteman of Shakespeare for whom we wired last evening arrived. Sent for Dr Brown, but was away. So Dr W. made a thorough examination of Mary & expressed his opin-

ion that she had Typhoid fever without a doubt, this [knocking?] Dr Brown's theory on the head. My opinion of Dr B is that he is neither a gentleman nor a physician & not near what some people think him to be. Dr W. further told me of Mary's very dangerous condition & that I should let her know it & inform her friends. I told him that from the first she did not think she would get better again having told me so twice either on Monday or Tuesday & that even today she stated so to me thinking she is too weak to recover. I asked him "How long may she live." He replied, "If she does not speedily improve she cannot live over 3 days. She cannot live till Thursday." (8 May 1887)

The Victorians did not shrink from death or from describing the deathbed, as we do. They had a natural curiosity and were happy when someone made "a good death." It was also a matter of course that people were informed when they were approaching death, since it was essential that they had time to compose their souls.

Drs Ling & Moorhouse held an examination and consultation telling poor Aunt Fanny that her cause is one of extreme danger and of holding out no hope of recovery. She has taken it very quietly and calmly. (Diary of Alice Patterson, 14 July 1881)

Dr Ling came in the afternoon and told her that her suffering would not be long. Dr Ling's kindness and candor have been a great comfort to her. (27 July 1881)

In our own day, there is a revival of the Victorian habit of people being with a dying person in their last moments. For a number of decades, people were often left alone or with medical personnel only. But a century ago the family gathered to make their final goodbyes, and to provide emotional support to one another and the dying person.

Tonight he went over to see how Mr Benham was. He found the family assembled and expecting him to die before morning. All his daughters were there. (Diary of Ann Amelia Day, 11 March 1879)

A strong faith in God appears to have been an essential component in achieving a peaceful death during Victorian times. If that element existed, the dying person was able to relinquish worries about what was to become of those left behind. During her illness, Mary (Staebler) Wagner said to her husband: "I am so glad that I attended to my soul long ago. If I would have to do it now it would make me crazy."

> At about 2:30 a.m. I went in to her to bid her good night when she asked me to pray with her, so I knelt down besides the bed, as I had often done during previous sicknesses of my dear wife at Hespeler & prayed for her and our dear little Louis Jacob Gordon. She also prayed very earnestly & tenderly for me that I might so walk as to be an example to others & never do anything but the Lord's will & live for him &c. then for her little darling son that I might train him up in the fear of the Lord & that he might grow up an honor & glory to His cause. This made her very tired so I left her when she said Amen & she slept a little. I retired about 3:00 a.m. & slept well till mother called me at 7:00 a.m. (Diary of L. H. Wagner, 8 May 1887)

On the day that his wife died, L. H. Wagner wrote about some of the things she had said during her illness.

> During her sickness I did not once hear her pray for herself. She seemed fully resigned & willing to abide by the will of the Lord. How glad I am that it was so. Once she said to me "I am sorry to leave you & the baby. I'd like to be with you yet but there'll be a way." (10 May 1887)

When their children were ill, mothers tried any remedy they could get their hands on.

> Stuart has sore throat ....put burnt alum on his throat & he gargled with salt water. We are burning sulphur. (Diary of Frances Tweedie Milne, 23 January 1882)

The scourge of young adults was tuberculosis. It was not uncommon for more than one member of a family to die from this disease, which spread relatively easily. For those with money enough to ensure that

Frances Tweedie Milne, diarist, ca. 1876.
Photo by J. Bruce & Co., Toronto.
Collection of Margaret Haist

they had a well balanced diet, the chances of contracting tuberculosis were slightly less than if they were poor. However, it often seemed to strike indiscriminately. On 3 September 1873, Robert Cullen died from this disease.

I was at the death of one of Collins' boys. what a blessed thing to die in the Lord. how he spoke to them all. till the very last he sung "Rock of ages" and "Jesus lover of my soul." That night he died. he would have liked (to) live longer if it had been god's will but he was ready to go. hoping they would all cling to some rock for safety. (he said) "I did not think when I was well the peace that was (mine) believing on the lord Jesus except now one and all of you may live without it, but you cannot die without or you will perish for ever. Mother, keep them in mind of [the] end." Mrs Lambert and me dressed him, a perfect skeleton. It was consumption and there are [the] other two of them will go the same way.[101]

Mrs Wyllie was right about the Cullen brothers. Robert's brother Adam died the following year at the age of 28, and Thomas Cullen died in 1878 aged 26. The treatment of consumption was nothing more than experimentation. As recently as 1902 the following was suggested.

A German physician recommends to consumptives the sulphur treatment. This consists in the patient living in rooms where one or two drams of sulphur are melted daily on a hot stone. The first ten days there will be felt increased irritation and cough. These soon decrease, and improvement is rapidly felt, and complete cures are often effected if the disease is not too far advanced.[102]

The care of poor people stricken with this disease was often provided for through the benevolence of the wealthy.

> ...At 3 I went with Mrs Eaton to see a consumptive girl she seems to belong to a family of gypsies. a "bad clan" as Mrs Eaton with her strong way of putting things—says. They all seem poor & worthless, idle and unthrifty. We are going to do something for the sick girl by removing her from their hovel to begin with. the atmosphere in all respects is dreadful. (Diary of Lady Macdonald, 25 April 1868)

Respiratory ills were especially prevalent. Sometimes peculiar treatments were devised. The rather old-fashioned medical practices of cupping and leeching continued well into the second half of the century. In Lindsay, Dr. A.W.J. de Grassi treated William Eliot of Fenelon on 24 March 1875: "visit & cupping Wm. $1.00"[103] after having made four previous visits to leech him that same month. Leeches are small wormlike animals with heads at each end. They pierce the skin and suck the blood. Their use to draw out blood and bad humours was also an ancient medical practice, part of that system of bleeding and purging which doctors felt would rid the body of disease. What it actually did was to weaken the already ill patient. Leeching was so common that "leeches" is a slang term for doctors.

> A lovely day. Andrew away all day collecting the ministers Salary. nothing particular happened. I have felt sick all day with a bad pain in my side. (Diary of Frances Jones, 19 February 1878)

> A snowy day, Will took me to Prescot to see Bill, he says I have pleurisy and cupped & blistered me. Andrew in the woods all day. Bella better. (20 February 1878)

Cupping was an ancient medical practice where a cup or horn was heated, then applied, hollow side down, to the skin (often to the back). The heat inflamed the skin, and as the air cooled, it drew the flesh up into the cup. This caused an inflammation or blister, and was thought to draw the blood away from the sick part of the body.

Although both cupping and leeching are still practiced in specialised circumstances today, they were no longer fashionable when

Dr. de Grassi was using them in Lindsay in the 1870's. The heyday of leeching had been in the 1830's, when it was a fashion based in Paris. Cupping had been gone even longer. The country doctor in nineteenth century Ontario was not necessarily worried about keeping up with latest developments, and might continue using the techniques of his youth throughout his career.

Eliza Bellamy was much troubled by illness in her family during 1855.

> Satturday. rain which is much wanted busy this morning. made cakes and pies. done some mending and preparing to go to Eliza who is not getting better. surely there is nothing in this life worth liveing for, when we think we are within reach of the object we most wished to obtain, a blight comes and all is gon. Oh! May we so live that when the dread summons comes, we shall have nothing to do, but, obey. (Diary of Eliza Bellamy, 2 June 1855)

> Cool, gloomy weather. some rain every day. last Satturday Father look to Eliza. Much trouble there. She had been with doctor Edmondson who operated on her throat, where the cause of her complaint was, and which would end fatal, if not immediately attended to. I pass'd a lonesome Sabbath. Isaiah and Eliza went to the Dr in Brockville has to go every second day. I read the word with the dear children, they reading also. (7 July 1855)

> Some time and much trouble has pass'd over me since I last pen'd a few lines here. My grand child Emily Wright was a second time attack'd with inflamation on the brain which was more severe than the first. I have been there with others attending day and night a weeke her poor mother constant and little less her Father. few expected she would be spared but God in His wisdom has raised her. I came home Yesterday evening with my Husband who was Kind and attentive. (14 July 1855)

> Sabbath. cool. Doctor Edmondson has been here three times during the past week he Lanc'd or cut open Luther legs, from which an immense quantity of Matter flowed. the opperation

was severe both to the patient and those who assisted. I was the prenciple help. it was a trial Luther is very feeble yet, not able to be up. (2 September 1855)

Illness and death often came suddenly and unexpectedly, bringing great sorrow and sadness, especially when the deceased had been considered to be hale and hearty.

Received a shocking telegram from William Pearse, Winnipeg, "Henry died this morning of pneumonia." Our poor Henry who left us two weeks ago in such good spirits to make a home for himself in the far West. Aunt & I went to see poor Aunt Mary in her sore sore bereavement. (Diary of Alice Patterson, 5 May 1881)

Highly infectious diseases were naturally cause for great alarm. Caregivers, unless they had already had the illness, were usually at great risk of contracting the disease.

Beautiful mild day. Went for a drive in the afternoon, but the horse tumbled & broke the shafts and we had to walk home. it was caused by too small a collar. Mrs Geo. Frothingham died last night from diptheria which she took from nursing her son. (Diary of Janet Hall, 14 December 1876)

Sometimes an illness took a turn for the better, surprising everyone, including the patient.

Aunt Breithaupt was very weak this evening. Johney and I had to go and fetch Doctor Bowlby. We brought Aunt Brahler along out. When we came home Aunt Breithaupt had given them all a farewell in this world, she thought she had to die, but she got better again. (Diary of L. H. Wagner, 2 January 1873)

Sometimes alternative methods of healing were sought. In Waterloo County, "charming" was used to some extent. This was a type of faith healing practiced by certain individuals who claimed to have the gift. One advantage of "charming" was that it could be done at a distance. It did not necessarily require that the patient actually meet with the healer. Many thought it the work of the devil, so steered clear of it, but others vouched for its effectiveness.

While visiting in Toronto, Gertrude Nicholson learned a little about faith healing.

> Mr Salmon believes in faith healing & once when Connie lived with them she was very ill & nearly died of diptheria & they never had a doctor near her all the time. Uncle Fred was very vexed about it. (Diary of Gertrude Nicholson, 20 June 1896)

Hysteria seems to have been a generic term for some sort of failing in the female sex. It is probable that a large number of ills came under this general heading.

> In the forenoon I called on Katie I was informed yesterday afternoon that she had taken suddenly ill so I called over to see her immediately. She pressed me so hard to call today that I could not refuse. she is sick for certain, with hysteria. (Diary of Matilda Bowers Eby, 9 July 1863)

When Helen Grant Macdonald visited friends in Lakefield, she had the privilege of meeting the venerated author and naturalist Catharine Parr Traill. Mrs. Traill had some reservations about current medical practice:

> She is 91 years old. Had Grippe [influenza] last winter and was recommended during convalescence to take brandy and water, which she did not do. Explained afterwards to Mrs Tate that she was afraid of contracting a bad habit. (Diary of Helen Grant Macdonald, 23 August 1891)

Oysters were a very popular food. Surprisingly, they were often served to invalids during convalescence.

> After dinner we came up to see dearest Mamma we found her much better and she took some Oysters for her dinner which she relished very much. (Diary of Sophia MacNab, 21 January 1846)

> This morning I made some Oyster soup for the Dr. got him to

eat a plate full through the day. I am glad he is taking a little to eat again. (Diary of Matilda Bowers Eby, 24 April 1867)

Mrs Dale came. I asked her to stay all night and she is here still. I don't know what I shall do when she leaves, for Citty will not be with me all the time, and I find it very fatiguing going from room to room only waiting on myself. I have had enough to weaken me but all the bad symptoms have left, pain in my side entirely, and the cough is nothing to speak of. Night sweats, etc gone, and my appetite pretty good. Those little oysters in the shell from Thomas, Dr Jukes said, were nearly as useful as the cod liver oil, and a sponge bath every morning, has done more good than all the quinine, etc. (Diary of Catharine Merritt, 28 November 1859)

However, perhaps the most novel food was that enjoyed by the young Mary Frances Cleveland, once her appetite had returned.

Have been crocheting edging all day except a couple of hours that I took to visit Mrs Haynes and in which I had a *large* time. Brought some boiled dry corn home with me. Pa went shooting this morning and shot two pluvers and a black squirrel. While over Mr Haynes, Old Jack Tragus came to do a small work for them and Pa came home with the squirrel and wanted me to help skin it, and of course I was sent for and on arriving at home found the said squirrel skinned which was very pleasing. Had squirrel soup for supper. Received my certificate for entering high school this evening while busy mending my stockings. (Diary of Mary Frances Cleveland, 18 October 1882)

Got up this morning (as usual) and ate a whole black squirrel along with about three slices of bread. Never saw the beat for I was about as hungry when I got through as when I commenced. (19 October 1882)

The last twenty years of our own time have seen a resurgence of interest in herbals—those gentle medicines which generally have a calming effect. The Victorians were very aware of the more common herbs and their properties. Some of them were used in a regular way to soothe or provide rest.

Was up about 8 o'clock this morning and forgot to take my
tansy before breakfast. (Diary of Mary Frances Cleveland, 22
October 1882)

I had some ginger tea and slept well all night. (Diary of
Catherine Bell Van Norman, 23 February 1850)

I have commenced to drink almost daily hoarshound tea
which I think is highly benificial to my health. (Diary of
Matilda Bowers Eby, 24 August 1863)

Horehound lozenges, originally for medicinal purposes, began to be
seen as a popular sweet. As early as 1855 in Mrs. Gaskell's *North and
South*, her heroine offers a horehound candy to a friend. Although
rarer today, horehound candies still exist.

   Although there were a growing number of patent medicines, people still depended on the homemade remedies, many of them herbal
in origin, which had been handed down through the centuries. People shared the ones they liked the most. Late in the century Mary
Cain of Manvers shared this ointment with her niece, Lulla Lunn.

Oil of Gladness

| 1 quart of raw Linseed Oil | 1 ounce Orrigawin Oil |
| 2 ounces Gum Camphor | 1 ounce Hemlock Oil |

Mix the Oils thin. pulverize the Camphor, add it to the Oils,
if required it will mix in five minutes. inwardly a dose for an
adult from fifteen to thirty drops.

"Inwardly" means taken by mouth, probably in some water. These
medicines—the sort with linseed or camphor as primary ingredients—smelt strongly, and would not have had a pleasant taste. Unfortunately, Mrs. Cain does not tell us what the Oil of Gladness cured.[104]

   Salves were also commonly made at home. The basic protective
salves still marketed by Watkins and Raleigh, which consist of
beeswax and something herbal, undoubtedly have their origins in
homemade concoctions. Their continued use is a mark of their success. They protect hands against possible injury from small pricks and
cuts, as well as insuring that nicks already present on the hands do
not become infected with dirt.

Other homemade salves had active healing properties. One which is still in use by Old Order Mennonites in Waterloo County consists of beeswax, resin and raccoon lard melted together, with a bar of castile soap added when the mixture is removed from the heat. The resulting salve keeps for a long time.

> If you do not have raccoon lard easily available at home, you can ask your neighbours who might be going "cooning" to bring you some. It is easily rendered, similar to chicken fat. It does not smell, and neither does the salve, which is good for healing cuts and sores.[105]

Both patent medicines and home remedies were suggested for many ailments which we apparently no longer have today. Women had the vapours and children had brain fever.

> About 5 o'clock Miss Proudfoot came with Mrs Dill and we had tea and a nice chat. Mrs Dill is up for her nerves. (Diary of Mary Coldwell Butcher, 23 September 1918)

One of the most common afflictions was "impurities of the blood," for which this home recipe was the cure:

Dr. Tuckwell's Receipt for
all impurities of the blood

one oz. Magnesia
one oz. cream tartar
one oz. Epson Salts
one oz. Milk of Sulphur
one inch of ginger slightly bruised
one nutmeg sliced
the rind of a large lemon, pared off as thin as possible

Over these ingredients pour one quart of boiling water. Stir it up, let it stand 48 hours, then slice the lemon into it and let it stand one day. Pour off the liquid and add one pint of best Holland Gin. Dose: one wine glass full for a grown up person, diminish according to age.[106]

The basic ingredient of this cure, the pint of gin, is typical of many remedies of the period. They were heavily alcoholic; Lydia Pinkham's popular mixture, for example, was 18 per cent alcohol. It is interesting to think of this and remember that the temperance movement was, at the same time, so powerful. The use of alcohol as a medicine continued for several more decades, causing teetotalers some distress when faced with medical advice which contradicted their usual practices, as in the case of Mrs. Traill.

A few Home Remedies

To cure hiccoughs: place your two little fingers in your ears and hold your breath.

To stop a nosebleed: chew a newspaper.

To cure rheumatism: a raw salt herring with the bone taken out, applied to the neck tying a handkerchief over it and keeping it on all night.

To cure whooping cough: put a trout's mouth into the patient's.

A cure for diabetes: take a deer's bladder. Stand it in a quart bottle, and fill it with good Madeira wine. let stand 48 hours, then drink three or four times a day, half a gill at a time.[107]

Dentistry was at its most primitive.

I am most sick with toothache. It will have to be extracted. (Diary of Catherine Bell Van Norman, 27 February 1850)

My dear husband extracted my tooth with hawksbills or nippers. (28 February 1850)

My Dear undertook to extract a tooth for Harriett Emory, but did not succeed. She was much frightened. (4 March 1850)

For those who could afford such things, false teeth were available. However, getting such work done often required that a person travel a fair distance in order to find a dentist with sufficient skill.

In the evening my Mother Agnes & I went to the village called at the Mitchells we found poor Miss M in rather low spirits caused by the absence (with out leave) of one of her front teeth she is thinking of going to Toronto to have it replaced which I strongly advised her to do. (Diary of Mary Hallen, 2 July 1852)

It was only in the 1870's that organized training for dentists became general in Ontario. The dental college was small and inadequate; those wanting qualification to call themselves "doctor" had to go to the United States. The result was a very small number of dentists in the population, and most people neglected the matter completely.

Mr Brymer came to pull my tooth but could not. George got me some stuff to put on it. (Diary of Mary Coldwell Butcher, 13 November 1894)

Remedy for black teeth. Take equal parts cream of tartar and salt, pulverize it and mix it well. Wash the teeth in the morning and rub them well with the powder.[108]

Funerals and Mourning

Her end could not be anything but triumphant
for her life was a constant victory over Self and sin.
DR. HELEN E. (REYNOLDS) RYAN

THOUGHTS OF DEATH were never very far from the minds of Victorians. Young Matilda Bowers was no exception.

> This day passed away like all the rest gone before, day after day passes by and brings us nearer to the grave. What a solemn thought, but why should we be afraid of death, the Lord has made the way plain enough that we can all find, if we only seek, and if we seek and do the will of the Lord, we need not fear death. But how many of us do not seek the Lord as we ought to do. Often "the spirit is willing but the flesh is weak." (Diary of Matilda Bowers Eby, 19 February 1863)

She was eighteen years old when she wrote this entry in her diary and, though still very young, would have experienced the death of friends and relatives many times. Life expectancy was not high, and one constantly lived with the knowledge that defence against illness and disease was often negligible. When one reads the tombstone inscriptions in old cemeteries, it does not take long to find cases of entire families of children who died from illness within the space of a few weeks. For everyone, the hold on life was tenuous. Despite the frequency with which one faced the loss of a loved ones, the pain became no less intense.

> On looking at the date, the thought struck me that this day was the third anniversary of my dear companions death. Oh! The thought recalls back the past to my mind as had it been but yesterday. I can still see her in imagination her smiling cheerful face and those heaven blue eyes, which spoke volumes, at times. It was a trying time to me when the hand of disease laid her low and in two weeks death closed those deep azure eyes, and the vital spark had fled. Oh! the thought that I never could behold those eyes and smiling countenance in this world never should hear her voice this side the "valley of death," again. all this made me feel very sad for a time. Time has changed my sadness into joy, when I consider that she has been rejoicing in the Saviour's bosom where sorrow is unknown, while I had to contend with adversity, trials and temptations, and none but my heavenly Father knows what sorrow and trials may be in store for me ere my Heavenly Father will call me to the judgment seat to give an account of the deeds done in the body. (Diary of Matilda Bowers Eby, 19 August 1863)

As illustrated by Matilda Bowers Eby, death brought a very deep sadness to the bereaved. But coping was aided significantly by a strong religious belief. For the Victorians, there was also another important element for dealing with a bereavement. This was a very strong sense of etiquette surrounding mourning. Because the rules of behaviour for a bereaved family and their friends and acquaintances were clearly defined, each knew what was expected of them and acted accordingly.

Generally there were three stages of mourning. During the first stage, the immediate family would enter a period of "heavy mourning," which lasted for six months. During this time, the women wore black clothing devoid of jewellery or any other ornamentation. In addition, a long veil was worn, covering the head and extending all the way down to the knees, front and back. Veils such as these were rather cumbersome things, which were only removed in the presence of the immediate family. Young children were dressed in white, sometimes embellished with black trim. It was considered perfectly acceptable, on special occasions, for a young girl wearing deep mourning to set aside her dark clothing and wear an all-white gown.

Men's clothing did not differ, to any great degree, from that worn normally. Most garments for men were cut from very conservatively coloured material, making them suitable for any occasion. However, some may have added a black arm band. Others, such as distant relatives and close friends, may have chosen to wear "complimentary" mourning clothes. These consisted of standard black garments and were worn for three months.

After the first six months of heavy mourning were up, a period of "middle" mourning was entered. This lasted for twelve months. At this time, women had the option of wearing jewellery. Jet, because of its dark colour, was the most popular. The veil was also changed from a heavy crepe to a lighter one of lace. All clothing, including underwear, remained black.

Eighteen months after the death, the period of "light mourning" commenced. The only visible difference between middle and light mourning was the addition of a second colour, white. White lace was added to the collar and cuffs of the garments, and the black bonnets & hats could be replaced with white ones. In all other respects, the styles of the middle mourning period remained unchanged. The widow at this point also had the option of returning to her regular clothing, if she did not wish to remain in mourning.[109]

To ensure that all members of the family were dressed suitably upon the death of an immediate family member, the assistance of a friend was often required. The duties of this person would be to make whatever arrangements were necessary for the purchase of mourning clothes, possibly shopping on behalf of the bereaved family or hiring a seamstress. Families without sufficient funds to hire somebody to sew for them would do the work themselves.

> Bright and pleasant. Peter Cameron brought the crepe cloth for our dresses...brought home my crepe bonnet. (Diary of Alice Patterson, 8 August 1881)

As with other aspects of social behaviour, the higher up the social ladder one climbed, the more stringently one observed these rules. Queen Victoria, at the pinnacle of society, set very high standards, particularly in mourning.

Obviously, the extent to which one observed these rules depended very much upon one's economic situation. For example, a young widow, with several small children to raise, might have been forced to remarry because of economic reality. She would have needed somebody to help. In such cases, society did not frown but understood the implications. Similarly, a widower might seek a new wife to run the house and look after children. "There are no weeds that wilt so quick as the weeds of the widower," says an old proverb.[110]

In small towns and rural areas, neighbours were inclined to offer assistance to the bereaved family immediately upon hearing of a death. News of this sort usually travelled very quickly. Those in areas without the convenience of a daily newspaper posted notices of death in a local store or post office. This way, word spread very quickly throughout the region.

As today, neighbours would have taken food and drink, or perhaps helped by running errands on behalf of the family. In many communities, it was common for funeral wakes to be held. These often attracted large numbers, which helped to give the mourners a strong sense of support in their sorrow. However, for those in high society, things were a little different. No member of the immediate family of the deceased would leave the house between the time of the death and the funeral. Friends, although they attended the funeral, did not make calls of condolence until about a week later. Acquaintances called within a month. No calls of condolence were made while the dead remained in the house.

Upon making one's first call of condolence, it was permissible to ask to see the family only if you were a very close friend. Others left cards or short notes of condolence. Calls from distant friends and acquaintances were not repeated until they had received a card of acknowledgment from the family. It was customary for friends to wear sombre colours when making their calls. The bell knob or door handle was draped with black crepe with a black ribbon tied on, if the deceased were married or advanced in years; and with a white ribbon if young or unmarried. A wreath on the door was always a sign of a death in the house. Decorative wreaths such as those used at Christmas time would be hung at a window, so there was never any confusion.

The Roman Catholic Irish woman who used to wash for her shewed her love for her in the only way she could by tying crepe on the door where Mrs Rennison used to live and on

her own door too. She was loved by every one who knew her.
(Diary of Belle Kittredge, 4 December 1891)

The traditional helper when someone died in the household was an
older woman, perhaps a relation but not always. She would bathe the
corpse and dress it or wrap it in its shroud, preparing for the period
of mourning and funeral. In some communities, there would be a
woman whose job this was; she was also sometimes the midwife. The
most famous literary example of the woman who laid out the dead is
Sarah Gamp, Charles Dickens' ghastly creation. But more likely these
women had a respected place in the community, and knew how to do
their job well. As this task was gradually taken over by the undertaker
(whose position grew out of his owning the furniture store which sold
the coffins), these women were no longer needed. It is interesting to
reflect that there have always been a few woman funeral directors,
even in that early twentieth century period when women had so few
acceptable jobs. This can perhaps be traced to the memory of those
women who came in to lay out the dead.

When a person died during hot weather months, there was an ur-
gency to bury the body quickly before it began to decay. Cracked ice
was sometimes used in an effort to preserve the body until the time of
the funeral. Later, embalming techniques would remove the necessity
for this.

As soon as the patient has stopped breathing and death is certain, straighten the limbs and place the arms by the side or
across the chest as desired. Close the eyelids and keep them
closed either with your fingers or by placing something upon
them. If false teeth have been worn they should be place in
the mouth soon after death before the jaws have set. Then
close the mouth and tie a handkerchief under the jaw after
first putting a pad under the jaw. Tie the handkerchief on top
of the head, tight enought to make the mouth close and look
natural. Comb and, if a woman, braid the hair; also wash and
dress the body if so desired and at the same time change the
bed linen. Tie knees and ankles together with a broad ban-
dage. You can also bind the hands in place if necessary. Make
the body look natural and comfortable and cover with a
sheet. If the body is clean I never could see the use of washing
it after death. It seems a needless exposure and an unneces-

sary annoyance to the relatives. Call an undertaker but do not let him use an injection until death is an absolute certainty. If you are not certain of death keep the body until signs of decay are seen before you allow any injection or preparation to be used. Not many people have been buried alive but some have been, so keep your friends til death is certain.[111]

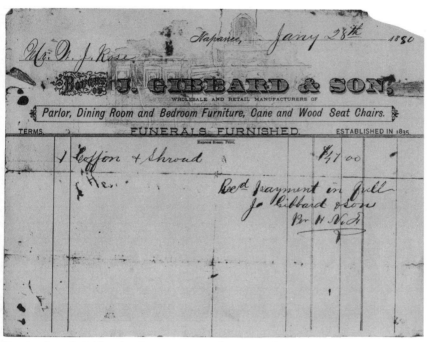

Invoice from J. Gibbard & Sons, Napanee, for one coffin and shroud, dated 28 January 1880. *Queen's University Archives*

Should the funeral services be at the home, guests would have been greeted by a close friend of the family. The immediate family members, having taken their last view of the corpse before the arrival of guests, would not appear until shortly before the service began. The coffin lid remained open. As the guests arrived, they were requested to look at the corpse before sitting. The lid was not closed until the conclusion of the service.

I had a letter from Sarah poor Mrs Jansen died on 11th Saturday & Mr Jansen on Tuesday at 2 o'clock in the morning. Mrs J. was ill some time & she remarked she was worn out &

wished that she & Mr J should be buried in the same coffin, at the time he was in his usual health & I said that could not be but in the same grave, he had a stroke & was not consious when Mrs J died. The three Drinkwaters were at the funeral the coffins were of polished wood were placed in the drawing room all were invited to see them there was glass showing the faces & busts there were 65 vehicles besides numbers on horse back & foot. They were much respected & had lived there so long. Mrs J was I think 83 & Mr J 90[?] She always took the lead & they were a happy couple. I shall really miss going to see them when I go to Orillia. (Diary of Mary Hallen 20 April 1874(?)

Perhaps writing about his wife's illness and death was of therapeutic benefit to the Rev. Louis H. Wagner. His diary contains extensive details about her illness. On many days, he made several entries describing changes in her condition. After her death he wrote:

Dave & I immediately took dinner, after which we undertook to wash the poor lifeless body of our beloved Mary. We laid her out dressed in a chemise & nightgown. Tore down the bed & disinfected things generally. During her sickness we put water and a little diluted "corrosive sublimate" into the pot which thoroughly killed all bad odors, much better than "chloride of lime" or [blank] (Diary of L.H. Wagner, 10 May 1887)

Once the funeral was over, he wrote the following description of the day's activities.

Aunt Mary had sent a bunch of calla lilies which we placed inside the casket 2 & a leaf with white satin ribbon in her hand, one at each side near the shoulder & face & one into a button hole on her bosom. The effect is very beautiful. A pillow of white flowers got by her brother Dave, & relatives with "Our Mary" in coloured flowers lay on a table at the head. A "crown" of flowers adorned the centre of the casket & a "cross" the foot end. These latter two emblems I had ordered for the occasion for it had always been her motto. "No cross, no crown." The casket stood in the hallway. When all was ready Rev D. Kreb of Berlin read a chapter spoke a few words & sang. Rev. D. Dippel of Elmira leading in prayer, after which following Rev. Brethern took up the bier acting as bearers, this change being affected only 20 min previously, according to the wish of Christian & Dave & some of the other relatives.

2:15 p.m. the procession moved down Foundry & up King Sts. to Mount Hope cemetery in the following order. Revs. D Krebs & S.L. Umbach, buggy, hearse Pall Bearers. Walked to King then riding, myself & mother & her children in carriage. Staeblers & carriage...

At about 4:30 p.m. the services were over having begun at the house about 1:45 p.m. I feel thoroughly tired. We with many of the friends retired to Father Staebler's house where we partook of some refreshments & by 8:30 p.m. the house was again left to its usual occupants. (Diary of L.H. Wagner, 13 May 1887)

Today Mary & I would have been married 3 yrs. (20 May 1887)

One of the comments made regularly after nineteenth century funerals concerned the length of the procession following the coffin from house to cemetery. At great ceremonials, people walked, which they still do today at the funerals of kings and presidents. For ordinary people, where several miles might need to be covered before the burial, the number of carriages following were counted. The number would then be a source of comment in the community, "evidence of the esteem in which the deceased was held," as the saying went.

Mr Mathiesons funeral of over sixty rigs. (Diary of Laura McMurray, 12 April 1899)

The funeral took [place] at two o'clock, a great many 63 teams I stayed, all the others left. Ann & I busy at tea. 25-30 [people served]. (Diary of Frances Tweedie Milne, 5 February 1868)

The first carriages in the funeral procession always contained the clergyman and the pallbearers. This was followed by the hearse, which was immediately followed by carriages of close relatives. More distant relatives, friends and acquaintances followed in appropriate order. If a society or Masonic body were to take part in the funeral procession, as they did in the case of the funeral of Frank Whitelock of Innisfil township, they would have preceded the hearse.

> A lovely day but the roads were in a very bad state. A very large crowd. At the house the hymn page [blank] was sung and the organ played "Tune" "Dennis" West Ferguson made a very impressive prayer and Mr Sanderson gave out the hymn. the Forresters and the Temperance Societies were there and wore regalia and badges. At the church—Both Gilford and Ebenezer choir sang as he was a member of both. Voluntary—"We are pilgrims looking home"—Mr Ferguson preached from the text, "Thy word is a lamp unto my feet and a light unto my path." as this was the one he selected before dying. Three burial services were read at the grave. The church service read by Revs Ferguson and Sanderson, Forresters service, read by Paul West and Ernest Bennett. Temperance Service read by Charlie Mattenley, Mr Neilly and Ed Rothwell. Come back to Bradford from funeral. (Diary of Annie Boyes, 5 March 1894)

The Foresters were a benevolent lodge, founded in the English Midlands several decades before, to ensure that poor people received a respectable funeral. They continue today, both as a lodge and a means of insurance for the working classes.

With the arrival of the railway, it became possible for the remains of those who died far away from home to be returned to their families for burial.

> Mama & I went to Dr. Jones service at 10. I received no visitors—tho' some 60 left cards. Sir John did not wish it, as Mr Blairs funeral left this afternoon for Woodhill & he was one of my husband's colleagues! Sir John went to the station with the Body it was a gloomy day as the few dark sleighs swept over the white white earth dimly seen thro the heavy falling snow....(Diary of Lady Macdonald, 1 January 1868)

In remote areas, it was sometimes necessary for a person to officiate at the funeral of a member of his own family, simply because there was nobody else available to do it.

> Preston came with the sad news that my poor dear Mother had died at 5 o'clock. It was a fearful shock to me as us all. I set off at once for Penetang, arrived after they were in bed. (Diary of Sarah Hallen Drinkwater, 1 February 1864)

> It is a sad trial for my Father as no one realized she was really ill and Mary was sitting up with her while my Father went to bed, she seemed to die in her sleep. John and the boys arrived, poor boys saw their dear Grandmama and were much upset. George got here at daybreak. At three my dear Mother was laid in her last resting place, my dear brothers all assisted to put her in her coffin and carried it into the sitting room where we all kissed her for the last time. My brothers screwed the coffin down. Mary had cut out a cross and covered it with artificial flowers and put it on top of the coffin. My dear boys went with their uncles as mourners. My poor Father read the service, a fearful trial. John and the boys returned to "Northbrook" after the funeral. I shall remain with my dear Father for some time. (Diary of Sarah Hallen Drinkwater, 2 February 1864)

If there were no clergy available, a lay person would perform the duties.

> Attended Mrs McCraigs funeral…Solemn occasion, crowded house. Felt the occasion, and preached sermon earnestly… Went with the remains to Sundridge solemn service at the grave. Much weeping. (Diary of James Geddes, 24 February 1890)

Because of Victorian social mores, incidents which appear bizarre to modern eyes sometimes occurred. The following was reported in *The Daily Evening Journal*, St Catharines, on 30 December 1863.

> The Ayr Observer relates the particulars of a disgraceful charavari in Douglas village two weeks ago, which was followed by the birth of two illegitimate still born children by a young

woman, daughter of the man whose house was serenaded. The burial rites of the children are thus described by the *Observer*—The father of the girl went to a clergyman in the village, carrying with him in one hand a jug containing whiskey, and a coffin, in which was the body of one of the infants, in the other, followed by another individual, similarly freighted, minus the whiskey. The clergyman was requested to read prayers over the dead previous to interment. This the reverend gentleman refused to do, and very justly too.—The men still entreated his reverence to perform the service, but the gentleman remained deaf to their entreaties. Determined not to bury the young McKeys without religious services, the men proceeded to one of the churches, which they found unlocked and entered. The reverend gentlemen followed the pair into the church on tip toe, remaining a silent spectator of the proceedings. After entering the church the coffins were laid down, but not so the jug of whiskey, for one of the men went up into the pulpit, read an appropriate chapter, made a long prayer, and then came down again, holding on to the jar all the while, as he was afraid, evidently, that his companion would get hold of it, in which event he would not even get a taste of its contents. All things being now done to their satisfaction, the men left the church buried their dead, and returned home, spending a pleasant evening over the contents of the aforesaid jar. The affair has created quite a sensation in the neighbourhood, and not a few are to be found who give the story even a higher colour than we have done. Such proceedings are a disgrace to any civilized community.

The death of a public figure would be the opportunity for mourning even by private individuals. When Queen Victoria's husband, Prince Albert, Prince Consort, died on 14 December 1861, it had more than passing interest even in Hamilton, Ontario:

Slight mourning for Prince consort—some by crape on arm, others on hat, with Black Gloves. (Diary of Forbes Geddes, 11 January 1862)

Christ Church hung in black out of respect for Prince Consort. (12 January 1862)

Draping of the church might also be carried out for some funeral services.

> The service was very sad indeed. The coffin was carried to the chancel steps and placed there on the stand resting on a black mat. The church was draped in black that is the communion table had a skirt of black & the railing was loosely twined with black cloth. The Reading desk, Pulpit &c. were also draped and the lamps were burning owing to the darkness caused by the rainy weather. (Diary of Belle Kittredge, 3 December 1891)

A rather morbid fixation plagued the minds of some Victorians. This was the fear of being buried alive. They worried that the vital signs might be so faint as to go undetected, and therefore a person might be pronounced dead before the event occurred. This frightening notion was encouraged by articles such as the following.

> *The Constitutionel* states that the cases of premature interment prevented by fortuitous circumstances in France since the year 1833, amount to 94. Of those, 35 persons awoke of themselves from their lethargy at the moment the funeral ceremony was about to commence; 13 recovered in consequence of the affectionate care of their families; 7 in consequence of the fall of the coffins in which they were enclosed; 9 owed their recovery to wounds inflicted in sewing their winding sheet; 5 to the sensation of suffocation they experienced in their coffin; 19 to the interment having been delayed in consequence of doubts having been entertained of their death.[112]

As fantastic as this notion seems to us today, it was a very real concern for the Victorians. For without the aid of sophisticated equipment to monitor vital signs, a person could indeed be pronounced dead when still alive. A noisy wake was considered to be a good precautionary measure. The belief was that anyone other than a dead person would be roused by the noise.

An unsavoury activity occurred in some parts of Ontario during the Victorian era. In 1859, Dr. Friedrich Christ, a physician who lived in Waterloo from 1853 until 1866, and his accomplice, Hugo Werthman, spent three months in jail for robbing graves. Werthman stole the bodies and Dr. Christ reduced them to skeletons which he sold. Although this was a highly distasteful matter, Dr. Christ's standing in the community did not seem to be greatly affected. After his release from jail, he continued to live in Waterloo. Later he moved to Michigan where he died from an overdose of morphine in 1875.[113]

Naturally, a story such as this was picked up and published by newspapers far and wide. The following is from the *Huntingdon Herald*,[114] of Quebec.

> A distressing investigation was held before the Magistrates of Berlin, on Wednesday, involving the character of one of the medical gentlemen of that town, another residing in Elmira, and a gentleman closely connected with the first-charged offender. It seems that for some time suspicious hints and circumstances, and smells, had indicated that the resurrection trade was being revived in Berlin, and that the remains of certain bodies had been conveyed to the premises of a medical gentleman, and, after dissection, the flesh had been consumed by boiling. The circumstances were so pointed that the magistrates deemed them sufficient to issue warrants for the arrest of the parties accused, and search warrants were also put into the hands of the officers to examine the Doctor's premises, and there accordingly they found the mutilated remains of several human bodies. Among these were the remains of a fine young lad named Eby, the son of Mr. Abraham Eby, of Bridgeport. The youth had been accidently killed at a soiree at Bridgeport a week or two ago, and his body interred, amid the heartfelt sorrow of a multitude of friends. A portion of his body was found on the premises of the accused, and they were sworn to by the afflicted father from certain marks. Portions of two other bodies were found, which the accused stated were those of certain persons; the tale was found to be false. The bodies appear all to have been taken from a graveyard in Berlin.

Although not so serious a matter as losing a dear family member, the loss of a pet could inflict tremendous sorrow.

> My dear old puss died to-day, had been sick since Sunday and ailing a few days before—nearly eight years old; she came to

me a baby kitten in Fall of 1879. I never cared for any creature like her even my little turtle stood second. Her box was moved outside early this morning. I attended to her as usual and was hurrying up with my work to go out again. Just as I got out I saw her walking off a little piece, then she laid down & drew her poor legs up in agony "poor darling" said I & just as I spoke such an agonized cry she gave—I turned away for I could not bear to see her dying agonies and a real cry to God went up that my poor puss should be spared much suffering—and indeed I think she died then. It is well, for she had some swelling on her side for a year or two & has been subject to illness both before and after. I was so afraid they would insist on having her killed & now she has died without suffering very long. She purred to the last. Just before I started my work I went to her box—she looked at me purring. So clever and yes, a bad temper—how she would hiss, even at me, but the next moment was over her pet. Could open the kitchen door, very tiresome we found that trick especially on a cold winter day. Other cats I may have and love them too, but never will I care for one like my old black puss. Lonely for a long time I will be for puss was a companion. She lies buried by the playhouse. (Diary of Emma Laflamme, 26 May 1887)

Many years earlier, Mary Hallen wrote about the day her pet dog died.

My father & Edgar buried poor old Fido on the grass between the cottage & summer house. Edgar kindly made a box for him. Loosing him I am almost ashamed to say has been a great trial to me but he has been my constant companion through joys & sorrows for 13 years & the feeling you have for a dog is different to other animals they are so companionable. (Diary of Mary Hallen, 31 December 1849)

Obituaries often included an elaborate account of the death of an individual. When read today, it is sometimes difficult to appreciate the seriousness with which some were written. The following is an excerpt from the obituary of the mother of Mr Forbes Geddes.

She had left the family circle in perfect health and cheerful spirits and was putting on her apparel to go with them in company to the House of God but the bell which summoned the earthly worshippers was her summons to the world of spirits—to those heavenly courts where the worshippers go no more out....[115]

When people died in the pioneer era, faraway relations might not be informed for months, if at all. Illiteracy would prevent communication between separated branches of families. Therefore, it was a frequent duty, after a death, for those who could write to compose letters on behalf of others. It must have been truly heartbreaking to inform one's own relatives, often thousands of miles away, that a loved one had died. Robert Scott Sr, wrote such a letter in 1834, upon the death of his daughter Margaret Govenlock.

I must let you know where we have buried your sister. I have taken up a burial place on our own ground, a little below us on the river side. A fine dry spot four square and we have it railed in. It will hold us all when we are gathered to our people.[116]

In the later 19th century however, the growth of education and the penny post ensured that everyone would know of a friend's death. This resulted in a new form of communication: the letter of condolence. In our own age, this is one of the most difficult of notes to write, but our ancestors had a greater facility. In the first place, they shared a universal religious background, where so much about the next world was taken for granted. As well, most of them had learned at school the proper form for every social letter they would need to write. In fact, these forms were so thoroughly impressed on the brain that they were repeated as if by rote. The result might be less than heartfelt, as M.E. Loane describes them, "Epistles stiff and empty at the beginning, affectionate and incoherent at the end, and with little but the address to mark one from the other."[117]

This was not, of course, always true. Sometimes the beauty of true sentiment shines through the piety. For instance, Amelia J. Robb wrote to her cousin on the death of his wife: "she is now with her Saviour singing the song of the redeemed."[118] It might not be what we would write today, but it spoke to the bereaved husband of 1886.

When Dr. Ada Funnell died at the age of 40, her medical-college chum, Dr. Helen Ryan, wrote from Sudbury to Ada's mother that she had not seen her friend for fifteen years, but the link between them was undimmed:

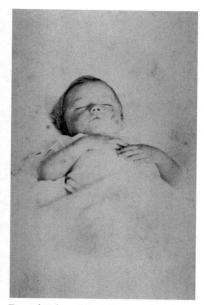

...Ada and I slept together, talked and laughed and enjoyed each other thoroughly... Her end could not be anything but triumphant for her life was a constant victory over Self and sin—to be ready to live is the surest way to be ready to die.[119]

It was especially difficult to cope with the death of a family member who was far away. Perhaps the most tragic was that of a wife or child dying, while the father was working a great distance from home.

Daniel Edward Breithaupt of Berlin, a posthumous portrait taken in July 1871. *Breithaupt-Hewetson-Clark Collection, University of Waterloo*

Last Monday poor Mrs Brown became much worse she has not been moved since she is expected to die every hour. She told my Father this morning that she wished to see Agnes & myself. We went it was a great trial to me as I have not been accustomed to visit sick people. I often wish I had the poor woman looked very very ill almost as if she was dead she knew us & asked us to sit down & said "Good bye dear" when we shook hands with her. It is a dreadful abuse that she is dying of. She has been ill 5 months, ever since her last child was born. She is so thin that in many places her bones as through her skin. Her husband is a sailor on board the Mohawk he has not been able to come and see her but my Father has often written to him in her name & he has written to her. (Diary of Mary Hallen, 14 August 1850)

Mrs Brown died on 17 August. The sad duty of informing Mr Brown, who was away at sea, probably fell to the Rev. George Hallen, Mary's father. As a member of the clergy, he would have been relied upon to bring comforting words to mourners. This task would have been especially difficult when his own daughter, Eleanora, died.

> This day always brings back very melancholy recolections dear Nora died this day 6 years. She was indeed a loss to us in *every* way. How different to me though we always agreed in every thing & I think I should have been very different if she had lived to what I am now. I never remember having one uncomfortable word with her she always tried to please me & I did her. We were "Two hearts in unity that only death unbound." (Diary of Mary Hallen, 26 May 1852)

Placing flowers on the grave of a loved one has always brought about some degree of comfort, even years after the death.

> Agnes and I walked up to the church where dear Nora is at rest & free from all the trials & miseries of this wretched world. We put fresh flowers on her grave as Agnes has done ever since we left, they are very scarce now I am afraid. We shall have soon to discontinue it which I shall be sorry for as it is a melancholy pleasure. (Diary of Mary Hallen, 1 October [year uncertain])

There were many ways in which the Victorians preserved memories of the deceased. One of the more unusual was coffin plates.

It was an old English custom to affix engraved plates to the coffins. They gave the name, date of death and age of the person inside. This tradition may have come from the days when coffins remained in church crypts for years after someone died, and had continued when burial became more common.

Some people found that the idea of burying the valuable coffin plate did not sit well with their frugal natures, so they took it off before the burial. The plate was then kept as a memento of the dead person. It might even be displayed in the parlour.

When their infant son Osten died, Lulla and Jack Cain of Manvers township had his coffin plate framed and hung in the best bedroom of their house. It remained there for almost ninety years, long after those who had known little Osten were gone themselves. By such means, the bereaved could come to terms with death.

Entertainment

*Father was to town, he brought me
a "Petersons Magazine" from the past.
I perused it with great gusto.*
DIARY OF MATILDA BOWERS EBY, 5 FEBRUARY 1863

I N THE DAYS BEFORE POPULAR ENTERTAINMENT, what did families do
with themselves in the evening? A letter from 1853 describes one
family's activities.

> As to our family I will begin at the oldest & that you know is
> grandpa he is on the bed blessing his soul & dont know what
> to do no more than the ded—Grandma is quietly seated in
> her room smoking her pipe I am at the table writing and
> when I get up I go off limping on three legs for my knee trou-
> bles me very much this fall. Julia Ann & Harriet ar by the
> table picking Chickens, Augustus quartering apples. Brigham
> & Julia are coming, but stop out of sight out of mind. Pheby
> is on the bed taking one of her oldfashioned comfortable
> snooses &c—Robert must not be forgotten he has got his lit-
> tle yankee notion mashine pareing apples with a where to it
> that is all.[120]

For most, there were no places of entertainment—no theatres in the
countryside, nothing of the kind we know—and so fun came from the
family, and much diversion originated with the church.

We all went to the Cathedral where we had a clergyman both worth hearing & seeing (as much as there was to "see"). Am afraid he struck us unanimously as odd for the giggles were more than audible. (Diary of Marion Chadwick, 26 June 1892)

As well as two or three services on Sunday, the church provided a variety of suppers and teas, often for charitable purposes. Women congregated for working groups which sewed or cleaned the church building. There was also the chance to sing in the choir, which required a midweek practice, giving a further chance to visit.

It was choir practice night too and we have an anthem on for Xmas (Diary of Belle Kittredge, 11 December 1891)

Church attendance on the sabbath was of paramount importance to most families. When visiting far from home, folks often took advantage of the opportunity to visit as many churches as possible.

A beautiful morning and my heart is full of love. We all go to the Methodist Church except Joseph. He kept the children. We had a lovely sermon. How I was wishing my Willie was there. I saw several familiar faces. Among them Mrs. G. McGill and Thos. McKitrick. They look very natural. In the evening Joseph and us were at the Prespitarian church. Heard an excellent discourse and nice singing and we came home feeling refreshed and a days march nearer home. (Diary of Catherine Miller, 24 August 1890)

Among the diaries are very few mentions of "keeping the Sabbath" as a day of no work and little activity. Even the most religious of the women had a relaxed attitude toward what was permissible on that day, although for many at the time even the most innocent of games and light reading were forbidden.

Late in the century, the missionary movement which would constitute much of the focus in many churches for the next fifty years led to the formation of women's missionary societies ('The Ladies' Aid'). As well as doing good works, these groups provided outlets for women to socialize, and gave them the opportunity to get away from their lonely farm outposts. It was a short step to the Women's Institute, founded by Adelaide Hunter Hoodless and others as a means of educating rural women in matters that had practical application to their daily lives.

For the young, the Sunday evening church service was an important event. Courting couples could sit together (on Sunday mornings they had to sit with their parents). The walk home afterwards would probably take much longer than necessary. Groups often visited churches other than their own for this service, where there were opportunities to meet new people. For those whose weekdays were largely spent isolated in the country, Sunday provided the same outlet as the weekly visit to market: the chance of a social occasion.

> Queen St Metho[dist] in morning (after long hunt)—Manly Benson, good, plain speaker—Metrop[olitan] S[unday] S(chool) home by way of Jarvis & Bloor In evening to Bloor St Pres[byterian] Mr W very fine man (prays for those in trouble & who have loved ones sick) (Diary of Bessie Mabel Scott, 3 November 1889)

We have already seen that visiting provided a major chance for entertainment, simple as it was. The extended family group would sing, play games, read aloud and interest themselves intensively in the community around them. Since there was so much work to do, the combining of play with everyday tasks—as in the McEuen family evening at the beginning of this chapter—was common. Preparations for a big occurrence such as Christmas, a wedding, even a local dance, were almost as much fun as the event itself, given the excitement they generated.

The day-long 'bees' which we mentioned earlier could also lead to that combination of work and play. After the day's work was completed, everyone could gather for an evening of fun. Ann Amelia Day prepared for a 'raising' (possibly a barn-raising) which led to a dance.

> Had dancing in the driving house until 10:30 when we had tea. Everybody seemed to enjoy themselves. Pa and Ma came home at dark. Dan Talbot took Emily home and then came back for Jenny and me. It was 1:20 a.m. when we got home. (Diary of Ann Amelia Day, 22 June 1878)

Throughout this period, the temperance movement affected the way people viewed public entertainments. The Victorians viewed the chance of improving oneself, either personally or professionally, as of the greatest importance. Inexpensive, easily available liquor might prevent people from getting ahead, through their own weaknesses.[121] The solution was to educate people not to use liquor. So the temperance movement was born in the early 19th century. It quickly turned into an prohibition movement however, and gathered religious overtones.

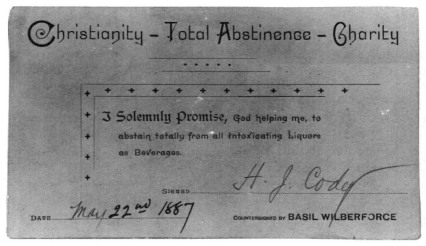

A temperance pledge of 1887. *Archives of Ontario*

> I wish they had ambition enough in this neighbourhood to form a society of the "Sons of Temperance," so that the folks would get home on time, as it is not very pleasant to be up all night. (Diary of Catherine Bell Van Norman, 16 April 1850)

Mrs Van Norman was right up-to-date in her wish, for the Sons of Temperance had only come to Canada in 1848. Eventually there were many groups whose purpose was to abolish the liquor traffic. They succeeded in cutting down the consumption of liquor in Canada, but there was always an element of class war in the struggle, for alcohol remained one of the few accessible pleasures of the working classes. It was unlikely that they would willingly give it up for any high-minded reasons. Mary Brown and her friends, however, planning a large public function in Hamilton in the 1880's, were firm that no alcohol be served. Because they were in charge, their wish prevailed. The stern reaction of the temperance advocate in the face of the enemy became a comic staple which had its origin in real life. It can be summed up by this admonition from *The Ladies' Journal* of February 1890.

> Don't sanction wine drinking when out to parties or weddings. Your simple act of declining the proferred glass may act as a check upon your companion. Tacit disapproval sometimes does more good than the most eloquent temperance lecture.

The Temperance movement was always more attractive to members of the evangelical churches. The head of the Hallen family was an Anglican priest who felt that signing the pledge was redundant to a true Christian's life. His children made irreverent remarks to those who had taken the pledge.

> ...who having joined the temperance society would not take a glass of wine but eat a piece of rich cake with great relish although I kindly informed him there was brandy in it. (Diary of Eleanora Hallen, 1 January 1845)

If there was an ambivalence on the subject, it can be summed up in one of Eleanora Hallen's vignettes.

> the cousin was much amused at the glass of tody [toddy] that George made for Aunty she discreetly looking another way during the mixing of it and seeming to appreciate its taste very much on tasting it. It was late when they departed. (29 January 1845)

The other side of the coin was benign happiness when someone turned away from sin.

> Mama says she is glad to have the opportunity of welcoming you in the stand you have taken on the side of temperance.[122]

The temperance movement remained politically powerful for decades into the twentieth century. Its significance in the Victorian era was in part that it was a sphere in which women could wield power, while being refused the vote and influence elsewhere.

Alternatives to beer were often proposed by the temperance movement, but they had little success. The flavour often combined ginger and lemon with a shortlived fizz.

A temperance Drink: Put a pint and a half of water to four teaspoonfulls of ginger, a table spoonful of lemon juice, sweetened to the taste with syrup of white sugar and turn it into a junk bottle. Have ready a cork to fit the bottle, a string to tie it down, and a mallet to drive down the cork. Then put into the bottle a heaping teaspoonful of the sugar, carbonate of soda, cork it immediately, tie it down, then shake the whole up well, cut the string and the cork will fly out. Turn it out and drink immediately.[123]

The explosive dangers of this drink are coupled with a sickly taste. It is hardly surprising that temperance drinks did not become popular. It is likely, however, that the invention of the now universal cola drinks resulted from this movement. The fizziness inherent in most temperance recipes, put there to make the dull drinks more interesting, made their cork-popping qualities a byword.

Even with temperance drinks, the message was not to drink too many. In its recipe for "Sham-Champagne, A Purely Temperance Drink." *Mother Hubbard's Cupboard*, a Canadian cookbook of 1881 warns, "Be sure and not drink over three or four bottles at one time."[124]

Not everybody held with temperance views.

Mr and Mrs Hamilton called. My Mother had some cake & wine brought but of course neither of the temperance creatures took any. great lack of conversation. Mr H. said he saw in some paper the reason the Great Briton [struck?] on the coast of Ireland was the Captain had been *drinking*. My Father told him it was not at all likely to be true. (Diary of Mary Hallen, 11 November [year not indicated])

There were plenty of activities, other than consuming alcohol, to engage those with leisure time, even those fortunates like Marion Chadwick who led a busy social life. She was never at a loss for some sort of entertainment.

Commenced the day very profitably by attempting to take my first photograph...In the eve. I tried to develop the photograph which needless to say turned out a complete failure. (Diary of Marion Chadwick, 1 January 1892)

This evening we had a sort of party. The Robertsons—Mac—etc. played Jenkins, hot potatoes & hide the thimble. a very successful eve. on the whole. (15 January 1892)

We went to the theatre to have charades I recovered sufficiently to recite "Little William & the peaches," "Billie's breakfast," "How I committed suicide," etc. all of which "took" tremendously. I am not sure that sentimental poetry could amuse our audience but "the tomato can"—& did. (4 March 1892)

Ethel & Mac came up for tea & supper. None of us went to Church. We sat around the fire in the dark & told stories & each of us gave a description of his or her "Ideal" (20 March 1892)

In aft, Dad Dick & I went to see the first parade of the "Kilties" All Toronto was there with his girl in her Easter Hat. Never saw such a crowd...(24 April 1892)

And on a snowy day, what more perfect way to pass the time than to gather a group of young people together and have

Mesmerism, will power, dancing—table manifestations, Planchette-isms all aft. Miss Barton is an amateur "medium" She brought up the ghost of Josiah Wallace. & we heard all about the lost fortune etc. It was really wonderful. (Diary of Marion Chadwick, 9 April 1892)

Marion and her friends played many games. People in the country found these made for a diverting winter's evening.

Willie & his wife & Mick & young Forly came had checkers & nations. they stayed untill 11.30. (Diary of Annie Elizabeth Cragg, 28 January 1889)

Evening parties were popular year round and were the most common form of entertainment:

Busy preparing for large party in honour of Lieutenant Riddel. Harry & Daisy working with energy, to have the drawing room ready for dancers. Upwards of fifty visitors arrived at eight o'clock and a very delightful evening we had, the garden being very attractive, so cool, & moonlight. Broke up about mid night. (Diary of Mary Brown, 1 August 1881)

Went to the Ball at the Crawford House. Great sucess—wore new black velvet—214 guests.—Mrs Wilkinson made claret cup—20 gall. 10 galls native wine 3 doz claret 8 lemons. (Diary of Frances Julia Davis, 2 January 1891)

Card-playing, which would be a universal passion after the turn of the century, had already taken hold in Toronto. For the Chadwicks, any excuse was good enough for a few hands.

In evening had a party—a euchre 4 tables (Diary of Marion Chadwick, 27 Sepember 1898}

in aft to a girls' Euchre party at Mrs Arthur's—a *really* dinky one (28 November 1898)

In evening all went to the Fullers & played cards (16 December 1898)

In the evening Mother had an impromptu euchre—7 tables (17 December 1898)

Modern eyes might widen at an 'impromptu' party that needed at least 28 people.

Some card parties turned into rather elaborate affairs, requiring a great deal of preparation and organization.

...Played cribbage & whist—supper at 11 pm. 1 turkey 11 lbs, 1 Ham. Corned beef. Salad. Trifle. Jelly [illegible] 2 qts. Mince pies. Jelly Tarts. Scalloped Oysters. Bananas 38, Oranges, Cake, Coffee, Sherry & port ale—Pine Apple. Ladies fingers 12¢ Sponge Cake, 6 tarts, cards. (Diary of Frances Julia Davis, 18 April 1888)

Another way of varying an evening's entertainment was to have a 'progressive dinner.' In later years this meant travelling from house to house, eating a course in each place, but it was much less strenuous in 1896.

> The progressive dinner-party has suffered a revival this winter and is once more established in fashionable favor. As 1896 is a leap year the dinner is now arranged so that the men remain in their original seats throughout the meal, while the women progress with the courses. The first announcement that the dinner is in any respect different from the ordinary ceremonial meal of society, is in the appearance at the host's place of a small silver bell, which he rings at the conclusion of each course....The rule to be observed by the hostess is that she must have as many courses for her dinner as she has couples present. This is made necessary by the fact that the progressions are made with the courses, and that the round must be completed with the end of dinner.[125]

Very welcome at these get-togethers was the man of all talents, musically inclined and with a stock of funny stories.

> Mr Davis made his appearance he had come up to go with Drinkwater the next morning to the meeting in Oro. It was delightful to here him lay on the pianoe. he also sang several pretty songs and one with words of his own composing in ridicule of a dinner party he was at in this neighbourhood. We had several hearty laughs at various things and it was late when we went to bed. (Diary of Eleanora Hallen, 7 January 1845)

Wintertime provided ample opportunity for entertaining, since people were less busy.

> Johnson and I attended to the kitchen stove. Beautiful clear day with sun. Ther.r [thermometer] 10 at 8 am. Very busy indeed taking off druggets [floor coverings] in dining room and drawing room. Evening Party. A sleighing party of 10 from Ancaster arrived at nine o'clock. We had 27 altogether. Sandwiches, cakes and tea and coffee were the only refreshments.

Plumber came and put new basin into the W.C. (Diary of
Frances Gay Simpson, 4 February 1881)

Busy all day preparing for our evening. Everything went off
well, we were 55 altogether. Dancing & cards. Mrs Trilly &
Mrs Field came to wash up. (6 December 1881)

Dancing was a pleasure which required only a little space and a musician or two. "House dances" were common. Larger gatherings in the
summer might use part of a barn's loft. Sometimes these outings became rather raucous.

They all (reared and pitched) a little, that is what Al said
when they went out to play the wild Irishman and I think
there was one gentleman that had a bowl of bread and milk
with a stick in it. (Diary of Louisa Bowlby, 1 January 1862)

The 'stick in it' was a tot of rum or whiskey.[126]
   It is interesting to note that all but the youngest in the family participated in these parties. The small children would go up to bed, but
adolescents, parents and the very old were all part of the group. The
segregation of age groups which we know had not yet taken place.

After tea we amused ourselves with waltzing dancing and
what we call coochy coochy which is crouching down and
hopping along as fast as you can round the room. I do not
know when I have laughed so much. (Diary of Eleanora
Hallen, 30 January 1846)

In mixed groups, there is always the danger that the natural levity and
irreverence of the young will offend the old. In Victorian times, when
'propriety' was more strictly enforced, the danger was all the greater,
but the outcome was the same.

Mr McKibbon did recite a ridiculous address from a visitor to
some Sunday School children. There was a mention in it to
Elijah's bald head which displeased Mrs Gibbs. She wouldnt
smile at all & when her satellites so [saw] her of course they
pulled down their faces, tho' before noticing her they had
been enjoying it with the others. Mrs Gibbs didnt get over it

all evening & after it was over spoke to Mr McKibbon about it. Then Mr McKibbon got mad. He said he certainly wouldnt have given it if he had though it wrong at all and said privately some[thing] to the effect that Mrs Gibbs might be hanged (Diary of Belle Kittredge, Thursday, undated [late January 1892])

Once a girl was finished school, there was an awkward period, before she came out or took to housekeeping full time, when there might be little for her to do. Helen Grant Macdonald spent her time on charity work, but for others it might be a time to live entirely for pleasure. Perhaps realising that with childbearing and housekeeping, they would never have the luxury of days full of free time again, their mothers granted them a few months of liberty.

The early diaries of Marion Chadwick of Toronto represent one of these free periods. Her high spirits and enjoyment come through on every page. An ordinary day in her life at this time began with a morning spent sewing, for herself or her family. Often she assisted the travelling seamstress, who visited the house about once a month. Then she might go shopping or visiting friends and relations in the afternoon, take a music lesson and practice the violin, write, sing or rehearse.

We have a vision of languid Victorian maidens who might not have the energy to cross the street alone, but Marion and her friends do not fit into that category. They take Physical Culture lessons in the winter, and then form a "Ph.C." club at their summer home in July. They play tennis, row, canoe, sail, swim—even have a cricket league. The Chadwicks lived on Howland Avenue in Toronto. But in the summer, they packed up the children, furniture and chickens, and moved to the Island in Toronto harbour, where a large community of friends had formed the Island Amateur Aquatic Association. Here they competed regularly.

Percy R & I set off in canoe for Sports at 3. The first race we were personally interested in was a tandem under 15 George & Ford came in second by half a canoe. The next was a Ladies single Ladies Tumble I call it...I was 3 feet from the finish & two canoe lengths ahead when I put my paddle over. Took a header into four feet deep of water. (Diary of Marion Chadwick, 16 July 1892)

The results of the Sports were published in a newspaper the following day, including the news of Marion's dunking. It is interesting to see how freely the boys and girls mixed with each other. For example, Percy R. and Marion regularly go canoeing all over the Island, but he makes no other appearances in the diary.

Marion's principal interest was the theatre. She wrote plays, which were produced by her friends to great acclaim, with reviews in the Toronto newspapers and paying audiences. Her comic acting was regarded as of professional standard, and her rendition of "Clementine" brightened many a dull journey or evening party.

When one of the greatest actresses of the day came to town, Marion and her friends were there.

> ...went to see Julia Marlow in "As You Like It." Oh my! she is sweet. She has as Pink puts it "a smile you can go home & think about." (19 March 1892)

Minstrel shows were popular amateur events, and Marion participated in a rather ramshackle version during the winter. The next morning she wrote:

> Have just come home from the Cathedral. It was amusing to see four boys in the choir with half the black on their faces after last night. (10 January 1892)

Her plays were one-act farces on popular themes—misunderstood wives, society gossip, soldiers—which later graduated to full plays. The characters had fantastical names. The troupe of actors were close friends who shared Marion's high spirits. After giving two farces in Toronto on separate occasions, they were invited out of town.

> Queen's Birthday & such a birthday. We left the House at 6.30 bound for the train. arrived at city hall 7.30. train left at 8. Were fortunate enough to secure a parlour car practically to ourselves. Had bango [banjo] soloes, songs, etc.—Arrived in Barrie 11.30 or thereabouts. Went to the theatre for a practice—Had lunch about 2. After which we went to see a match. It was raining so we returned at 4.30. Mr Strickland "borrowed" a violin & we amused ourselves till 6 o'clock. arrived at the theatre at 7.30 after having been stared nearly out

of our sences by the astonished town folk on a walk down. Citizens Band at Theatre playing outside till the show commenced. Every thing went "splendaciously.."..

The evening consisted of their two farces opening and closing the show, with recitations and a banjo solo between.

After we got back to the Hotel we had some music & Mrs Boddy recited 4 or 5 more things…Mr Schott gave us a Yankee piece. The Hotel people gave us the cold shoulder (it was now about 11.30) Finally went up—but not to bed. We girls kicked up a terrific row & The Men a terrific-er & that fiddle the terrific-est. It went till 2 a.m. (about 1.30 we had cheese sandwiches). Got to sleep towards 3 on top of mice & rats in abundance "Oh that night, that night to memory dear." (24 May 1892)

"But what a difference in the morning." We all awoke between 6 & 1/2 past. (25 May 1892)

Theatrical events of every kind provided exciting outings.

We Rossie Beatrice Helen Frankie & I went to Pinafore. acted by the Operatic Club ameturs. We took 25 ct Gallery seats it was lovly the deck of the Pinafore and the Sailors sang…in between acts Rev Normans pupils danced Daisy St George among them (Diary of Ethel Chadwick, 21 April 1897)

Shopping was already a diversion for young woman, especially those who lived in the towns. One Canadian retail institution was present to add to the pleasure.

Go down Yonge St to Eaton's, buy a belt & come home. (Diary of Bessie Mabel Scott, 8 November 1889)

For those, such as Catherine Miller, who lived in remote parts of the province, a visit to such a place was exciting.

we go to Eatons great Establishment. I never saw anything to compare with it. We choose some beautiful carpeting and oil cloth and are in a great hurry to catch the 4 oclock. (Diary of Catherine Miller, 31 July 1890)

For young ladies of fashion, there was the possibility of 'coming out' in imitation of the formalities of English court life. In Toronto in 1892, it was not so formal, but had the same purpose, an announcement that the young lady was now an adult, ready for grown-up society and the possibilities of marriage. For many, it would have been exciting, but not for everyone.

> Miss Hawthorne & I busy all morning making my 'coming out dress' as they call it. (Diary of Marion Chadwick, 24 October 1892)

> In eve. I 'came out' at a party at Mrs Moss'. Mamie and I went with the Robertsons. They all say I should have said, "I had a glorious time," But I never had a glorious time at an old dance in my life & never expect to. Met nearly all new men. (27 October 1892)

As a result of her new status, Marion's mother left her to receive afternoon callers alone, which Marion found disconcerting at first, but later enjoyed. A few days before Christmas, she had a surprising time of it, however.

> I received (nobody) alone in the afternoon. (Diary of Marion Chadwick, 22 December 1892)

Although she lived in an isolated village on the north shore of Rice Lake, and had a household to care for, Annie Cragg was addicted to reading. She kept a list of books read. It shows the tendency of her thoughts.

> Ten books read by Annie Cragg in 1889: *The Fatal Glove; The Baron's Will; A Family Secret; An Extraordinary Wooing; At War With Herself; Lady Diana's Pride; Lady Gwendoline's Dream; Adventures of a Bachelor; Guy Kenmore's Wife* (2nd reading); *A Young Girl's Wooing.*

Many girls had an autograph album, in which friends and relations inscribed their names and small verses, funny or inspirational. The results would be treasured throughout life. Here are two examples from Edith Adams' album:[127]

There is nothing but death	There is a word in language
Our affections can sever	known to Friendship very dear
And till life's latest breath	In English tis "Forget me not"
Love shall bind us forever	In French tis "Souvenir"
Anna C. Framson	John K. Appelbe
Northampton Mass.	Trafalgar
Feb. 11th 1881	4th August A.D. 1882

A great many houses had a small piano. The ability to play it was a basic social accomplishment for young ladies. Many young men could also play. Playing and singing were great pleasures for performers and listeners. They may have had few additional opportunities to hear music, other than the organ on Sunday.

> Ma & I stayed home. It was Dull I played & sang for a while but it was dry & wretched work & lonesome singing alone. (Diary of Bertha Harnden, 14 June 1895)

> we went in to sing for a while & we did it with a vengence. Ma heard us down to the root field she thought some one was squeezing us so she said. (24 June 1895)

The danger of being known to play was that you might be asked when unprepared.

> I am to open the programme with an instrumental solo...The piano is an old pan so the only thing I play that would sound well on it is "Tam o'Shanter." I am afraid the people will think "rats" but it can't be helped. (Diary of Belle Kittredge, 16 December 1891)

If a really talented amateur visited, the resulting music thrilled the audience to a degree which we find hard to appreciate.

> Last night he & Aunt Maggie came up to the house. He plays

beautifully better than any non-professional I ever heard. The music he had with him was all new & he played it at sight with as much expression & feeling as if he had been studying it for some time. (Diary of Belle Kittredge, 27 April 1892)

The genteel tinkling of young girls on the piano was not to be compared to a professional musician's playing.

Professor Rosenburg the grand music teacher favoured us with a call the other day and came very near tearing our piano to pieces with his grand fandangoes. (Diary of Hellen V. Bowlby, 1 May 1868)

When music was heard only occasionally, it had a greater effect. The Fiske Jubilee Singers, a famous group of black music-makers, came to Port Arthur in the winter of 1892.

John Richard Harris' woollen mill, Rockwood, a watercolour from the diary of Gertrude Nicholson. *Collection of Clair C. Chapman*

The four male voices sang a quartette. It was an invitation to the dance in Waltz time. I simply couldn't keep still. It went right through me. (Diary of Belle Kittredge, 29 January 1892)

Such experiences were rare, even for those who lived in the cities. Most of the music they heard was of the amateur variety. As most everyone contributed at some time, they were tolerant of their neighbours' foibles.

> Mrs Gibbs had a musical for young people...We had singing, instrumental music & recitations and a good supper on lovely china...I think the Port Arthur people are very good natured. They will listen to people attempt to sing who make terrible attempts at it and keep asking them to sing two or three times. No one things [thinks] Miss Clarke can sing yet they ask her to bring her music always & Miss Jocelyn sang several times last night & really her medium notes are nothing but a whistle of wind in her throat. (Diary of Belle Kittredge, 19 February 1892)

The invention of the phonograph sounded the death knell for these amateur performances, as it brought a new standard of singing and playing into everyone's home. In the last decade of the century, the rich were having their first glimpse of this toy.

Residence of J.R Harris. Rockwood.

John Richard Harris' house, Rockwood, a watercolour from the diary of Gertrude Nicholson. *Collection of Clair C. Chapman*

After our meeting some men came in and Dr Birdsall had hired
a phonograph for the evening. It is the first time I have ever
seen one. We listened to bands, speeches, solos &c. It seemed
like a music box. (Diary of Belle Kittredge, 9 December 1891)

Another popular indoor pastime was painting. For those who were
conscious of the importance of a well rounded education, instruction
in drawing, painting, and the appreciation of art was considered an
essential aspect of a young woman's development. Reverend George
Hallen, though not a wealthy man, tried his best to instill a degree of
artistic ability into his offspring. Eleanora, Sarah and Mary were each
blessed with a natural talent. As youngsters they spent a great deal of
time at this occupation. For reasons unknown, Sarah, who was particularly talented, did not continue drawing once she reached adult-
hood. Work by Eleanora has survived, but the collection is not large,
for she died when still young. Mary, who lived to a great age, made
quite a name for herself, her work being frequently displayed. Not
surprisingly, in the 1840's the Hallens were often frustrated because
art supplies were hard to come by. One interesting substitute for
paper was the half-moon shaped fungus which grew readily on the
sides of trees. Drawing on them was like etching. Once they dried, the
picture was permanent. They made attractive gifts.

> After dinner Mary and I went to look for fungus to draw on I
> found a very large one on an old trunk on which I copied a
> landscape. (Diary of Eleanora Hallen, 2 October 1845)

> then I will go to my painting. How I love it. Drawing and
> Painting cultivates the mind so much & the taste also. (Diary
> of Louisa Bowlby, 16 January 1862)

> I went in the morning & took a sketch of J.R. Harris's house.
> It was rather hot sitting out on a hill top with no shade—
> However, after a while Edgar came out to pay me a visit & I
> got him to go & get me a parasol which I held up with one
> hand & painted with the other. (Diary of Gertrude Nichol-
> son, 13 August 1896)

Games, both indoor and out were very popular. Croquet was one of
the most popular summer pastimes.

Min was over this afternoon and we had tea early and after tea we played croquet for the first time this year. We had splendid fun at it. (Diary of Hattie Bowlby, 8 May 1874)

Em said Will Seldon wanted her to go down & play croquet when I came back. We are not going untill he gives us a special invitation. I have not had an introduction to his lord-ship yet nor the squinteyed Col Campbell either. (13 May 1874)

A rule for which sporting activities were acceptable for young women was that they appear to be gentle. If too much running around was required, the game would be deemed unfeminine. If they seemed quiet, they were admissible. Croquet was tolerated, and so was canoeing.

Thursday evening Flora Powley and I went out in a canoe for a paddle…It was a glorious night. (Diary of Belle Kittredge, 4 June 1892)

Swimming was not popular. It required an immodest costume, and in living memory, it had been habitual to swim in the nude (men only, of course). Within two decades this attitude would change. But in the meantime, women still had to contend with long, concealing clothing.

We went quite a long walk in the evening. We came to a place where a lot of boys were bathing & cousin Will went on a bit ahead to warn them some ladies were coming. He said one fellow got out & began trying to get into his clothes with frantic efforts. He told him he need not do that as long as he kept under water. It was most amusing when we walked past. Trying to look so solemn they would keep making remarks to each other such as "Here they come" Keep down can't you" Get under the bridge" etc. All the way back we were walking along through some rather thick cedar woods when a voice suddenly shouted out "Good night girls." (Diary of Gertrude Nicholson, 7 August 1896)

Summer time would not be summer time without the picnic, an event which provided a respectable opportunity for young people to get together.

A riverbank picnic in Waterloo county, ca. 1895. *Breithaupt-Hewetson-Clark Collection, University of Waterloo*

This morning the boys sent some twenty invitations to girls and boys. We are going to have a Pic-Nic on Saturday if the weather is favorable, because Aaron is going away on Monday. I think it will turn out rather a respectable affair. (Diary of Matilda Bowers Eby, 13 August 1863)

The day before the picnic Matilda busied herself baking raisin, lemon, and apple pies. She rose at 5 a.m. on picnic day to make sandwiches, cakes, nectar cream and lemonade. No doubt this picnic turned out a great success. However, another picnic, attended by Matilda and her brother later in the month, was not entirely pleasing to her.

This afternoon Jacob and I attended a "Pic Nic" having had an invitation from Mr S.E. Moyer. It was on the banks of the river two miles below Breslau. We were the last, they had already commenced their games. On seeing such a large party of buoyant lads and lassies I anticipated a gay time but after all it turned out rather a dry affair. The greater part of them acted as if they never had been to a "Pic Nik" before. If they all had acted their part as they ought to have done it would have passed off more satisfactorily. Mr Joseph B Bowman played the violin, and Mr Hunsicker played the accordeon. I liked the music better than the dancing. It is very little like dancing when they dance without a platform or something

similar so that you can hear the noise. According to my estimation there were about fifty present, about an equal number
of both sexes. The eatables made a splendid show after we
had them managed. My cake was pronounced the best, not
knowing, to whom the complement belonged. I heard a good
number express their opinion as such. With regard to the
"Pic Nik" speech it was abruptly brought to a terminus by
some young urchins upsetting the bench upon which the
speaker, Sammy, was so beautifully exalted. The speaker after
having informed his audience that they had lost an excellent
discourse quietly took the hint and resumed his seat on natures green carpet....(5 September 1863)

For those fortunate enough to live close to the lakes, sailing often became a passion. The Hallen family at Penetanguishene spent a great
deal of time exploring the islands of Georgian Bay. Visitors were also
treated to these excursions. The boat would be packed with food so
that picnics could be enjoyed. Mary Hallen made the most of these
outings, often taking along her sketch pads. Not every trip went according to plan.

We set off about 10 o'clock on the Hodgett's boat 18 in number two Miss Hodgetts 3 Miss Mitchells Mr & Mrs Hunter a
Mrs MacGleson a friend of theirs a most vulgar looking lady
that can be imagined but the picture of good nature...& two
men to pull. We sailed nicely to Blueberry Island where we
dined the only thing of interest that occurred was a puff adder
being killed & Miss Michell's parasol being burnt she had
hung it in a tree & the fire spred we left the Island early but as
the wind was against us & higher we were obliged to land on
"Picnic" Island & much to our horror remained the night.
There was a good deal of singing though poor Agnes had a
cold & cold [sic] not sing with her usual spirit. Mrs McGleson
amused us highly by seating herself on a large stone (by refusing to lie on a sail where all we poor creatures were striving to
make ourselves as comfortable as we could but the wind was
cold & there was as usual a lack of shawls) with a table cloth
wrapped round her she remarked she was a great big fool for
coming to such a place she kept a book in her hand and pes-
sisted that she did not get a wink of sleep all night but what

would make her nod & start appeared rather a mystery to every one. Poor Miss Hunter looked truly wretched there she lay her head resting on a stone looking very like a wax doll her dress was any thing but suitable her bonnet being a translusant one of the thinest discription trimmed with gause ribbon a white lace viel barage deep short sleeves & tucked to the waist ribbons on her wrists & a thin shawl. The moon rose beautifully there is much to admire in being out all night the dark water & the starry sky nature had perfect beauty in glowing colors on these islands. Soon after sunrise & we had performed the dutys of the toilet by the lake shore we started home & arrived at the Barrack Wharf at about 10. My Father then met us & asked them all up to breakfast & imediately they left Mr Hunter amused us by relating many anecdotes. (Diary of Mary Hallen, 13 July 1848)

A rather different sort of boat trip was undertaken by Catherine Miller in July 1890. She was travelling from her home at Thessalon to

A painting class, taught by Mr. Gilbert in Toronto. Photo by Notman & Fraser. *Archives of Ontario*

southern Ontario, and spent two nights on board the Baltic, sailing across Georgian Bay. The voyage provided her with many interesting observations:

> We have 6 Priests on board looking sheep's eyes at the girls and smelling very strong of Wisky."...One young Priest especially gave some beautiful songs. (Diary of Catherine Miller, 25 July 1890)

Catherine enjoyed the singing and remarked that there were many fine voices amongst the passengers, both male and female. On the following day, she suffered some sea-sickness.

> The ladies Maid Mrs Miller is very kind. She brings me a Tray laden with choice dishes but some how my stomach refuses. Even a cup of Tea ceases to be a comfort. (26 July 1890)

Poor Catherine was not in the mood for kicking up her heels, but for those with sea legs, there was no lack of entertainment.

> 10 o'clock the dancing begins and I am afraid they danced in the Sabbath. (29 July 1890)

Rackets were very popular among the men in Hamilton, but they did not welcome women into the club.

> The Misses Thomas and Mrs Rose were at the Racket Court. It is proposed to have a Lady's Day at the Court, so that the Gentlemen may not be caught "dishabille" to use a mild term. But many think it is not a proper place for the soft sex. I agree. (Diary of Forbes Geddes, 22 February 1862)

Badminton was thought to be a more appropriate racket game for women, as it required less exertion.

Only occasionally does male prejudice against women make its presence felt in this way in the diaries. Another noticeable example is the remarks made by the professor of mineralogy at the University of Toronto, when Bessie Scott first went there in 1889. Women students had been granted the right to earn degrees only in 1884, and the professor had not reconciled himself to the change. Naturally, he refutes the charge of discrimination.

Prof Chapman,[128] very funny dear old man—denies that he objects to ladies (Diary of Bessie Mabel Scott, 30 October 1889)

However, he is caught out when the eight women normally in the class are late arriving because they have trouble disposing of their coats.

Prof Chapman an old fraud, said the other day he was glad we girls were not there, when we walked in there was a row... (29 November 1889)

In afternoon go alone to Egmont (last lecture) & Geology Poor Prof Chapman overcome at sight of 8 girls. (29 January 1890)

The woman students were regularly treated to comments and songs as they walked in and out of the lecture halls. Their accommodation in cloakrooms and lounges was also difficult. Bessie Scott makes light of these matters, concentrating her comments on the joy of knowing the other female students.

A popular winter time amusement was ice skating. For those who could afford a pair of skates, there was no shortage of ice.

When we came home after dinner a large party of us went out on the bay for a skate. It was lovely. The ice was like glass. There was quite a wind one way so we skated up the wind & then I opened my Jacket & it blew me down to the running water. It was splendid but warm. Isn't that a strange weather mixture. We had a little crack the whip. (Diary of Belle Kittredge, 16 December 1891)

Went to the Skating rink with Mrs Drysdale. Lady Dufferin was on the rink she skates very nicely. (Diary of Janet Hall, 31 January 1877)

Lady Dufferin was noted for her skating parties in Ottawa. In Hamilton, skating became a popular pastime by mid-century.

The Officers had a space cleared on the Bay for skating where some of them enjoyed themselves daily. Rackets however the principal amusement. (Diary of Forbes Geddes, 19 February 1862)

By the next season, the Officers wanted something more comfortable than the Bay to skate on.

> A skating rink will be constructed in Hamilton this Autumn. This will be the Aristocratic Resort. Another one for the "unwashed" is talked of to be constructed at the East end of the town open. The first named will be roofed in, lit with Gas for Evening amusement. Lady skaters are springing up in all parts of Canada. In Quebec and Montreal rinks were in vogue 5 years ago...It is another capital "stand" in the matrimonial world these skating rinks. Many a match has resulted from attentions first received there. (Diary of Forbes Geddes, 22 October 1862)

> First Skating on rink at East End. (Diary of Forbes Geddes, 18 December 1862)

The snow offered other amusements.

> Mr Stratton and Mr Egger were engaged in the sensible amusement of sliding down the hill on a tobawgan (Diary of Eleanora Hallen, 8 March 1844)

Janet Hall, diarist. *National Archives of Canada*

> We had Oyster soup and coffee for the Tobogganers after a very cold tramp home from the slide. (Diary of Mary Brown, Ash Wednesday 1888)

> went to the Curling Rink. There was a match on between Ft Wm & P[ort] A[rthur]. It is only the second time I ever watched curling. But soon got to understand enough to make it interesting...we tried throwing the stones in a part of the ice not in use. It looks so easy to watch the men slide them along but when we tried it is not quite so easy. I did not slide mine but threw it and was very much frightened by the crack

it made when it touched the ice. I thought the stone was broken & it would take more than a months pay to replace it. (Diary of Belle Kittredge, Friday undated [late January 1892])

One annual cause for excitement was the local fair.

went to the Exhibition.—We four Girls & George "did the Fair" in State. Saw every big show & every side show and all the free shows & finished up on oyster Soup. (Diary of Marion Chadwick, 15 September 1892)

Whether it was as large as the Canadian National Exhibition in Toronto or represented the efforts of a tiny village, it was welcomed enthusiastically by the population. It was a chance to see new things, visit with your friends, and even enter a competition.

Many of the contests were for men, but women had their own sections which reflected their domestic interests. The 1893 fair at Williamstown was the 82nd there, the oldest fair in Ontario. The women's events included a great deal of needlework.

worked blankets	quilting
woven cloth	a suit of clothes
coloured and white flannel	wincey
woollen carpet	knitted or crocheted
rag carpet	bedspread
knitted mitts	(spinning) woollen yarn
knitted socks	knitted stockings
hearth rug	plain sewing (for girls
sofa cushion, embroidered or not	under 14)
various embroidered items	table covering

It is interesting that so many of these crafts would not be included in today's fair events, which are usually seen as reflecting traditional handicrafts. The most unusual 1893 entry (to modern eyes) is for "an example of darning on a sock."

The food events for 1893 include canned fruit (raspberries, strawberries, plums, pickles, jelly, catsup), raspberry or currant wine, bread, biscuits and handmade hard soap. Cakes, pies and cookies are absent.[129]

Travelling entertainments, such as the circus, provided an outlet and talking point when they came to town.

> A circus in town—band, wild west show, and a number of ladies(?) & clown—the cowboys & women rode horseback through the place headed by band in chariot—it looked tolerable. (Diary of Emma Laflamme, 21 July 1888)

However, when one circus came to town, tongues wagged.

> There was a Circus here yesterday. It was a kind of a nasty thing and we do not go. The procession passed here so we saw all there was to see.... There was a girl performed at the Circus with nothing but tights on and a little wee shirt tail. she was a Damsel in more ways than one. (Diary of Hattie Bowlby, 13 May 1874)

Although it cannot strictly be said to be an entertainment, the effects of living in the magnificent Canadian landscape were not lost on many women. Perhaps this especially affected new immigrants. Victoria Campion frequently comments on the beautiful land and sky in her part of Hastings County. Belle Kittredge had only been at the Lakehead for a few months. The effect of living in view of Lake Superior was still a novelty.

> There was a big sea on outside. We could not see the Giant but could see the rolling waves a long way out until the earth & sky met. I like to see the big sweep of water, no land to be seen. (Diary of Belle Kittredge, 3 December 1891)

Aside from all the entertainments which might be regarded as strictly fun, such as circuses, fairs and sports, much diversion in the nineteenth century had a pedagogical flavour. The idea of improving one's mind by learning and discussion was very current. Groups formed to assist this process, whether it was intellectual or religious.

> Held Bible class. Quite a number of good men & women present. Can I do them good? Help! (Diary of James Geddes, 9 November 1889)

Travelling lecturers came to town and gave their speeches on whatever topics were of interest. People flocked to hear them, but became experts on methods of lecturing and were not uncritical.

> tuesday night Birdie & I treated ourselves to a Scotch lecture and didn't think much of the treat. I am not Scotch & I have come to the conclusion that it needs Scotch blood to appreciate the Scotch character...his delivery was bad. (Diary of Belle Kittredge, 19 February 1892)

Groups could not depend on too many outside speakers, so they worked up debates among their own numbers. In Port Arthur, the Society to which Belle Kittredge belonged tried to provide a varied evening.

> We decided to have another public affair before Lent this time it is to be a debate & concert & no refreshments & a nice piano so I hope it will be good. (19 February 1892)

Topics such as "Resolved that Wellington was a better General than Napoleon at Waterloo" were the order of the day. At first, only the men were allowed to debate and the women listened. In January 1892, the topic of the debate was whether women should be allowed to participate. Each team consisted of a man and a woman. The first to speak had a difficult time.

> Maria had to open. She had her part written out as an essay and hadnt time to do any more. When she got up she began to laugh and could not stop. She stood there and laughed & laughed until the whole audience (30 or 25) followed suit and we had a laughing party for a time. (Thursday undated [January 1892])

Belle herself took part in the debate, but spoke against women's participation. One reason was the hypocrisy which courtliness made necessary.

> Dr Birdsall tried to attract people by witticisms & compliments to the ladies. I hate that complimenting business. (11 December 1891)

The society obviously chose to continue having women participate, for in April of that year, the debating team consisted of women only.

The chance to dress up was always attractive. Before Lent 1892, they held a Carnival in Port Arthur.

> Last night we went to the Carnival. Flora Powley & I wore our regiment dresses and Eva wore Frank's gown, cap & LL.B. hood. Eva looked so sweet. She has an intellectual face & the costume suited her. Poor girl she would love to own such a costume in reality. Her great wish is to go to the University. (13 February 1892)

As Belle's reference makes clear, once again the presence of an army regiment affected society. For weeks before, there had been preparations for a regimental concert, celebrating the presence of the 96th Battalion Algoma Rifles in town. There was singing, both solo and in groups.

> The singers always saluted when coming on the stage instead of bowing. The whole concert was intensely military & therefore very attractive. (6 February 1892)

A more unusual part of the show was a group of young women (Belle included), who did a display of military marching and close order drill, wearing mock uniforms and carrying wooden arms.

A rather important form of amusement which was enjoyed by most diarists was to get their "likeness" taken. Photography became popular by the 1860's. Most people took advantage of the many studios available. Sometimes the result was not all one desired.

> Pollie and I took Mabel and Milton down to get their Pictures taken. Two darlings they are. We got ours taken too. But what a scarecrow I am in a picture. Death on a mopstick. (Diary of Catherine Miller 11 August 1890)

Celebrations and Holidays

we girls ate apples and drank cider
and talked nonsense.
DIARY OF ANN AMELIA DAY, 25 DECEMBER 1878

T HE ROUND OF THE YEAR, with its special days, regulated the Victorian's lives as it does our own. The first day of the year was a new beginning, full of hope.

> Our dear Lord has premitted us to see another year enter. May his loving spirit be with us to the end. Uncle Arthur & family all came over for New Years supper. We had two turkeys. All went off pleasant. (Diary of Margaret Emma Griffiths, 1 January 1900)

> Formed many good resolutions which I hope to keep. (Diary of Annie Boyes, 1 January 1894)

For society people, the first day of the new year was devoted to visiting by gentlemen. By tradition, the women stayed at home to receive guests and offer refreshments. According to Etiquette in Washington (1857):

> The time of visiting on this day began as early as ten o'clock,

and continued until three, or later. The lady remained at home to receive her visitors, who are usually gentlemen, She partook of some refreshments with each: wine and cake, or coffee, which is placed conveniently on a table.

As with so many old customs, it had a solid basis in practicality.

Each visitor leaves his card, and remains but a few moments. The day furnishes an opportunity of healing up any estrangements or differences which may have arisen among friends, and is one of great hilarity.[130]

We see a survival of this habit in the levees still held by politicians on New Year's Day.

Mr Poper & Papa & Willy paid 41 visits in a sleigh. I received 27 kind visitors. Went at 8 p.m. to Henry McLarens to spend the evening. (Diary of Mary Brown, 1 January 1872)

We had about twenty visitors, some before lunch. (Diary of Marion Chadwich, 1 January 1894)

My brothers went their usual round of calls we had two Hodgetts, Dr Stevens & 6 people from the town & some Indians. (Diary of Mary Hallen, 1 January 1852)

Dear old Willy Allan brought five books for the younger children. Mr Carmichael opened the New Year by reminding us of the "love of the Father." Adam stayed at home after paying a few visits. Thirty two gentlemen young & old called on me. Mr Poper arrived the night before attended the midnight service with us & went out to pay visits with Harry....(Diary of Mary Brown, 1 January 1880)

New Year's was a special time for family celebrations. The Brown family of Hamilton organised a splendid event.

Daisy & Lily & I busy with preparations for the family gathering at night. Daisy having brought me silver spoons for our use. The table was placed diagonally in the second drawing

room having decorations of green silk with two lovely maiden
hair ferns swathed in green silk & dessert on the table à La
Russe, grapes of Hilly's giving & all looking very pretty, 12
seated at the long table. Ann Small came to cook the dinner
whilst Mary & Agnes waited. Daisy had indeed done her ut-
most to make the table look well. Dinner served at 7:30 pm.
(Diary of Mary Brown, 2 January 1893)

Some New Year feasts were rather more unusual.

The Indians had a big Feast today. We were all afraid we
would not get an invitation & while we were talking about it
Mr & Mrs Fox from near Hastings came, commenced to get
dinner for them when our invitation to the Feast came. took
the Foxes with us. Had a fine time. (Diary of Annie Elizabeth
Cragg, 2 January 1888)

The frivolities of Groundhog Day may seem far from our serious-
minded ancestors' usual habits. But the basis of looking for our shad-
ows is solidly agricultural. When we found a reference to it, the
groundhog was absent and another animal took his place.

Just a gleam of sunshine enough for the bear to see his shad-
dow. (Diary of Mary Ann King, 2 February 1893)

Bruin saw himself and it has been storming ever since. (Diary
of Mary Belle Eberts, 2 February 1896)

Some people were unable to make up their minds about St. Valentine's Day.

On Valentines day the "Captain" and his two sons took a
number of Valentines to the post office one of which I received but burnt it without looking at it some of them who
did read it said it had rather a religious tendance & was evidently an original....(Diary of Mary Hallen, 18 February
1852)

Agnes & I contrived to trudge down to call on Mrs Keating &
the Miss Hodgetts at the latter place there was a great deel

talked about Valentines which they seem to think very amusing things & write a great many themselves. (Diary of Mary Hallen, 12 February 1853)

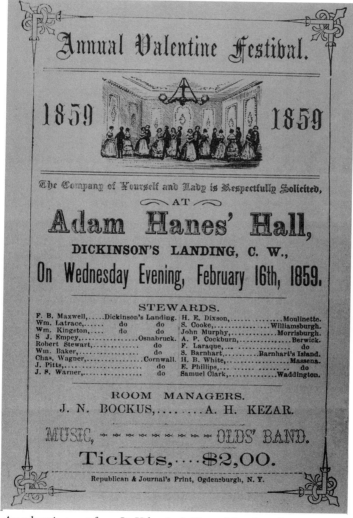

An advertisement for a St. Valentine's Day celebration of 1859.
Upper Canada Village Library and Archives

In the post bag there were three stupid valentines. One for me was from Barrie and the other two put in here for Edgar & Preston. I got a piece of coloured note paper & wrote one for

Richard as he is here getting wood. The fun lines I got hold of were "Is there a man that never loved" & at the end I put Adieu pour jamais, Chacun à son gout, they were the only [illegible] I could get hold of as I expected Richard in every minute & when sealed & put with the others it looked quite natural. It was great fun to see my Mother & Richard looking at it & not the least suspecting it. (Diary of Mary Hallen, 15 February 1853)

This was St Valentine's day. I am glad that I did not get any, at least so far, neither did I send any. I don't believe in such nonsense. (Diary of Matilda Bowers Eby, 14 February 1863)

After due consideration we came to the conclusion that we would sew today, and wash tomorrow. At about ten O'clock Mrs Lennet came, she came to pay us a visit. She stayed till two. Mother gave her two chickens and a large piece of pork, so that she left with a merry heart. She appears to be contented. We made three more patches today, one more then we have twelve. This evening Lydia Reist came from school with Malinda. Joseph brought home two Valentines, one for Maria and one for me. The one I got is by far the prettiest. It is the nicest I ever received, I can't imagine who sent it. (17 February 1863)

Despite the fact that Matilda claimed not to believe in such nonsense, she was not above sending a Valentine card, in jest.

This evening Father brought me several letters, on opening I found that one was a note from Aaron stating the reason why he did not call. I would not have been hard on him even if he had not told me because I could guess the true reason. The other was the Valentine I had sent to J.F. He is rather ahead of my time—sent back the identical thing. I could not help having a hearty laugh on reading the contents over. It must have been too pointed for his sensitive nerves. By all appearances he must be highly insulted. I did not intend to insult him by no means. I have only one way to get out of the scrape. He sends his eternal thanks. Quite thankful, I am sure for such a great favour. (18 February 1864)

After marriage, Matilda washed her hands of the whole affair.

> This was the great St. Valentine's day. I have given up dealing
> with the like of that before today. I consider it rather a low
> piece of business. (14 February 1868)

St. Patrick's Day has long been an important festival for the Irish. In
Penetanguishene, pensioners resident at the garrison marked this day
in their own fashion.

> Agnes & I drank tea at the Mitchell's & being St Patrick's day
> we met tipsy pensioners. I do wish they were all out of the
> place they will never do any good. (Diary of Mary Hallen, 17
> March 1853)

Birthdays have always been reason for celebration. For the young,
they hold a special excitement.

> Today I am Sweet Sixteen and I never was so old before...For
> my birthday presents I got a pair of kid gloves from Ma this
> little journal from Hellen & Charlotte gave me a lovely print
> apron to wear in the mornings when I go down to Mrs Ger-
> mans....I got all my presents on my breakfast plate this morn-
> ing...I have been so smart today that I suppose I will have to
> be smart all the rest of the year. (Diary of Hattie Bowlby, 11
> April 1874)

> Yesterday babys birthday no time to make cake so gave her a
> molasses cookie. (Diary of Margaret Emma Griffiths, 4 Sep-
> tember 1900)

Some parents had more leisure time, and were able to ensure that
their offspring were treated in "royal" style.

> Jack's twenty second birthday. Papa gave him an Oyster Sup-
> per. (Diary of Avice Watson, 8 March 1888)

> A little more snow. Dear Philips birthday (18). Made plum
> pudding. (Diary of Frances Gay Simpson, 22 March 1881)

Harley's birthday (his 25th). Father and I took an opportunity to let Harley know that he had never in all those years given us an hour's anxiety or worry since he could walk. (Diary of Mary Brown, 23 June 1888)

In true Victorian fashion, birthday presents needed to be useful and instructive.

I do not know what to E would be most acceptable. She reads a great deal & is always glad to get a book. Would not a mate for the pigeon be nice & a faithful source of pleasure in the eggs the hatching of which would not only delight in the realization but in the anticipation.[131]

The elderly made much of birthdays too.

My birthday is past, 64 years old. It is possible I have lived to be an old woman. (Diary of Catharine Merritt, 4 August 1857)

Had fat hen and iced cake for M's birthday. (Diary of Margaret Emma Griffiths, 29 April 1900)

Wedding anniversaries were celebrated in elaborate manner by those who mingled in society. The Davis family home, located on the banks of the Detroit River at Windsor, presented a splendid view of the July 4th fireworks in Detroit.

16th Anniversary of our Marriage. 60 Guests to view fire works from our veranda. Refreshments, Sandwiches—Ice cream, Strawberries, Cake, Lemonade. Warm but pleasant evening. (Diary of Frances Julia Davis, 4 July 1888)

Mrs Davis paid $5.50 for three and a half gallons of ice cream. $1.50 for fifteen boxes of strawberries, and to the servant, Annie Stewart, 70 cents for waiting on table.

The first of April was noticed.

...yesterday which was the first of April. I went with ma to see Jane, She was very sick on Sabbath...when we went there she was washing dishes. She made us an April Fool, for we expected to find her in the bed. (Diary of Catherine Bell Van Norman, 2 April 1850)

April Fool Day. Mr Preston [the clergyman] was here. We had great fun fooling one another. I fooled him several times. (Diary of Mary Victoria Campion, 1 April 1863)

This is a lovely morning and E- is very busy April fooling every one.[132]

Lent, the period of self-denial before Easter, has never played as large a part in the English speaking world as it did in continental Europe. But it was still noticed.

Good Friday. We went to Church there were a good many people there. As usual made cross buns. (Diary of Mary Hallen 9 April 1852)

It was considered wrong to marry during Lent, and frivolous activities were abandoned as well as some foods. Once Easter came, normal life resumed.

Lent is over & dancing has begun again. (Diary of Belle Kittredge, 20 April 1892)

Gave the boys a holiday...I started for a drive with Jim, Teddy & George. broke the whipletree &c. returned by the orchard, waggon stuck in the lane. (Diary of Agnes Leacock, 14 April 1879)

This, of course, serves as a reminder that spring sunshine and solid ground are not always evident at Easter time. However, everyone knew that Spring was just around the corner.

The coming of spring would have special meaning in some communities, when some event would indicate to the populace that a new season had arrived. It was a time for rejoicing, throwing off the shackles of winter and enjoying the warmth. In Port Arthur, the harbour cleared of ice and the first boats came up from the south.

The dock was crowded with people who had come down to

welcome the first boat. The flags are flying in the town in honor of the event. (Diary of Belle Kittredge, 2 May 1892)

A little later, each individual would have a momentary satisfaction in donning summer's lighter clothing.

...threw off flannels put on muslin dress (Diary of Frances Tweedie Milne, 8 June 1867)

Nowadays, the 24th of May is a holiday without a reason, but a century ago it was The Queen's Birthday. The Queen herself, so distant and forbidding, was venerated by almost everyone. Her birthday was pleasingly placed in the calendar as a time to welcome the first really warm weather. It marked the beginning of summer, when light-coloured clothes could first be worn. The celebration was heartfelt.

I will say at once, for the reminder to persons living in England, that the twenty-fourth of May was the Queen's birthday. Nobody in Elgin can possibly have forgotten it. The Elgin children had a rhyme about it—

> The Twenty-fourth of May
> Is the Queen's Birthday
> If you don't give us a holiday,
> We'll all run away.

But Elgin was in Canada. In Canada the twenty-fourth of May *was* the Queen's Birthday; and these were times and regions far removed from the prescription that the anniversary "should be observed" on any of those various outlying dates which, by now, must have produced in her immediate people such indecision as to the date upon which Her Majesty really did come into the world. That day, and that only, was the observed, the celebrated, a day with an essence in it, dawning more gloriously than other days and ending more regretfully, unless, indeed it fell on a Sunday, when it was "kept" on the Monday, with a slightly clouded feeling that it wasn't exactly the same thing. Travelled persons, who had spent the anniversary there, were apt to come back with a poor opinion of its celebration in the "old country" ...Here it was a real holiday, that woke you with bells and cannon—who has forgotten the time the ancient piece of ordnance in "the Square" blew out all the windows in the Methodist church?[133]

Sara Jeanette Duncan's characters in *The Imperialist* are in a state of great excitement about the Queen's Birthday, and their celebration is long and dramatic. For many of our diarists, the day was much like the others—work came first. Whether they celebrated or merely worked however, the notations in the diaries always begin, "Queen's Birthday," indicating that they were aware of the importance of the day itself. Perhaps no holiday in the modern calendar retained the same universal mystique, except Christmas.

> Queen's birthday. Had a pretty dull day washed all the forenoon besides chasing pigs, cows and horses got dinner ready & had a quarrel with both Edith & Ma about the Almighty doing all things well. He hasn't done anything for me so I said so & got in a Devil of a row after dinner. (Diary of Bertha Harnden, 24 May 1895)

At Hamilton, the Brown family entered the festivities with great enthusiasm.

> Queen's birthday. Daisy & young people went to Floss Falls, taking dinner, ret. to tea and fired off crackers till after ten. (Diary of Mary Brown, 24 May 1881)

> Queen's birthday rose bright & fine but as usual clouded up & rained in the afternoon. We went to the pic-nic but had to go in the hall. However enjoyed seeing all our friends as it is probably the last pic-nic we shall be at here. George is at the Mill tonight. (Diary of Mary Coldwell Butcher, 24 May 1892)

In 1863, the celebration had to be put off a day, so that the festivities would not take place on Sunday, especially as it was Whitsun.

> This forenoon I spent by reading and strolling about which was all very pleasant. After dinner Jacob, the girls and myself took a drive to town to see what was going on there. The

Queen's birthday was celebrated today, Whit Monday, the games were the same as on former occasions. We were on the ground about two hours when we concluded to go down town. In the meantime we fell in with some friends...(Diary of Matilda Bowers Eby, 25 May 1863)

Queen Victoria celebrated her golden jubilee in the year 1887 and Ontarians made much of this event.

Jubilee services in church this day which I enjoyed so much. All hearts seemed to join in prayers for our Queen. (Diary of Avice Watson, 19 June 1887)

Jubilee celebrations all over that day & very grand doings in every city in honour of Her Majestys long reign. May she reign Many years still....(Diary of Avice Watson, 21 June 1887)

Ten years later, her diamond jubilee was even more of an event in Ottawa.

Jubilee Day. We have the house fixed with flags and big red ensine an Irish American papal union jack naval white ensine etc I had breakfast in bed as I had asthma badly last night at 8 oclock in the morning all the church bells Began to ring for half an hour I heard them all ringing at 10 the Children from the Schools sang on Parliment hill. (Diary of Ethel Chadwick, 22 June 1897)

Despite her illness, Ethel was allowed to see a military drill at the armouries, to ride to the Experimental Farm (but forbidden to get out of the carriage), and to see a bicycle parade. Cycling was still something of a novelty in 1897. In the evening, there were illuminations on a downtown street.

In Norfolk County, young folk of the Quaker Community organized a picnic near Otterville to mark the Queen's birthday. On the way there, they stopped to walk in the woods to hunt for ferns and wild flowers. For this group of youngsters, the highlight of the day was tea time.

Then we had tea which was laid out on a long table. Two of

the girls brought lemon juice in jars with screwed tops & one of the gentlemen went & got a pail of nice cold water. They put the lemon in & some sugar & made lovely lemonade. One lady brought tea & got some made at a house near by. There were meat & lettuce sandwiches, ham ones, potted meat, egg, skinned salmon & cold beef sandwiches. Then all kinds of nice cake, jam tarts, pickles, gingerbread & lemon pie. It was a real good spread & everyone seemed to enjoy themselves. We started home pretty soon after tea. We had a most lively time all the way home. Fred drove us under a locust tree & we got some branches of the blossom. It is just like white laburnum & smells very sweet. We all put some in our hair & Mr Henry had a flag (Union Jack for Queen's birthday which was kept as holiday on Monday instead of Sunday). He tied it to the end of an umbrella & waved it about all the way...The conveyance in front of us had the horses which are usually used for the hearse & we had the wagon which is used to take the pall bearers to funerals in. We enjoyed the picnic very much especially the drive & the tea. (Diary of Gertrude Nicholson, 25 May 1896)

Some families chose to commemorate events which were rather unusual.

Edgar put some oak boughs at the door in memory of the Restoration of King Charles in 1660 which we have always had done. (Diary of Mary Hallen, 29 May 1850)

The Dominion Day celebrations in Hastings in 1872 took on an extra dimension, when a committee decided to have a picnic. Money was needed for the cemetery, so the picnic was a natural place to raise funds. There would be food, drink and boat rides.

The committee evidently felt that the bar would be the great moneymaker. They ordered the following:

30 tumblers	10 gallons of rye whisky
1/2 dozen of ale	1/2 dozen port wine
1/2 dozen or porter	1 pail and 2 taps
1/2 dozen of brandy	

at a total cost of $31.60. This was supplemented with two half-barrels of beer. The food included the following.

45 pounds of ham	oranges and lemon
biscuits	cheese
gingerbread	candy
cakes	

The receipts totalled $372 (of which about two-thirds came from the bar), and the costs $150, leaving $222 for the cemetery.

It was at this time—in the 1870's—when many places were establishing community-based cemeteries, instead of churchyards or private burying grounds. The growing population made it necessary and it was easier to control the large municipal plots.

There was already a growing temperance movement in Ontario, and it is interesting that it does not seem to have had any influence on the Dominion Day celebrations in Hastings in 1872.[134]

The Bowlby sisters lived at Port Dover, and had the advantage of enjoying the excitement not only of Dominion Day (now called Canada Day) on 1 July, but the American 4th of July as well.

Nothing of importance happened untill Monday the first of July when we had a holiday, of course, it being the birthday of the New Dominion. We had quite exciting times in Dover. The Gunboat was here and the volunteers from all the surrounding towns. the Doverites gave a free dinner to the volunteers. Well I was bound to have a good time so I asked every person I knew (that is, agreeable ones) over to dinner. We had Dr Harrison and his wife, Mrs Joe Douglass and two children Bell and Charlie McCall, Charley B, Jim McCall, Ned Carpenter, Clem York besides 20 of our family, of course including the school girls (a total of 31 people!). (Diary of Hellen Bowlby, 3 July 1867)

Yesterday was the 4 of July. There was an excursion from Erie [Pennsylvania] over here. They came in on a splendid schooner. There were 1,400 on board. It made quite a stir in Dover for a short time. they brought a splendid band along played God Save the Queen coming in & Yankee doodle going out. (Diary of Hellen Bowlby, 5 July 1867)

One holiday which we scarcely remember today is the 12th of July. The parade which took place on that day commemorated the Battle of the Boyne, the final defeat of King James II of England by William of Orange. It ensured that the monarchs of England would always be protestant. The Orange Lodge was an Irish society which remembered this anniversary each year with a noisy procession. The lodge came to Canada in 1825 and quickly established chapters in many Irish communities.

> mother and I alone all day. they all went out to the 12th (Diary of Mary Victoria Campion, 12 July 1861)

Eliza Bellamy also made note of the 12th of July.

> On the 12th The Orangeman passed through our Village at an early hour bands playing and Banners waveing to the glorious memory. (Diary of Eliza Bellamy, 14 July 1855)

The parade, known as 'the Orange walk', was a large social occasion for some Irish. Much of the population would use the day as an excuse to visit and carouse, but for those who had Orange connections, it was a holiday with a great importance. The walks continued into the 1950's and even later, but were much more sedate affairs than those of a hundred years earlier.

> It rained near all day Pa and Thomas and Johny and Eliza went out to see the orangemen walk (Diary of Susanna Whaley, 12 July 1865)

> Pa and I went to Alliston to Orange Walk had a splendid time. (Diary of Laura McMurray, 12 July 1899)

The difficulty of the Orange Walk in the early days was that it was also an occasion for rowdyism. Some had too much to drink. Others remembered the religious prejudice inherent in the day and tried to frighten their Roman Catholic neighbours.

The pioneer Orangemen were so rough in their celebration that an act was passed in 1843 which outlawed the parade. In 1844 the Protestant Irish of Toronto were determined to have their fun. Between four and five hundred set out on a steamer bound for Niagara, where they had advertised their illegal party. When the boat reached

The Ouse Club of Berlin (now Kitchener) on a riverside outing in Waterloo County, 12 August 1898. *Breithaupt-Hewetson-Clark Collection, University of Waterloo*

Queenston, it was met by magistrates who said that between 1500 and 2000 Roman Catholic Irish were waiting to fight those on board. As the Protestants had brought sixty muskets with them, their intentions cannot be said to have been entirely honourable. After some negotiations, all Orange memorabilia was left behind and the party continued unmolested.

On the same day, in Toronto, the forbidden parade took place. An alderman tried to stop it and was assaulted. The Riot Act had to be read to disperse the participants and twelve people were charged. It was a far cry from later, more orderly celebrations.[135]

Civic Holidays provided the opportunity for much needed relaxation. Those living in urban areas would make the most of the day, often planning excursions to escape the heat of the city. On a hot summer evening, what could be nicer than a seat on the lakeshore?

Went to Beach with Father by 7 P.M. Train with Lily & the Misses McLaren. sitting on a Bench close to the edge of the Bay, our party…enjoyed the display of Fireworks from the long line of Yachts & craft & thought it very beautiful. (Diary of Mary Brown, 20 August 1889)

Thanksgiving was institutionalized in Canada in 1879. Prior to this time, it was customary for the Governor General to set apart a day in each year as one devoted to Thanksgiving. In 1865, Matilda Eby was celebrating Thanksgiving in October, as we do, but for many years it occurred in November, closer to the American holiday. By then, the harvest which it was meant to mark would have been long past in Ontario.

> This was Thanksgiving day and was observed as a public holiday in this place. I was surprised to see such was the case, ungodly place that it is. It seems to one it must be the most wicked spot in the world. It is heartrending. (Diary of Matilda Bowers Eby, 18 October 1865)

> Thanksgiving day! and a glorious fine day, makes one feel glad to be alive a day like this—Oh! so much I have to be thankful for such a year as this has been...retired soon after pumpkin pie...(Diary of Bessie Mabel Scott, 1 November 1890)

> Thanksgiving Day—A fall of snow last night. I went to church with Mary & Nelly & enjoyed the service. Came back to dinner of roast goose which George came just in time for. The little ones are very good. We had some music in the evening. (Diary of Mary Coldwell Butcher, 10 November 1892)

Hallowe'en has invariably provided an opportunity for mischief. The youngsters of 1862 were no different from today in high spiritedness.

> The Youth of Hamilton amused themselves and annoyed householders by carrying off gates, wheels of vehicles &c. A sound thrashing to each juvenile would be a benefit to the community. Pumpkin Lanterns, Ducking for apples &c are all very well—harmless—but injuring property or annoying householders should be promptly punished...Evening at Allen's, girls dressed as boys for a lark. (Diary of Forbes Geddes, 31 October 1862)

> ...Edgar & Preston attended them home and I belive had a good deal of fun one of the young ladies let *out* that on all Hallowd eave they went into Dr Bautree's garden at night to pull cabbages. (Diary of Mary Hallen 12 November [year not indicated])

This is hallowe'en and the children are making a great noise outside. There are processions of them with big pumpkin lanterns. Hellen and Will are coming over very soon to have some Hallowe'en fun—popping corn, cracking nuts, eating apples etc. I don't know whether we will duck for apples and tie one up by a string as we did last year—we would if you were here wouldn't we, Appins?[136]

Marion Chadwick's busy life centred around her family, as did that of most of the diarists we find here. As she prepared for Christmas, she made many of her presents for her brothers, sister and parents herself, with a special one for the baby, Bryan.

Janie Bowlby as Little Red Riding Hood. *Clement-Bowlby Papers, University of Waterloo*

It was a wet snowy day so we didn't go out. I read & sewed at Christmas presents, all day. (Diary of Marion Chadwick, 28 November 1892. on holiday in Albany, New York)

Made presents all morn. (13 December 1892)

Made Bryan his first knickerbockers in morn. (14 December 1892)

Christmas Day. St Albans in morn. The church was decorated by Mrs Arthurs & looked quite great—the singing was—...the kids had their stockings today...we were 19 in all...—We danced skirt dances etc. & played on all the musical instruments that the kids got at the tree. I forgot to say we had a tree but it was a very small one. Mother got dozens of things for the house & a diamond ring—I got 22 articles of various descriptions, a great card case from G Br. a writing case—pin—pictures—a rocking chair. (25 December 1892)

When he married Queen Victoria in 1840, Prince Albert had brought the Christmas Tree from Germany to England. By the end of the century, it had become universal in Canada too, crossing the ocean with English emigrants such as Mary Brown.

Small Christmas tree in spare room for Harry's sake. Mr & Mrs & 3 Misses McLaren kindly came down just during the lighting. (Diary of Mary Brown, 24 December 1864)

The glittering candles on the tree must have been a thrilling sight, although very dangerous. Harry Brown was an invalid at this time, confined to bed with a hip ailment.

Perhaps the great attraction of Christmas was the day off from the regular working schedule.

we killed six fowls and two geese after we got home. (Diary of Mary Victoria Campion, 23 December 1861)

I was making pies, cakes, fried cake [doughnuts] and cleaned upstairs preparing for Christmas. (24 December 1861)

A beautiful day for Christmas day...We spent a very pleasant day all alone with the exception of Tommy being her[e]. Esther Effie & I took a long walk down the Creek. We had a goose, plum pudding for dinner. I had a sleep after dinner and part of the day. (25 December 1861)

Whatever form Christmas took, the basis for the season was the same as it is now.

All well here. No trouble getting the Xmas Spirit with five children in the house.[137]

We are preparing for Xmas & I am getting the children's clothes ready for Whitby. Blowing from the East like a storm. Hung up the children's stockings tonight. (Diary of Frances Tweedie Milne, 23 December 1875)

It is so nice to see the children looking forward to & believing in Santa Claus. (Diary of Belle Kittredge, 26 December 1891)

we all went to church, roads not good. this church beautifully decorated [illegible] and for dinner we had an immense turkey. so glad we are all together. (Diary of Sarah Hallen Drinkwater, 25 December 1846)

Christmas of 1889 was celebrated by the Browns of Hamilton with the knowledge that their elder daughter Daisy would be married in less than a month. She would not be with them the next Christmas, and was allowed to try her hand at the traditional delicacies, in preparation for her coming role as lady of the house.

Harley with us at Sacrament, Daisy, Father and I after 11 Service. Family gathering in the evening, dinner at 6:30 P.M. Arthur & Harold coming in to dessert. Ann sent the dinner up very nicely, the pudding excellent. Daisy's cake magnificent with icing & almond over it, well made, her mince pies also. The children were very happy dancing about & enjoying themselves till 10 P.M. (Diary of Mary Brown, 25 December 1889)

The *Ladies' Journal* for December 1889 suggested this menu for Christmas breakfast: Toast, breaded sausage, canned tomatoes, baked potatoes, oatmeal fritters with maple syrup, coffee or cocoa.[138]

And for Christmas dinner, *The New Galt Cookbook* (1898) suggested the following meal: Oyster soup, roast turkey, cranberry sauce, mashed and browned potatoes, onions in cream sauce, tomatoes, chicken pie, rice croquettes, plum pudding, foaming sauce, mince pies, lemon tarts, salted almonds, celery, crackers, cheese, fruit and coffee.

There is no doubt that preparing for the Christmas season meant extra work in the kitchen. Fortunately, some of the special foods could be prepared well in advance. Plum pudding was often made in November, giving the pudding time to ripen and develop a moist richness. In many places, the last Sunday before Advent was considered the best time to make the pudding. Some folks called this day "Stir Up Sunday." It was a time when the whole family would get together and take turns stirring the pudding mixture. Legend suggested that a wish made while stirring the Christmas plum pudding would come true.

Another time to make a wish was when eating one's first mince pie of the Christmas season.

This morning I made a lot of mince pies to last over the holidays. (Diary of Matilda Bowers Eby, 23 December 1868)

For many families the most exciting time of the Christmas season was Christmas Eve. Children, filled with excitement and anticipation, bubbled over with glee, as families played out their own traditions.

Xmas Eve!…children greatly excited over Santa Claus. Nan, poor child, doesn't like Xmas nearly as well since Miss Allen so kindly(?) told her there was no Santa but Edith & Mac are still ignorant—in evening Auntie, Mother and the boys prepare things for the tree and Pa puts them on—seven stockings hung in a row—at 12.35 Nan wanted to take hers but went to sleep again and at last about 6:30 we six hudled into our bed as we used to do but it is now rather hard for six to squeeze in as we are not as small as we used to be—After breakfast we went into drawing-room and had distribution—Mother rec'd chair from Father over which last night we had lots of fun getting it in—I rec'd *boa* from Auntie & Uncle Geo., *Jewel Case* from Auntie M & A, *slippers* from Maude, *brush & comb* case from Aunt Marrie, needlecases from Hal & Ben—In the evening Mabel came in and we roasted marshmallows—lots of fun. (Diary of Bessie Mabel Scott, 24 December 1890)

Kissing under the mistletoe was always an entertaining business. Since mistletoe was not available in many parts of the country, other plants or evergreen boughs were substituted. An English custom dictated that a single man who refused to kiss a lady under the mistletoe, must, at a later date, present the lady with a new pair of gloves. However, Mary Hallen's remarks indicate that not all English people were familiar with the mistletoe tradition.

> There was a piece of hemlock, a substitute for mistletoe hanging in the drawing room most inviting truly for the gentlemen but as they did not enter into with proper sport Miss Hodgett was obliged to *prevail* on Edgar to salute her by first kissing him herself. Preston was also *honored* in the same way. How strange it is not English I am sure nor Canadian, perhaps it is a wild Irish custom. The scandal of it at breakfast by Preston cause poor Edgar's face to resemble the rising sun on an Indian summer morning. (Diary of Mary Hallen, 30 December 1852)

Charity was at the forefront of many minds during the Christmas season. Those who were less fortunate were often treated to meals. The Hallens helped to provide some festivities for local children, and provided them with a meal each Christmas.

> My Mother not well. We got up by candle light we made a large plum pudding before breakfast as the pensioners children are coming to dinner. Sarah, Drinkwater, the children & I made an attempt to get to the town in the double sleigh but were obliged to turn back at Bradleys the road was so soft & snow so deep. The children all assembled about one o'clock 50 in number they dined in the cottage which was decorated with wreaths of evergreen & pictures. We went to see them all at dinner the variety of faces was amusing they behaved well & after a game of play they dispursed to their homes. (Diary of Mary Hallen, 29 December. 1851)

The week after Christmas continued the celebrations, with much visiting, dining with friends, and hilarity.

Much to do this week yesterday kill'd six geese and two turkeys...(Diary of Eliza Bellamy, 29 December 1854)

It was also the time for the Christmas Concert, put on by the school
or the Sunday School. Children performed their songs and recitations, and had a Christmas tree. The whole community attended the
joyous occasion.

> We swept the Sunday School out twice put up a Xmas tree
> made tables & set them, cut up cake, spread bread & butter
> & wrote the fly leaf in nearly all the prizes. Such quantities of
> cake &c as we had and all so nice. there was lots left. After tea
> the children played about till it was time for the concert to
> begin. It was Bedlam let loose. The noise was deafening. But
> it was their day so the [they] had full liberty. The concert was
> all their own. They recited & sang thirteen different Selec-
> tions. After the concert the Prizes were distributed. Mr Reni-
> son was presented with Parkman's works & Frank was pre-
> sented with a family bible. It was too much for Frank. He
> took it but did not reply. His feelings were too much for him.
> After the prizes we had a magic lantern of jumping horses,
> dancing men & funny things. the children each got a bag of
> candy & an orange from the tree. (Diary of Belle Kittredge,
> 30 December 1891)

And then the new year came, with its sense of hope and renewal, and
the cycle started again.

Acknowledgments

We are grateful for the welcome accorded us in the libraries and archives of Ontario while we read the diaries. In particular, we would like to thank:

Susan Bellingham, Doris Lewis Rare Book Room, University of Waterloo; Gail Benjafield, St. Catharines Public Library; Susan Bennett, Ontario Agricultural Museum; Linda Brown-Kubisch, formerly of the Kitchener Public Library; Bonnie Callen, Wellington County Archives; Bernadine Dodge, Trent University Archives; Mary E. Groocock, Norwich and District Archives; George Henderson, Queen's University Archives; Susan J. Hoffman, Kitchener Public Library; Margaret Houghton, Hamilton Public Library; Mark Jackman, Town of Clarington Archives; Tom Kuglin, Macaulay Heritage Park; Stewart Renfrew, Queen's University Archives; Jack I. Schecter, Upper Canada Village, Mark G. Walsh, Windsor Public Library and Municipal Archives and Leon Warmski, Archives of Ontario.

The authors are indebted to the following for permission to quote from works whose copyright is in their control:

Gladys Arnold for the memoirs of Mary Hutchinson Orr; Norah Bastedo for the diaries of Sarah Drinkwater and Mary and Eleanora Hallen; Gail Benjafield and Keith Geddes for the diaries of James and Jessie Geddes; Linda Brown-Kubisch for the quotation from the Waterloo Historical Society 1992; Gwynedd Brundrett for the diary of Margaret Emma Griffith; Margaret (Ketchum) Catto and Penny Sanger for the diary of Josephine Ketchum; Clair C. Chapman for photographs of Gertrude Nicholson's diary sketches; Gayle Cooper for the diary of Forbes Geddes and the letters of William and Ann C. Macaulay; L. H. Cragg and Jack Stone for the diary of Annie Elizabeth Cragg; Zan Critelli for the diary of Susan Agnes, Lady Macdonald; Tim Cumming for permission to quote from *The Huron Expositor*; Florence Duncan for the diary of Fanny Goodfellow; Glenbow Archives for the diary of Mary Victoria Campion; Catharine Gray for the diary of Frances Gay Simpson; Margaret Haist for the diary of Frances Tweedie Milne; Major G. Michael Henderson for the diary of Elizabeth Van der Smissen; George M. Hendrie for the diary and letters of Mary Brown; Mark Jackman for a quotation from his *In Repose*; Kitchener Public Library for the diaries of Matilda Bowers Eby and Rose Eby and permission to quote from oral history interviews of Tusie Zurbrigg, Lucinda Allendorf, Joseph Zinger, and Roger Weiler; Lenore Law, for permission to use the photograph of Louisa Cowell; Alister Littlejohn for the diary of Alice Patterson; Diane Mackinnon and Queen's University Archives for an extract from the Burleigh Papers; Ann de Grassi McIntosh and Winnett Boyd for the diary of Lillian de Grassi; Thomas R. Merrit for the diary of Catharine Merritt; Joan Phillips, for a quotation from *Threshing and Other Delights*, by David Phillips; Mary Oliarnyk for the diary of Catherine Miller; Carol Sharer for the diary of Ann Amelia Day; Paul R. Sheppard for the diary of Agnes Emma Butler Leacock; The Chatham Kent Museum for the diary of Mary Belle Eberts; *The Dictionary of Canadian Biography* for the quotation on Sir John A Macdonald; The Metropolitan Toronto Reference Library for the diaries of Sophia and Thomas Adams, Mary Coldwell Butcher, Mary Frances Cleveland, Emma Laflamme and Helen Grant Macdonald; The Niagara Historical Society for the diary of Mary Ann King; The Pennsylvania German Folklore Society for *Granmother's Washday Receet*; The Waterdown-East Flamborough Heritage Society for the recipe for purifying the blood from the cookbook formerly belonging to Alma Reid; The Waterloo Historical Society for extracts from the William Gladstone Letters; University of Pittsburgh Press for *The Cormany Diary;* Florence Thomas, and Queen's University for permission to quote from letters in Dr. Ada Funnell's collection; Christine Tremeer, for permission to quote from *From Forest to Thriving Hamlets* by Isabelle Campbell; Gordon Wagner and the University of Waterloo for the diary of L.H. Wagner, and Norma J. Whitney for the diary of Eliza Bellamy.

While every effort has been made to secure permission, it has in some cases proved impossible to trace the heirs of the diarists. We apologize for any that have been missed.

It is a pleasure to thank Ron Lambert for his continued support of this project and for his many helpful suggestions. We thank John English and Ken McLaughlin for reading the manuscript. Also, for keeping the car running, for always being there with words of encouragement, and for assisting in so many ways, thanks are due to Peter Hoffman.

Biography

Thomas Adams (1831-1928) and his daughter Sophia (b. 1868) farmed near London. Sophia wrote the entries in the early diaries, perhaps dictated by her father. Later, he kept the journal himself. Their brief entries are largely concerned with agricultural life.

Eliza Bellamy wrote an interesting account of family life in the mid 1850's. At the time of writing her diary she was middle aged and married to her second husband, Samuel Bellamy, mill owner and farmer at North Augusta, Grenville County. Her account of daily activities are beautifully detailed and her writing is frank.

The Bowlby Sisters: The three Bowlbys each kept their diaries for about one year only, when they were 17 years old. They lived at Port Dover, where they assisted at a small school and followed active social lives. Louisa (1845-1872) was later married to a Mr. Carpenter, and died at the age of 27. Hellen (1849-1939) never married, but worked as a teacher and was active in the arts. Harriett (1858-1876), known as Hattie, died at the age of seventeen, a few months after she stopped keeping her diary.

Annie Boyes lived in the southern part of Simcoe County.

Mary Brown was born in England, the daughter of Thomas Harley Kough, a barrister, and his wife Catherine. It was while visiting relatives in Hamilton, that she met Adam Brown, a widower with four sons. They were married in September 1862, and had seven more children. As the wife of a member of parliament, she had many social and charitable commitments. She died at sea in 1896 while returning from a year spent in England.

Mary (Minnie) Coldwell Butcher was the daughter of Ursula Gibson and John Holdsworth Coldwell. About 1888 she married George Charles Butcher. They lived in Port Sydney, Muskoka. For a brief time they also lived at Meaford. Her diary entries are primarily concerned with domestic activities such as dressmaking, as well as other types of sewing, baking, preserving, and also farming matters.

(Mary) Victoria Campion (b. 1839) lived in Hastings, north of Stirling. In the early 1860's, when she kept her diary, she helped her widowed mother keep house and care for her several younger siblings. She married Henry M. Fowlds (1825-1907) in 1864.

Ethel Chadwick (1884-1975) was born in Ireland but came to Canada as a child. She grew up in Montreal and Ottawa. Her diaries (1896-1971) provide a rich glimpse into the life of Ottawa's elite.

(Fanny) Marion Chadwick (d. 1905) came from a wealthy Toronto family. She wrote and directed plays which were well received. She married James Grayson Smith in 1898. High spirits are reflected in her diaries, which continue through the 1890's to the birth of her son in 1904. She died at the age of 34.

Mary Frances Cleveland (b. 1868) was the daughter of John and Nancy Cleveland, of the village of Glendale, Westminster Township, Middlesex County. Mary Frances was sick with malaria on her 14th birthday, the day she made the first entry in her diary. Although the diary covers a very short span of time her vibrant personality shines through.

Samuel and Rachel Cormany. Rachel Bowman, daughter of Benjamin B. and Mary Clemens, was born 12 April 1836 near Berlin, Ontario. She received her senior education in Ohio, and met Samuel Cormany when they were students at Otterbein University. After their marriage in 1860, they came to Ontario for an extended visit. It was during this time that Rachel gave birth to their first child. Samuel, a citizen of the U.S., eventually felt compelled to return. He did so with his family during the civil war. Surviving diaries cover the years 1858 to 1865, and have been published.

Annie Elizabeth Cragg (b. 28 Dec. 1859 at Wallaceburg), kept house for her clergyman father who was serving as missionary to the Indians of the Hiawatha Reserve on Rice Lake. When she was writing her diary in 1889, she was an unmarried woman. Her rather secluded life changed when she married E. B. Stone, a prominent lawyer in Peterborough. She had one son. She died in 1963 at the age of 104.

Frances Julia Davis (1844-1928) was the daughter of William Duperon Baby, of Sandwich, who served as sheriff of Essex and Lambton counties. She became the second wife of John Davis, who was elected mayor of Windsor five times. Frances was instrumental in the founding of the Hotel Dieu hospital at Windsor.

Ann Amelia (Minnie) Day (b. 1853) was the daughter of Thomas Day, and Sarah Turner of Eramosa Township, Wellington County. Minnie's diary commences in 1878 when she was a single woman helping her mother to run the home. She discontinued writing the diary in 1879, shortly after her marriage to Noah Sunley.

Ida Lillian (Lilly) de Grassi (1858-1942) was born in Lindsay, Ontario, the daughter of Annie de Grassi and Dr. Alexander William James de Grassi. On 5 September 1883, she married Mossom Martin Boyd. They had seven children. Summers were spent at Bobcaygeon and winters usually in Toronto.

Sarah Hallen Drinkwater (b. 1818) Sarah, the eldest of eleven children, very likely kept a diary from childhood, as some of her siblings did. Unfortunately, many of the early diaries are missing. Her diary of 1840 began when she was living with her parents at Penetanguishene. Later that year she married John Humphrey Sumner Drinkwater.

Mary Belle Eberts(1819-1899) was born at Perth, Scotland and came to Canada in 1833. She married William Duncan Eberts, and had nine children. The Eberts family were among the earliest residents in Chatham, settling there in 1794. They are viewed as being instrumental in Chatham's prosperity and growth.

Matilda Bowers Eby (1844-1923) was born at Sweetbriar Farm, Berlin, Ontario, the daughter of Cyrus and Elizabeth (Craft) Bowers. She married Dr. Aaron Eby, M.D. They had seven children. Her diaries cover 1861-1873, and often give great detail of events and relationships.

Rose Eby (1865-1885) born at New Hamburg was the daughter of Matilda Bowers Eby and Dr. Aaron Eby. Following in her father's footsteps, Rose entered medical school at Toronto. She died before completing her training.

Forbes Geddes (1826-1904) was unmarried when he worked as a railway clerk in Hamilton in 1862. Part of a large and scattered family, he was intensely interested in social and sporting life. His gossipy observations are both acute and entertaining. He later became stationmaster elsewhere in Ontario, and died at Niagara-on-the-Lake. His sister was Ann C. Macaulay.

Jessie Geddes (1836-1920) and her husband James (1836-1908) were born at Wick, Scotland and came to Canada with their young family in 1877. They settled on the Magnetewan River near Burk's Falls. They had a small farm, but James was often absent preaching. His diary is largely an account of his religious services, while her brief entries are domestic in nature. They are not related to Forbes and Ann Geddes.

Fannie Goodfellow (1864-1941) trained in Barrie as a seamstress. She made clothing of every kind as well as crochet, knitting, tatting and quilting. Her fancy items—camisoles, pillow slips, buffet and table covers, all trimmed with lace—are still treasured. She was unmarried.

Margaret Emma Griffiths (1856-1915) was born at Decew House—the house to which Laura Secord is said to have walked to in order to give the message that the Americans were to advance on the morrow. Margaret married her cousin, Michael Griffiths, and at Decew House they raised their family and worked the farm.

Janet Hall (b. ca. 1858) went to live with her grandparents at Ottawa when only a few months old. Her grandfather, Alexander Workman, was mayor of Ottawa when work on the original parliament buildings was begun. Janet never married. She died 24 February 1933. Her diary was found in the basement of the old Workman store on Queen Street, Ottawa, which had been a family business.

Mary Hallen (1819-1908) was the daughter of clergyman, George Hallen, and Sarah Williams. Her sisters were Eleanora Hallen and Sarah Hallen Drinkwater. The Hallen children were encouraged to write journals from a young age, and continued this practice throughout much of their lives. In January 1875 she married W.A.R. Gilmour, M.D. The marriage did not last.

Eleanora Hallen (1823-1846) Her candid writing, which is often humorous, imparts a special sense of what it was like to live as part of a large Victorian family. Her untimely death, from tuberculosis, was a dreadful loss to the family.

Bertha Harnden was assisting her widowed mother and sister Edith run a farm in Darlington township at the time she kept her diary in 1895.

Frances Ann Jones (1841-1880) was the daughter of Ellen and Eliza Good of Myrtleville House, near Brantford, now a museum operated by Heritage Canada. Frances married farmer, Andrew Jones, of "Homewood," near Maitland, Augusta township. During the time of writing the diary, her health was not good. It is thought that Lucia, her daughter, wrote some of the entries, possibly dictated by Frances when she was unwell.

Josephine Anne Ketchum (1868-1887) was the third child and only daughter of Judge Jay Ketchum, of Colborne, and his first wife Mary Louisa Gilchrist. Her diary, begun when she was 17 years old, covers her last year of life.

Mary Ann King was a housewife at Chippewa, near Niagara Falls.

Belle Stuart Kittredge (b. ca. 1868-1959) was born and raised in Strathroy, but moved to Port Arthur in 1891 to work in a relative's office. She shared the family's active social life which she records in great detail in her diary, while longing for a chance at higher education. This she achieved, graduating from the University of Toronto, and then teaching kindergarten before marrying. She died at the age of 91.

Emma Laflamme (b. 1858) grew up in Winchester, southeast of Ottawa. She began her diary to record the preparations for her sister's wedding and kept it for only nine months. During this time, she kept house for her parents, who ran a store in the village. She did not marry, but continued to live there into her nineties.

Agnes Emma Butler Leacock (1844-1934) was born and raised in England. She married Walter Peter Leacock in 1867. Upon arrival in Ontario they settled near the village of Sutton in the township of Georgina, located on the shore of Lake Simcoe. The Leacock family consisted of eleven children. The most famous was the third child, Stephen Butler Leacock, writer and humourist.

Ann Catherine Macaulay (1806-1849) and her husband, William, (1794-1874) were married in 1829 and lived at Picton. William, a priest of the Church of England, was appointed first Rector of St. Mary Magdalene Church. Ann did not enjoy good health, a matter often mentioned in correspondence. She was an older sister of Forbes Geddes of Hamilton. She died childless.

Helen Grant Macdonald (1869-1942) was born into a wealthy family in Toronto. Her diaries from the 1890's, when she was a young woman, reflect her social and charitable pursuits, and include her interesting visits to friends in Muskoka and Lakefield. She later graduated from the University of Toronto, and taught for thirty years at Bishop Strachan School.

Susan Agnes, Lady Macdonald (1836-1920) was born in Jamaica, daughter of Thomas James Bernard and Theodora Foulkes Hewitt. In February 1867, she married John A. Macdonald. A few months later, on 1 July 1867, Sir John A. Macdonald became the first prime minister of Canada, and was knighted. His new bride became Lady Macdonald. They had one child, Margaret Mary Theodora.

Sophia MacNab (b. 1832) was the daughter of Mary Stewart and Sir Allan Napier MacNab. In 1855 she married William Keppel, Viscount Bury. Sophia's diary of 1846 mainly deals with home life in Hamilton. She speaks of her mother's illness and death.

Laura McMurray (b. 1880) grew up on a farm near Sunnidale Corners in Simcoe County. Her diaries cover twenty-five years, beginning in 1899. She later married a neighbour, John Wiggins, and spent the rest of her life in the same area.

Catharine Merritt (1793-1866) was born in the United States, the only child of Dr. Jedidiah Prendergast and his wife, Penelope Chase. In 1815, Catharine married

William Hamilton Merritt and settled in St. Catharines. During the years of her diary writing, her husband was Member of Parliament for Lincoln. Catharine's health was not robust, but she maintained a strong interest in her family and the lives of those around her.

Catherine (Kate) Miller (1847-1912) was born in Cornwall, England. In 1867 she married Samuel Harper with whom she immigrated to Canada. Shortly after their arrival, Samuel was killed in a mining accident. In 1869 she married William James Miller, a widower. They had ten children. Catherine's diary was written while on a mid-summer trip.

Frances (Frank) Georgina Agnes Tweedie Milne was born in 1848 northwest of Whitby. She was the youngest of thirteen children. Her diaries cover the years 1867 to 1871, and deal mainly with household matters. In 1869 she married Wm. A. Milne of Hillside Sawmill. They farmed on the Rouge River in Scarborough Township. In her forty-fifth year she developed pneumonia and died.

Gertrude Nicholson (b. 1869) was the daughter of Herbert Nicholson and Sarah Walker and was born at Norwich, Norfolk County, Ontario. The Nicholson family were part of the Quaker community. Gertrude's family went to live in Sunderland, England, about 1882. The diary was written when she and younger sister, Maud, returned to Ontario to spend a summer with relatives. Gertrude was also a talented artist and complemented her diary with numerous sketches.

Mary Hutchinson Orr (1850-1947) was the daughter of William Hutchinson, who had settled on Lot 12, concession 3, Nichol township, Wellington County. In 1940, Mary wrote her reminiscences of early farm life in the Fergus area. She died at Arthur.

Alice Patterson was born in the Blenheim area. Her mother died during her birth. Alice was raised by grandparents, Col. and Mrs Leslie Patterson, at Wallacetown, Dunwick Township, Elgin County. She never married and remained living on the Patterson property. She spent her adult life helping to look after elderly relatives.

Bessie Mabel Scott, later Lewis (1871-1951) grew up in Ottawa, and was the first woman from there to attend the University of Toronto. She had a long career after her husband's death, as librarian at Lisgar Collegiate in Ottawa.

Frances Gay Simpson (1821-1891) was the daughter of John Johnson Gay, of Alborough Hall, Norfolk, England. After the death of her clergyman husband in 1872, she moved her family to France. Later they joined her two oldest sons in Ontario, settling in Hamilton.

Edith Elizabeth Van der Smissen was the daughter of William Henry Van der Smissen, a professor of German at the University of Toronto, and Elizabeth Mason. At the time of writing her diary she was a young single woman.

Catherine Bell Van Norman (1821-1852) was the daughter of a doctor in Nelson township. She had five children before a debilitating illness forced her to accept an invalid's life in her late twenties. Her original diary for six months of 1850 is lost, but a copy had been made and it was published by the Burlington Historical Society. She died of consumption at the age of thirty.

Louis H. (L.H.) Wagner (1857-1945) was born at Buffalo, New York, and raised in Berlin, Ontario. He became a preacher of the Evangelical Church. On 20 May 1884, he married Mary Staebler, of Berlin, who died 11 May 1887. They had one child.

Avice Watson (b. ca. 1854—1892) was born at Windsor. Possibly orphaned, Avice made her home with the family of John and Mrs. Watson, of Cottingham Cottage, Guelph township. The diary began in 1886 and continued until two months before Avice's untimely death from consumption at 38 years of age.

Susanna Whaley (b. ca. 1847) in Markham Township, daughter of David Whaley and Eliza McLean. She was widowed at a young age. Susannah continued the family cheese factory while raising a family of several children.

Notes

1   12 January 1893, p. 2.
2   A discussion of the business lives of single women in the earlier period of life
     in Upper Canada can be found in Eleanor Margaret Glenn's essay, "Single Pi-
     oneering Women in Upper Canada," in *Families* (the journal of the Ontario
     Genealogical Society), v. 31, no. 1. (February 1992), p. 5.
3   Upper Canada Village, Commercial Records 11, Folder 6, Log of the Brig
     'Mayflower', 1860-1861.
4   Linda Brown-Kubish, "In Search of Freedom: Early Blacks in Waterloo
     County," *Waterloo Historical Society,* vol. 80 (1992), p. 51.
5   Municipal Archives, Windsor Public Library, Margaret Bowlby Collection,
     Box 17, Jim — to Edith Bowlby, 31 March 1897.
6   10 December 1847.
7   The Dumfries Reformer, 23 July 1873.
8   Private Collection
9   Hamilton Public Library, Brown-Hendrie Collection.
10   Pearl Wilson and Laura Morton, *Rural Gatherings 1857-1918.* p. 15.
11   There is no indication of when Sarah received this letter. It is copied into her
     diary and follows the entry for 5 April 1875.
12   28 October 1864
13   p. 232.
14   Municipal Archives, Windsor Public Library, Margaret Bowlby Collection,
     Box 17, Barclay Adams to Edith Bowlby, 30 April 1894.
15   Municipal Archives, Windsor Public Library, Margaret Bowlby Collection,
     Box 17, Edith Bowlby to Barclay Adams, 1 April 1891.
16   *Pen Pictures of Early Pioneer Life in Upper Canada*, by A Canuck of the fifth
     generation. (Toronto, William Briggs, 1905), p. 211.
17   *St. Catharines' Journal and Welland Canal, (Niagara District) General Adver-
     tiser*, 24 August 1843, no page. Reprinted from the *Simcoe Advertiser.*
18   Waterloo Historical Society, MC61. la. 18, Jane Pringle to Helen Gladstone,
     13 September 1873.
19   *The Ladies' Home Journal* (Philadelphia) March 1896, p. 39.

20   *The Dumfries Reformer*, 15 November 1876.
21   *The Cormany Diaries: A Northern Family in the Civil War*, Edited by James C. Mohr. (Pittsburgh, University of Pittsburgh Press, 1982).
22   *Charlottetown Constitutionalist*, 26 August 1846.
23   M. A. Crowther, "Childbed, death-bed", *Times Literary Supplement, 22 January 1993, p. 6. The new study is Death in Childbirth*, by Irvine Loudon. (Oxford, Clarendon Press, 1993).
24   *Newfoundland Royal Gazette*, 1 December 1840.
25   Toronto, University of Toronto Press, 1991, p. 127.
26   *The People's Home Library: Medical, Cooking, Veterinary*. (Toronto, R. C. Barnum & Co, 1910), p. 389.
27   *The Ladies' Book of Useful Information*, (London, Ont., London Printing & Lithographing Co., 1896), pp. 124-126.
28   Hamilton Public Library, Brown-Hendrie Collection, p. 802, Catherine Kough to Mary Brown, 5 April 1871.
29   Wellington County Archives, Correspondence to Mrs Joseph Rendall from her brother Peter and his wife Jean in New Jersey, 27 September 1886. A993-22 MU279.
30   *The Cormany Diaries: A Northern Family in the Civil War*, Edited by James C. Mohr. (Pittsburgh, University of Pittsburgh Press, 1982), pp. 192-193.
31   F.S. Verity, "Case illustrative of the difficulties to be encountered by the Practitioner of Midwifery in a rural practice," *Medical Chronicle* 2, 1854, pp. 160-62.
32   J. Worth Estes, *Dictionary of Protopharmacology: Therapeutic Practices, 1700--1850*. (Science History Publications, U.S.A. 1990), p. 175.
33   J. M. Pemwarden, "Barbarous Treatment by a Midwife," *Canada Lancet* 4, 1872, pp. 273-74.
34   *The Huron Expositor*, 5 November 1875.
35   Conversation with Velma Taylor, 19 March 1993.
36   Memoirs of Mary Hutchinson Orr, Wellington County Archives, A989.7, MU 102.
37   *The Finchley Manual of Industry no. 111: Female Servant Manual*. (London, Joseph Masters, 1867), p. 7.
38   *Miss Beecher's Domestic Receipt Book*. (5th ed.), p. 31.
39   *Huron Expositor*, 7 January 1876.
40   Memoirs of Mary Hutchinson Orr, Wellington County Museum, A090.7, MU 102.
41   David Phillips, *Threshing and other Delights*. (London, Phelps Publishing, 1989), p. 5.
42   Conversation with Velma Taylor, 9 December 1992.
43   Oliver Schmidt, *Schmidt diary* (Unpublished manuscript, Allen County Public Library, Fort Wayne, Indiana). The year of weaving was 1883.
44   *"Mother Hubard's Cupboard," or Canadian Cook Book*. (Hamilton, Briggs & Son, 1881), p. 57
45   *The Canadian Home Cookbook*. (Toronto, Hunter, Rose and Company, 1877), p. 10.
46   Pat and Frances Patterson, *Harvests Past*. (Erin, Boston Mills Press, 1989), p. 61.
47   Dorothy Rainwater, "Victorian Dining Silver", in Kathryn Grover, ed., *Dining in America 1850-1900*. (Amherst, University of Massachusetts Press, 1987), p. 182.

48 Audrey I. Armstrong, *Harness in the Parlour*. (1974), p. 42
49 Robert Yates Whitehead, *Records of an Old Vicarage*. (1906), p. 170.
50 *Tales of the Twenty,* (Kitchener, Pennsylvania German Folklore Society, 1979), p. 153
51 Memoirs of Mary Hutchinson Orr, Wellington County Archives, A989.7, MU 102.
52 Municipal Archives, Windsor Public Library, Margaret Bowlby Collection, Box 17, Ellen A. Adams to Robert Adams, 20 July 1877.
53 Tusie Zurbrigg, Kitchener Public Library Oral History Collection, OHT 133.
54 Interview with William Rusk of Coburg, conducted summer 1966.
55 v. 1. no 3, April 1854, pp. 58-59.
56 *The Canadian Home Cookbook*. (1877), p. 374.
57 Ibid., p. 367
58 Ibid., p. 379.
59 *The Cook Not Mad; or Rational Cookery*. (1831 reprinted 1984), recipe no. 266.
60 Lucinda Allendorf of Waterloo, Kitchener Public Library Oral History Collection, OHT 084.
61 Interview with Velma Taylor, 19 March 1993.
62 Interview with Robert Lovelock of Napanee, August 1964.
63 National Archives of Canada, Frances Gay Simpson Collection, MG 24 K48, file 15. A note on the back of an inventory from the home of Catharine Esther Gray.
64 Charles Elme Francatelli, *A Plain Cookery Book for the Working Classes*. (London, Routledge, Warne & Routledge, 1852, reprinted 1977 by Scolar Press), recipe no. 70.
65 Roger Weiler of Baden, Kitchener Public Library Oral History Collection, OHT 744.
66 Demonstrated by the late Viola MacKenzie Parrott.
67 *The Rideau Record*, 2 July 1907.
68 *The Cook Not Mad; or Rational Cookery*. (1831 reprinted 1984), recipe no. 116.
69 *The Ladies' Journal*, (Toronto, June 1891, p. 9.
70 Ibid.
71 Winnifred Pollock of Galt, Kitchener Public Library Oral History Collection, OHT 344.
72 *The Ladies' Journal*, (Toronto), June 1884, p. 8.
73 For the exact recipes for both pickled cherries and Canadian capers, see Blanche Pownall Garrett's *Canadian Country Preserves and Wines*. (Toronto, James Lewis & Samuel, 1974), pp. 49 & 46.
74 This is recipe no 195 in *The Cook Not Mad: or Rational Cookery* which is generally available in libraries in the 1984 reprint from Cherry-Tree Press/Government of Ontario. A modern and still potent version appears in Blanche Pownall Garretts, *Canadian Country Preserves and Wines*. (1974), p. 100
75 *"Mother Hubbard's Cupboard,"* or *Canadian Cook Book* (1881), p. 60.
76 She was nineteen years old.
77 *The Dominion Illustration*, (Montreal), 14 July 1888, p. 31.
78 Hamilton Public Library, Brown-Hendrie Collection, Correspondence, Catherine Kough to Mary Brown, 9 February 1867.
79 Archives of Ontario, Macaulay Papers, F 38, Ann C. Macaulay of Picton to her mother-in-law Mrs Ann Macaulay, Kingston, 20 April 1847.

80   Ibid., Rev'd. William Macaulay to his brother John Macaulay, 23 August 1847.
81   Diary of Eleanora Hallen, 17 December 1845.
82   Archives of Ontario, Macaulay Papers, F 38, Ann C. Macaulay of Piction to Mrs Ann Macaulay of Kingston, 1 December 1847.
83   Queen's University Archives, Burleigh Papers, Box 16, file 20a, Amherst Island Diary.
84   Harry Graham, *Ruthless Rhymes for Heartless Homes*. (London, E. Arnold, 1899?)
85   quoted in M. Loane, *The Queen's Poor: Life as they Find it in Country and Town*. (London, Edward Arnold, 1910), p. 119
86   Joseph Zinger of Maryhill, Kitchener Public Library Oral History Collection, OHT 825.
87   Municipal Archives, Windsor Public Library, Police Magistrate's Conviction Register, Sandwich, 1861-65.
88   Memoirs of Mary Hutchinson Orr, Wellington County Archives, A989. 7, MU 102
89   Ibid.
90   Memoirs of Mary Hutchinson Orr, Wellington County Archives, A989. 7, MU 102
91   26 October 1864.
92   Private collection.
93   unidentified newspaper clipping pasted in the diary of Marion Chadwick, 8 October 1898.
94   interview with Norman Wilcox of Bowmanville, 18 September 1965.
95   Queen's University Archives, Buchanan papers, coll. 2272, Box 1, Elizabeth Johnston of Brantford to her cousin, 23 December 1877.
96   Michael Smith, *The Afternoon Tea Book*. (New York, Collier Books, 1986).
97   Ivan R. Mackintosh to Annie de Grassi, 19 August 1915. Trent University Archives, Boyd-De Grassi Collection 88-011/21/1.
98   *The Berlin Daily Telegraph*, 12 April 1899 (no page).
99   *The Canadian Home Cook Book*. (1877), p. 378.
100   Waterloo Historical Society, MC61. la. 196, John Wyllie to the Gladstone family, date uncertain 1876.
101   Waterloo Historical Society, MC61. la. 17. Margaret Wyllie to Helen Gladstone, 18 September 1873.
102   *The Elmira Signet*, 17 April 1902.
103   Trent University Archives, Boyd-de Grassi Collection, 88-011/21.
104   Arthur's collection.
105   Recipe and advice courtesy of Old Order Mennonite friend who wishes to remain anonymous.
106   *Heritage Happenings*, the newsletter of the Waterdown-East Flamborough Heritage Society, September 1990, p. 9; the original from a handwritten cookbook dated 1852 and formerly belonging to Alma Reid.
107   Adelaide Hechtlinger, *The great patent medicine era*. (1970).
108   John H. Young, *Our Deportment*, (Hamilton, F. B. Dickerson, 1880), p. 390.
109   Mark I. Jackman, *In Repose: Victorian Funeral Customs & Practices*. (Kirby, Ontario, Clarington Museums, Clark Museum & Archives, 1992), p. 5.

110   From *Josh Billings Cook Book and Piktorial Proverbs*. (Toronto, Toronto News, 1880).

111   *The People's Home Library: Medical, Cooking, Veterinary*. (Toronto, R. C. Barnum & Co., 1910). p. 20.

112   *Weekly Herald & Conception Bay General Advertiser*, 18 March 1846.

113   A.D. Campbell, "Waterloo Body Snatcher", *Waterloo Historical Society*, vol. 77, (1989), p. 83

114   9 September 1859, p. 3, of Quebec.

115   Hamilton Public Library, Special Collections, undated newspaper clipping, death of Sarah Hannah Geddes, 20 December 1859, pasted in the back of the Diary of Forbes Geddes for 1862.

116   Isabelle Campbell, *From Forest to Thriving Hamlets*. (Seaforth, The Huron Expositor, 1968), p. 21.

117   M. Loane, *The Queen's Poor: Life as they Find it in Country and Town*. (London, Edward Arnold, 1910), p. 254.

118   Trent University Archives, Fowlds Collection, B-72-001/3/8/224, Amelia J. Robb to Mr (?) Fowlds condoling on the death of his wife, 30 January 1886.

119   Queen's University Archives, Dr. Ada Funnell Collection 2211.1, Dr. Helen E. (Reynolds) Ryan to Mrs Jesse Funnell Senior, 12 January 1906.

120   Upper Canada Village Library, Social History Papers, Folder 3, C. McEuen to Margaret...(?), 21 November 1853.

121   Graeme Decarie, *The Canadian Encyclopedia*. v. 4, p. 2129.

122   Municipal Archives, Windsor Public Library, Margaret Bowlby Collection, Box 17, Ellen A. Adams to Robert Adams, 15 June 1877.

123   *Guelph and Galt Advertiser*, 15 October 1848.

124   *"Mother Hubbard's Cupboard," or Canadian Cookbook*. (Hamilton, G. C. Briggs, 1881), p. 61.

125   *The Ladies' Home Journal*, (Philadelphia), January 1986, p. 21.

126   Information from Eileen Moodie.

127   Municipal Archives, Windsor Public Library, Margaret Bowlby Collection, Box 16.

128   Edward James Chapman (1821-1903), professor of geology and mineralogy, 1853-1895.

129   Queen's University Archives, Ewan Ross Collection, Series 111, #47 Fairs.

130   *Etiquette in Washington*, by A Citizen of Washington. (Baltimore, Murphy, 1857), p. 51.

131   Municipal Archives, Windsor Public Library, Margaret Bowlby Collection, Box 17, Ellen A. Adams to Robert Adams, 31 March 1873.

132   Municipal Archives, Windsor Public Library, Margaret Bowlby Collection, Ellen A. Adams to Robert Adams, 1 April 1873.

133   Sara Jeanette Duncan, *The Imperialist*,. (1904).

134   Trent University Archives, Fowlds Collection. 72-001/3/8/344.

135   *The Gobe*, 16 July 1844, p. 2.

136   Municipal Archives, Windsor Public Library, Margaret Bowlby Collection, Box 17, Edith Bowlby to Appelbe C. Adams, 28 October 1893.

137   Queen's University, Dr Ada A. Funnell Collection, 2211.1, Dr. Helen E. (Reynolds) Ryan to Dr Ada A. Funnell, 23 December 1905.

138   p. 9.

Bibliography

DIARIES

Thomas and Sophia Adams, Toronto Reference Library, Baldwin Room.
Eliza Bellamy, Upper Canada Village.
Harriett D. (Hattie) Bowlby, Municipal Archives, Windsor Public Library, Margaret
    Bowlby Collection. (Partial transcription at the Archives of Ontario, Margaret
    Bowlby Collection, MU 282, File 2).
Hellen V. Bowlby, Municipal Archives, Windsor Public Library, Margaret Bowlby
    Collection. (Partial transcription at the Archives of Ontario, Margaret Bowlby
    Collection MU 282, File 3).
Louisa Bowlby, Municipal Archives, Windsor Public Library, Margaret Bowlby
    Collection. (Partial transcription at the Archives of Ontario, Margaret Bowlby
    Collection, MU 282, File 4).
Annie Boyes, Simcoe County Archives.
Mary Brown, Hamilton Public Library, Special Collections, Archives File, Brown-
    Hendrie Collection.
Mary (Minnie) Coldwell Butcher, Metropolitan Toronto Reference Library, Baldwin
    Room.
Mary Victoria Campion, Glenbow Museum, Calgary. (Copy at Upper Canada
    Village).
Ethel Chadwick, National Archives of Canada, MG 30 D258.
(Fanny) Marion Chadwick, Archives of Ontario, MSS MS 573, Chadwick Paper
Mary Frances Cleveland, Metropolitan Toronto Reference Library, Baldwin Room.
Rachel and Samuel Cormany, *The Cormany Diaries: A Northern Family in the Civil
    War.* Edited by James C. Mohr. (Pittsburgh, University of Pittsburgh Press, 1982)
Annie Elizabeth Cragg, Archives of Ontario, MU 4734-7.
Frances Julia Davis, Municipal Archives, Windsor Public Library, Davis Diaries, Ms
    16/1-6
Ann Amelia (Minnie) Day, Wellington County Archives, A 981-92 MU 4.
Ida Lillian (Lilly) de Grassi, Trent University Archives, Boyd Family Papers, 88-011,
    Series E. Box 12.

Sarah Hallen Drinkwater, Archives of Ontario, MU 840 1-D.3.
Mary Belle Eberts, Chatham Kent Museum, Eberts Family Collection, 993.9.1.
Matilda Bowers Eby, Kitchener Public Library, MC 87 Aaron Eby & Matilda Bowers Eby Collection.
Rose Eby, Kitchener Public Library, Aaron Eby & Matilda Bowers Eby Collection, MC 87.
Forbes Geddes, Hamilton Public Library, Special Collections, Archives File.
Jessie and James Geddes, private collection.
Fannie Goodfellow, Simcoe County Archives.
Margaret Emma Griffiths, Transcription at the Archives of Ontario, MSS Diaries Collection 1-G-1, MU 841.
Janet Hall, National Archives of Canada, MG 29 C70.
Eleanora Hallen, Simcoe County Archives.
Mary Hallen, Simcoe County Archives.
Bertha Harnden, Archives of Ontario, MSS Van Buren Collection, MU 3062
Frances Ann Jones, Upper Canada Village.
Josephine Anne Ketchum, Private Collection.
Mary Ann King, Niagara Historical Society, MS 193, Series H V11.
Belle Stuart Kittredge, National Archives of Canada, MG29 C114.
Emma Laflamme, Metropolitan Toronto Reference Library, Baldwin Room.
Agnes Emma Butler Leacock, National Archives of Canada, MG29, C110.
Helen Grant Macdonald, Metropolitan Toronto Reference Library, Baldwin Room.
Susan Agnes, Lady Macdonald, National Archives of Canada, MS335, reel 217.
Sophia MacNab, National Archives of Canada, MG 24, B 17, A22, A305.
Laura McMurray (Wiggins), Simcoe County Archives.
Catharine Merritt, St Catharines Public Library.
Catherine (Katie) Miller, Private Collection.
Frances Georgina Agnes Tweedie Milne, Archives of Ontario MU 866, 111-9.
Gertrude Nicholson, Pickering College Archives. (Copy at Norwich Archives).
Alice Patterson, Archives of Ontario, MU 843 1-P.2.
Oliver Schmidt, Allen County Public Library, Fort Wayne, Indiana.
Bessie Mabel Scott Lewis, University of Toronto Archives, B80-0033/001.
Frances Gay Simpson, National Archives of Canada, MG 24 K48.
Edith Elizabeth Van der Smissen, University of Toronto Archives, B90-0014.
Catherine Bell Van Norman, *Her diary 1850.* (Burlington, Burlington Historical Society, 1981)
Louis H. Wagner, University of Waterloo, Doris Lewis Rare Book Room, Wagner Hailer Papers, GA 77, Box #1.
Avice Watson, Wellington County Museum, A988.5, Series 5. MU 84.
Susanna Whaley, Private Collection.

SPECIAL COLLECTIONS AND PAPERS

Boyd-De Grassi Collection, Trent University Archives, 88-011/21/1, Ivan R. Mackintosh to Annie de Grassi, 19 August 1915.
Brown-Hendrie Collection, Hamilton Public Library, Archives File, Correspondence, Catherine Kough to Mary Brown, 9 February 1867.

Buchanan Papers, Queen's University Archives, coll. 2272, Box 1, Elizabeth Johnston of Brantford to her cousin, 23 December 1877.

Burleigh Papers, Queen's University Archives, Box 16, File 20a, Amhert Island Diary.

Fowlds Collection, Trent University Archives, B-72-001/3/8/224.

Dr. Ida A. Funnell Collection, Queen's University Archives, 2211.1.

William Gladstone Collection, Waterloo Historical Society, MC61, Kitchener Public Library.

Macaulay Family Papers, Archives of Ontario, Macaulay Papers, F32, F38. Transcription available at Macaulay Heritage Park Museum, Picton.

Mary Hutchinson Orr. Reminiscences, Wellington County Archives, A989.7 MU 102.

Mrs Joseph Rendall, Correspondence, Wellington County Archives, A993-22 MU279.

Ewan Ross Collection, Queen's University Archives, Series 111, #47 Fairs.

Frances Gay Simpson Collection, National Archives of Canada, MG 24 K48.

Upper Canada Village Library, Social History Papers,

Folder 3, C. McEuen to Margaret —, 21 November 1853.

Oral History Collection, Kitchener Public Library: interviews with Lucinda Allendorf (084), Winnifred Pollock (344), Reger Weiler (744), Joseph Zinger (824), Tusie Zurbrigg (133).

OTHER PUBLICATIONS

Anglo-American Magazine, (Toronto).

Armstrong, Audrey I. *Harness in the Parlour*. (Toronto, Musson, 1974).

Canadian Illustrated News, (Montreal).

Campbell, Isobell. *From Forest to Thriving Hamlets*. (Seaforth, The Huron Expositor, 1968).

Duncan, Sara Jeanette, *The Imperialist*. (1904).

Estes, J. Worth, *Dictionary of Protopharmacology: Therapeutic Practices, 1700-1850*. (Science History Publications, U.S.A. 1900).

Etiquette at Washington together with the Customs adopted by Polite Society. (Baltimore, Murphy, 1857).

Francatelli, Charles Elme, *A Plain Cookery Book for the Working Classes*. (London, Routledge, Warne & Routledge, 1852; reprinted by Scolar Press, London, 1977).

Garrett, Blanche Pownall, *Canadian Country Preserves and Wines*. (Toronto, James Lewis & Samuel, 1974).

Godey's Lady's Book. (Philadelphia, January 1853).

Graham, Harry, *Ruthless Rhymes for Heartless Homes*. (London, E. Arnold 1899).

Guelph & Galt Advertiser and Wellington District Advocate, (Guelph, Ontario).

Hechtlinger, Adelaide, *The great patent medicine era*. (1970).

Jackman, Mark I. *In Repose, Victorian Funeral Customs and Practices*. (Kirby, Clarington Museums, Clarke Museum & Archives, Municipality of Clarington, 1992).

Josh Billings Cook Book and Piktorial Proverbs. (Toronto, Toronto News, 1880).

Larned, Linda Hull, *The Hostess of To-Day*. (New York, Charles Scribner's Sons, 1899).

Loane, M. *The Queen's Poor: Life as they Find it in Country and Town*. (London, Edward Arnold, 1910).

Medical Chronicle, 2, 1854.

Miss Beecher's Domestic Receipt Book. (5th ed.).

Mitchinson, Wendy, *The Nature of Their Bodies; Women and Their Doctors in Victorian Canada*. (Toronto, University of Toronto Press, 1991).

"Mother Hubbard's Cupboard," or, *Canadian Cook Book*. (Hamilton, G. C. Briggs & Sons, 1881).

Patterson, Pat & Frances, *Harvests Past*. (Erin, Boston Mills Press, 1989).

Pemwarden, J. M., "Barbaroud Treatment by a Midwife," *Canada Lancet* 4, 1872.

Phillips, David, *Threshing and other Delights*. (London, Phelps Publishing, 1989).

Pen Pictures of Early Pioneer Life in Upper Canada by A Canuck of the fifth generation. (Toronto, William Briggs, 1905).

St. Catharines' Journal and Welland Canal, (Niagara District) General Advertiser, (St. Catharines, Ontario).

Smith, Michael, *The Afternoon Tea Book*. (New York, Collier Books, 1986).

The Ayr News, (Ayr, Ontario).

The Barrie Magnet, (Barrie, Ontario).

The Bathurst Courier and Ottawa General Advertiser, (Perth, Ontario).

The Berlin Daily Telegraph, (Berlin, Ontario).

The Canadian Home Cook Book. (Toronto, Hunter, Rose and Company 1877; reprinted by Ontario Reprint Press, Toronto, 1970).

The Charlottetown Constitutionalist

The Cook Not Mad; or, Rational Cookery. (Kingston, James Macfarlane, 1831; reprinted by Cherry Tree Press/Government of Ontario, Toronto, 1984)

The Dominion Illustrated: A Canadian Pictorial Weekly, (Montreal, Quebec).

The Dumfries Reformer, (Galt, Ontario).

The Elmira Signet, (Elmira, Ontario).

The Finchley Manual of Industry no. 111: Female Servant Manual. (London, Joseph Masters, 1867).

The Globe , (Toronto, Ontario)

The Huntingdon Herald, (Huntingdon, Quebec).

The Huron Expositor, (Seaforth, Ontario).

The Ladies' Book of Useful Information, (London, Ont., London Printing & Lithographing Co., 1896).

The Ladies' Home Journal, (Philadelphia).

The Ladies' Journal, (Toronto, Ontario).

The Newfoundland Royal Gazette.

The New Galt Cookbook. (Galt, Ontario, 1898).

The People's Home Library: Medical, Cooking, Veterinary. (R.C. Barnum & Co., 1910).

The Rideau Record, (Ottawa, Ontario).

The Spirit of The Age & Canadian General Advertiser and Intelligencier, (Barrie, Ontario).

Verity, F. S. "Case illustrative of the difficulties to be encountered by the Practitioner of Midwifery in a rural practice," *Medical Chronicle* 2, 1854.

Weekly Herald & Conception Bay General Advertiser, (Conception Bay, Newfoundland).

Whitehead, Robert Yates, *Records of an Old Vicarage*. (1906).

Wilson, Pearl and Laura Morton, *Rural Gatherings*. (Printed by Floyd W. Hall, Lindsay, Ontario).

Young, John H. Our Deportment, or the Manners, Conduct and Dress of the Most Refined Society. (Detroit, Michigan and Hamilton, Ontario, Dickerson & Co., 1880).

Young, John H. *Our Deportment, or the Manners, Conduct and Dress of the Most Refined Society.* (Paris, Ontario, John S. Brown, 1883).

Index

"n" indicates "note" in index listing

About the Authors

FRANCES HOFFMAN was born and raised in the north of England. Some of her female relatives, particularly a great aunt whose home was a 350 year old farmhouse nestled in the Derbyshire Pennines, encouraged and set the scene for developing her interest in social history.

She came to Canada in 1966 and lives in a log house on the banks of the Grand River in the heart of Mennonite country near Waterloo, Ontario. It was while entertaining Old Order Mennonite neighbours, and in coming to appreciate the "old world" quality that pervades most of their lives, that the idea of writing *Hearth, Heart and Home*, was conceived.

Frances Hoffman is employed as an oral historian by the Kitchener Public Library. She is also a keen researcher of family history, and has lectured and presented workshops on these topics. Recent volunteer positions include: Editor of *Branch Notes*, the publication of the Waterloo-Wellington Branch of the Ontario Genealogical Society; Secretary to the Maryhill Historical Society; and Board member of the Waterloo Regional Heritage Foundation. She is also an active Hospice volunteer, working with people who are in the latter stages of terminal illness.

RYAN TAYLOR was born in Oshawa, Ontario, and is a graduate of Carleton University and the University of Ottawa. He has worked as a librarian since 1972, in Manitoba, Ontario and Indiana.

Ryan first became interested in family history in 1964 and since then has published a number of genealogies and biographies, both of his own and other people's families. He is the author of *Family Research in Waterloo and Wellington Counties* (1986) and *Important Genealogical Collections in Ontario Libraries and Archives: a Directory* (1994). Formerly a columnist with *Kitchener Downtown Alive*; since 1993 he has contributed a weekly family history column to the *Kitchener-Waterloo Record*.

A past chair of the Waterloo-Wellington Branch of the Ontario Genealogical Society, his long association with OGS began in 1982. During this time he edited the book reviews of the official journal *Families* (1984-1993), and since 1988 has edited the quarterly journal itself.

While at the Kitchener (Ontario) public library, he assisted genealogists and local historians and contributed to a number of regional publications. He has lectured extensively across Canada and in the United States, including at three national American genealogical conferences.

Ryan began the oral history programme at the Kitchener library in 1981. In ten years the programme recorded the memories of more than 600 individuals. He also broadcast the Library's book review programme, *Bookmark*, on CFCA-FM from 1983-1992.

Ryan Taylor is presently associated with the historical genealogy department of the Allen County Public Library, Fort Wayne, Indiana.